1000 HOSTELS: BRITAIN & NORTH EUROPE HYPER-GUIDE

Backpackers
&
Flashpackers

Hardie Karges

ISBN: 0988490544

ISBN 13: 9780988490543

Library of Congress Control Number: 2013946077

Hypertravel Books,
Los Angeles, California

Table of Contents

Preface:
Coming Around Half-Circle

This is the part where I typically get all philosophical and start talking about where we've been and where we're going (after all, people still ask me what I plan to do with my philosophy degree, so I guess now I know). Anyway, the initial project is about half over by now, so that means about half the world, approximately, and most of the Anglo-European world, fully documented in the four editions of the "Backpackers & Flashpackers" series so far in print, except that... Europe wasn't quite 'fully' documented, not then, and not the West, certainly. I intend to remedy that in this edition. If I was trying to be selective before, then I'm trying to be comprehensive now, and that means a lot more work. It means some other things, too.

It means that I don't have time or space to initiate novice travelers here, so I assume you're past all that. You realize by now that the weeks, months—even years—that some people spend preparing for travel—or not—is mostly unnecessary, or overkill, or even worse: an excuse to never do it. After all, most people are never going into war zones, or malaria zones, or high-crime zones, or any sort of danger zone whatsoever. They're just going to catch a few rays, catch a buzz, and catch a flight back home full of adventures to talk about for the next year, and then do it all over again... hopefully.

Even if you are going out of Europe's relative comfort zone, or the twenty or thirty Third World countries that emulate it well enough linguistically and culturally—and beat its pants off financially—the drill is not so much more elaborate, like so, more or less: 1) plan a tentative route; 2) book a flight; 3) get your visa(s), if any; 4) book a room, for the first night at least, maybe. Or just take one of my books. Or book a tour. Wait a minute. On second thought, take one of my books regardless. You're good to go now.

Of course the advanced traveler wants much more than a beach or a cocktail, or even a trek or a RTW trip, for that matter. He—or she—wants it all…but not necessarily now. Once it's a way of life, then travel is a state of constant preparedness, and constant awareness. The evening news inspires next month's trip; the end of one project signals the beginning of another. Conscious intentional preparation then becomes a case of processing information, not leafing through tourist brochures.

This book overlaps with some of the information in the previous books on Europe, with a couple of exceptions. While those were divided between East and West, the obvious cultural distinction, this book—and the next—are divided between north and south, the more obvious seasonal distinction… and likely path of travel. The problem is that it's hard to know where to draw the north/south line, so there are some anomalies here, but don't worry. Those other countries will be included in the next book on South Europe. The other difference is that this book is more comprehensive, especially for the western countries, so the end result will be twice as many hostels listed here.

If I started this project as a writer, then publisher, then marketer, then crusader, then geographer, I'm now playing the role of anthropologist, documenting a unique third-millennial phenomenon, that of hostelling, defined as shared accommodation, especially in wealthy developed countries, something that seems more logical as part of a poverty regime, so ironic. Though less celebrated than the rise of social media, it is probably just as important, and possibly related.

But I want to know how the story ends. I want to know exactly what the extent of the phenomenon is, whether it ever gets fully recognized—and capitalized—like FaceBook, or not. Stay tuned. But you just wanted to book a couple of hostels for your trip, right? Anyway, I'll assume anyone reading this is an experienced traveler, but not necessarily an experienced hostel fanatic. After all, I wasn't either, up until a few years ago. But I'll be brief. So please read on. BTW, did I mention that European hostel prices have dropped in the last year, in some cases by as much as half? Yeah…

Introduction

What is a hostel? Originally they were places, mostly in Europe, where students could sleep for cheap on extended country outings, frequently established at appropriate intervals over and about the landscape and which corresponded more or less to the amount of distance a student might hike or bike in the course of a day. Since those outings usually occurred in the summer when schools were otherwise uncommitted, the schools themselves became the logical place for seasonal conversion. That still happens sometimes, but not much.

The concept has expanded dramatically over the last decade, for a variety of reasons, no doubt; among them: rising hotel prices, rising restaurant prices, and — drum roll here, please — Internet. For the rise of Internet has not only made advance booking widely accessible for both hostel and traveler, but it also became a reasonably-priced accommodation where a traveler would almost certainly have access to that same Internet. This fueled an explosion which is still happening to this day, and has barely scratched the surface yet in many places.

What any good hostel should have, by my own current standards, are: 1) cheap dorm beds, 2) English language, 3) a kitchen, 4) storage lockers, and 5) easy access to Internet. Of course within each of those categories there exists significant margin for deviation, but a place of lodging should make the effort to at least offer something in each of these five basic requirements in my humble opinion (IMHO for short: critics please note that my use of common 21st Century shorthand is the result of a conscious stylistic decision, not bad editing).

Other things you can expect that probably wouldn't be considered "amenities" include DIY bedding (you know how to make a bed, right?) and the likely absence of a towel (though many have it, but charge a fee). For purposes of this guide I had to decide what ultimately defines a hostel, and for me that's the shared rooms. It's nice if they have private rooms also, but if they don't have dorms, then they won't be in this book. Nowhere else has the term been defined so concisely and precisely, to my knowledge. Just because a place calls itself a hostel is not enough for me.

This book is intended to be comprehensive, but I have to maintain some standards and criteria for inclusion, so there are a few issues to consider. The presence of dorms is not an issue; that's a definition. The main issues for me are age limits and websites. Most backpackers' hostels simply have no age limit, and that's the way it should be, I feel. Any problems can be dealt with on an individual basis. Another related problem is that in some cities hostel beds rank as decent long-term accommodations for some individuals and even families, who attempt to live there. Most hostels rightfully attempt to discourage this, as they should. Hostels are not transient hotels, after all.

I try to weed those places out of this guide and include only "real" hostels. With this guide you can contact hostels directly before committing any money, which is good. That way you can do some weeding, too, even at the last minute. You can't do that with most hostel-booking sites, which for some hostels is their only connection to potential customers. To do it right, then, a hostel must have a website with contact information. If they don't, then they won't be in this book (okay, on rare occasions I let one in that has a FaceBook page instead of a website, but not often). That tends to weed out shoddy operators, too. In general I also shy away from places that are only seasonal, but there's a sliding scale there, so many places with winter-only closure ARE included.

For better or worse, consolidation is setting in to the hostel scene rapidly, and the days of the "hippie hostel" may be numbered. The most obvious manifestation of this trend is the appearance of hostel chains, not only within a city or country, but in multiple cities across a region. I think that this in general is not a bad thing, as it establishes standards of services and expectations. The downside, that quirky little mom-and-pop operations may get squeezed out, is probably misplaced, since many of those places wouldn't rate very highly on my hostel-meter anyway, and the current "Air BnB" trend is probably more suitable to their offerings.

A word should be mentioned about HI, Hostelling International, which is often affiliated with YHA and such. This is the original hostel chain, and largely responsible for the existence of hostels, or at least their smooth transition from those early schoolboy barracks into modern backpackers' party hostels. They are a membership organization and you will need to pay an extra charge to stay there if you're not a member. When you've done this a half-dozen times or so, you'll be a member (current blurbs suggest you join in advance in your own country for best results).

But this guide is not about HI, though some are listed, particularly the ones that offer beds on the major hostel-booking sites and in the major cities. For better or worse, they tend to represent the old school of "youth hostels" more than the modern era of "backpackers." Check them out here and at *hihostels.com*. If you're looking for something out in the countryside, they may be best.

This book is intended as an introduction and complement to the vast online resources and hopefully a broader view. Still, hostel-booking sites are invaluable for feedback, specific information and special promotions, and I urge everyone to consult them. Two of the bigger ones that I know best are *hostelbookers.com* and *hostelworld.com*, though there are many others, and *hostelz.com* acts as something of a "kayak" for them all, so that's good. So what makes this book better than a website for booking hostels? That's like comparing apples and oranges.

For one thing, we give you the hostel's own website and/or e-mail address and phone number for direct communication. So, not only can we be more objective than a booking site that receives a commission, but a booking site may show a hostel to be full when a call or e-mail to the hostel itself will get you a bed immediately. For another, as mentioned before, we try to include only the "real" hostels, hopefully with good reviews.

Best Westerns and Ibises won't be listed here—unless they offer shared rooms. Don't laugh. It's happening. And DO NOT USE A HOSTEL-BOOKING SITE LESS THAN THREE DAYS BEFORE YOUR STAY! It's too late. You'll be standing in line there at midnight out by the Bangkok airport with a number, but no room. Contact the hostel directly. That's what this book is for, Internet optional.

By the way in some quarters a hostel itself is known as a "backpackers," short for "backpackers' hostel," I assume. Make a note. What's a "flashpacker?" That's me, I think, a backpacker who's grown up and has a little extra time to kill and a few extra bucks to spend on comfort, maybe increasingly oriented to the cultural offerings of cities rather than the raw wilds of the outback. I will try to give you at least a glimpse of those offerings here. Room and bed rates can be elaborate and confusing, and frequently changing, so are included here for comparison purposes only.

Some issues of previous concern have become less so recently. Thus, unless otherwise stated, and unlike previous versions, it can be assumed that the hostel provides Internet service of some kind, hopefully free WiFi, and if I know definitely that they do NOT provide that, then I will indicate so, most likely in rural hostels. Likewise it can be assumed that there is no curfew; if I know otherwise, then I will indicate it. Ditto for seasonality, per our previous discussion… and smoking, not an issue limited to hostels, but definitely an issue. If they permit smoking, I'll try to let you know. Did you know that once upon a time, hostels expected you to pitch in with chores? Don't laugh; it's been partially revived in some Scandinavian hostels who want you to clean up your mess or hire someone to do it. I'll discuss it more when we get there.

Hostels and their websites have some of their own vocabulary, and so do I:

Key to Symbols: Here are some symbols, shorthand and abbreviations used here:
--$bed = lowest price for a dorm bed that we can find for a typical day, for comparison only (they change with seasons, promotions, and currency fluctuations). Pvt. = private room, yes or no, multiply $bed by 2-3 for price, the number of people expected to share.
--B'fast = Breakfast (free or not or for purchase only); don't expect too much.
--c.c. = credit card, OK meaning they're accepted, +/% indicating a surcharge for use;
--cash (only) = even if you reserved with plastic, they want cash for the balance
--Recep = times when there should be someone to check you in. Don't press your luck.
--24/7 = they never close, supposedly. I suggest advising and confirming late arrival.
--HI, YHA, etc. are clubs that require a small fee; current recommendations are to join in advance in your home country, if you plan to use their services often.
--Y.H. = Youth Hostel (term I usually reserve only for organizations like HI/ YHA, etc.)
--central, center, ctr = hostel is centrally located in the city, generally a good thing…
--luggage room/bag hold = you can stash your luggage to pick up later, very handy

Introduction

--(used with Reception times) ltd = limited, / = midday break, // = long naps, /// = lazy

--party = they get down; partyy = they stay down; partyyy = they don't get up

--T/F = number for both phone and fax

--TF = Toll free number (usually only within the country; or Skype)

--lift = that's a bloody elevator, mate

--ETA = estimated time of arrival

--resto = restaurant

--CBD = Central Business District = city center = 'downtown'

--min/max = the minimum and maximum number of nights' stay allowed

--*Jack1Free@ hypertravel.biz/* (for example) = my way of contracting e-mail addresses contained within domains. The second half is the website address (add 'www' if necessary). All listings contain websites; some have forms inside for contacting, instead of e-mail addresses.

Note on telephone numbers: they are given here in several different ways, hopefully to show you how they work. Numbers that begin with a '+' should be ready for international use. Hold the '0' button down on a cell phone and the '+' appears, eliminating the need to know a country's international dialing code. The 2-3 digit country code then follows. For local use, drop that and **usually** add a zero, then the 9-10 digit local number. Where the local number is given, reverse that procedure. Add a '0' to the front if necessary. Some add no '0'; Russia and related systems add '8'. A picture is worth a thousand words.

Note on other related websites: you will also see a mini-UK flag on websites to indicate English language. That's the Union Jack, Jack.

Beware mid-day lockouts. That is the practice of some establishments of closing entirely for a specified period of time during the day, during which you will be forced to leave. This is much more common than seems reasonable and cheapens the whole movement.

Final note on hostel room and bed rates: in reality they are all over the place, depending on the booking site, the day of the week, the month of the year, current exchange rate, and general market conditions (prices in general seem to follow real estate values, I've noticed). Prices seem to be lower than the same period last year, so that likely reflects a maturing of the market. Numbers given here are for general reference and tend toward the lower range, though neither lowest nor highest.

Shop booking sites and the hostel's own website, especially if you plan an extended stay. Weekly rates might be negotiable. Prices are most erratic in the largest most developed markets, like London and Berlin. Off-season rates there of less than twenty bucks a bed are truly incredible, but not illogical, since cheap private digs have long been available for no more than forty. But do they have WiFi? The cheapest places don't always have the most satisfied customers. Now go travel. That's the fun part.

Part I: British Isles

The British Isles, as I use the term, encompasses the two sovereign countries of the Republic of Ireland and the United Kingdom, the latter of which includes Northern Ireland and Great Britain, the latter of which includes England, Scotland and Wales. Got that, or is it too confusing? Don't ask about islands. In addition to the two main ones of Ireland and Great Britain, there are countless others, including a few which are politically autonomous, domestically at least, like the Isle of Man and the Channel Islands, the latter of which includes Jersey and Guernsey. Whew!

Did I mention that the Republic of Ireland uses the Euro as currency? The UK is part of the EU, but still uses the pound sterling, as do its outliers, some of which print their own money, like Scotland and the Isle of Man. Avoid changing money or using ATM's there (I'll try to remember to remind you again). Fortunately corporations are less concerned with borders than governments (except at tax time), so transportation is fairly seamless, in the modern European fashion.

Buses connect seamlessly with ferries all over the UK, and now that Ireland is cooperating with its UK north, it's no huge deal, not for locals, at least, BUT… UK Customs officials can be real jerks to non-EU people, just like Canada, US, and Australia can be, since many illegal immigrants study English and nothing else, so usually prefer those countries. Ireland and the EU are usually no problem, until you pass the six month limit of residence for one year. Ireland is still a bit poorer than the others, especially with the 2008 recession unresolved.

This is where many Americans will get their introduction to independent international travel, so it's relatively painless, as these are the European countries most similar to the US. The language is similar of course (I'm half-joking); just lose the drawl and any assorted twangs. Get your tongue up front and speak from there instead of your throat, and you'll do fine; avoid the East End of London, or go with a translator. If you're lucky you'll even get to hear someone speak Welsh or Gaelic. You'll be surprised if you expect something like Scottish or Irish-accented English. If you go to Scotland, see if you can understand some Scots, a middle English dialect that got separated from the pack way back in the feudal era when the two countries were… uh, feuding.

Aside from any Anglo-American common culture and heritage, these are some of the coolest places in the world, and with one of the greatest proportion of hostels in the world, with the possible exception of Australia and/or New Zealand (or Spain/Portugal). Not only are the urban areas flashpacker central, with London topping out at seventy here, but the countryside is backpacker central, in the old-school sense, with hikers and bikers, and even surfers claiming turf.

It has long been the case that pubs offer some of the best deals in cheap rooms in Britain, usually upstairs, especially outside London. Now many of those are being converted to hostels, especially **in** London. YHA-affiliated hostels pretty much rule in the small towns and countryside. And the quality is good, with kitchens a standard offering, and bars quite common. Hey, you gotta' have priorities. But beware midday lockouts and limited reception hours, cash-only policies and over-cooked food. Enjoy.

1) England

England makes up the bulk of the United Kingdom (of England, Wales, Scotland, and Northern Ireland) and is the economic engine and dominant player — if not necessarily the heart and soul — of the Kingdom. But the history of the UK is first and foremost the history of England (and is fairly well known to most Americans, Commonwealth members, and Western Europeans, I assume, so I won't elaborate on the minutiae here): the Pictish aboriginals, the Gaelic immigrants, the Roman overlordship, the Anglo-Saxon invasion, the Danelaw, the Viking raids, the Norman Conquest, the Church of England, the Civil War, the Restoration, the Bill of Rights, the Empire, two World Wars, and perhaps the most incedible event of human history (still occurring to this day, so a drum roll, please)… the Industrial Revolution. This is probably England's greatest legacy to the world (I won't mention acts of enclosure and the highland clearances). Pounds sterling (GBP) are currency, English the language, calling code +44.

4 Hostels) BATH is famous for its baths, of course, since it first came on the scene as a Roman spa town in 43 AD. It is a UNESCO World Heritage site, with Celtic baths, Roman baths, and don't forget Thermae… ☺ The main landmark is the 16th C. abbey church of St. Peter and St. Paul. Then there are the 18th C. Pump Room, Queen Square, the Circus, the Guildhall, Lansdown Crescent, the Holburne of Menstrie Museum of Arts collection, and the Assembly Rooms, reopened in 1963 after destruction in WWII. Haile Selassie stayed here for four years.

St. Christopher's Inn- Bath, 9 Green St, Bath, Somerset; T:02086007505, *feedback@ st-christophers.co.uk/*; $16bed, Kitchen:N, B'fast:Y, Pvt.room:N, Locker:Y, Recep:ltd; Note: resto/bar/café, tour desk, bag hold, laundry, central

YHA Bath, Bathwick Hill, Somerset, Bath; T:08453719303, *bath@ yha.org. uk/*; $23bed, Kitchen:Y, B'fast:$, Pvt.room:Y, Locker:Y, Recep:7a>11p; Note: 5 night max. stay, resto/bar, c.c. ok, luggage room

Bath Backpackers, 13 Pierrepont St, Bath; T:+44(0)1225446787, *bath@ hostels.co.uk/*; $16bed, Kitchen:Y, B'fast:N, Pvt.room:N, Locker:Y, Recep:ltd; Note: tours, safe dep, c.c. ok, laundry, bag hold, tea/coffee, central, party dungeon

Bath YMCA Intl House, Broad St Place, Bath; *bathymca.co.uk/*, T:01225325900; $24Bed, Kitchen:N, B'fast:$, Pvt.room:Y, Locker:N, Recep:24/7; Note: central, café, gym, billiards, laundry, luggage room, maps

2 Hostels) BIRMINGHAM: If Manchester was the mill town of the Industrial Revolution, then Birmingham was the laboratory. The steam engine was invented here in 1776. That kept things running until petroleum and internal combustion took over, and without it the Industrial Revolution would've been impossible. Birmingham was a hotbed of small innovative workshops even before Manchester became the cheap-labor/mass-manufacture paradigm of industry. It was also the birthplace of heavy metal music, interesting symmetry. Now you know.

Birmingham is England's second most populous city today. Landmarks include the classical Town Hall, the Renaissance-style Council House, the City of Birmingham Museum and Art Gallery, St. Philip's Cathedral, St. Paul's Church, St. Chad's Cathedral (Roman Catholic), Centenary Square, the International Convention Centre, and the Bullring shopping centre, likely the first thing you'll notice.

B'ham Central Backpackers, 58 Coventry St. Birmingham; T:01216430033, *birminghamcentralbackpackers.com/*; $20bed, Kitchen:Y, B'fast:Y, Pvt.room:Y, Locker:Y, Recep:24/7; Note: nr Nat. Exp bus, bar, parking, bag hold, tours

Hatters Backpack Hostel, 92-95 Livery St, Jewellery Qtr, Birmingham; *hattersgroup.com/*, T:01212364031; $20bed, Kitchen:Y, B'fast:Y, Pvt. room:Y, Locker:N, Recep:24/7; Note: wh/chairs ok, bag hold, laundry, free tour/info, c.c. ok

9 Hostels) BRIGHTON is where you go to escape London, only a few hours away by train, and especially convenient if you've got business at Gatwick, home of the UK's second largest airport south of London. This is a party town; be forewarned. I suspect many of the guests are Brits from up-country. Double prices on weekends are not uncommon. It is also an art town, home of the annual Brighton Festival and its parallel Fringe Festival. Then there's the Soundwaves Festival, the Great Escape, Brighton Live, and the Brighton Pride festival for the LGBT community. It's irreverent; I warned you.

Kipps Hostel, 76 Grand Parade, Brighton, East Sussex; *kipps-brighton.com/*, T:01273604182; $24bed, Kitchen:Y, B'fast:$, Pvt.room:Y, Locker:Y, Recep:9a>2a; Note: bar, stairs, laundry, bag hold, coffee and tea, terrace, parties

Sobo House, 10-11 Seafield Rd., Brighton, E. Sussex; T:01273323097, *info@ roomsinbrighton.co.uk/*; $15bed, Kitchen:Y, B'fast:$, Pvt.room:Y, Locker:Y, Recep:24/7; Note: laundry, bag hold, parking, tea/cof, TV, dog, 2x$ on wknds

St. Cristopher's, 10-12 Grand Junction Rd, Brighton; *st-christophers. co.uk/*, T:+44(0)1273202035; $18bed, Kitchen:N, B'fast:Y, Pvt.room:Y, Locker:Y, Recep:ltd; Note: resto/bar/club, lift, late noise, close to pier, meals, maps, books

Grapevine North Laine, 29/30 North Rd, Brighton; T:01273777717

Grapevine, 75/76 Middle St, Brighton; *enquiry@ grapevinewebsite.co.uk/*; $18bed, Kitchen:Y, B'fast:N, Pvt.room:N, Locker:N, Recep:9a>6p; Note: luggage room, near waterfront, central, near bars/late-night partying

Journeys, 33 Richmond Pl, Brighton/Hove, E. Sussex; *visitjourneys.com/*, T:01273695866; $18bed, Kitchen:Y, B'fast:Y, Pvt.room:N, Locker:Y, Recep:24/7; Note: bar, laundry, luggage room, TV, curtained 3-deck bunks w/ socket & light

Smart Sea View Brighton, 9-12 St Catherines Terr, Brighton, E. Sussex; *svb. bookings@ smartbackpackers.com/*, T:01273227497; $15Bed, Kitchen:Y, B'fast:Y, Pvt.room:Y, Locker:N, Recep:24/7; Note: billiards, laundry, luggage rm, far

Seadragon Backpackers, 36 Waterloo St, Brighton/Hove, E. Sussex; T:+44/1273711854, *Info@ seadragonbackpackers.co.uk/*; $24Bed, Kitchen:Y, B'fast:Y, Pvt.room:Y, Locker:Y, Recep:10a//6p; Note: bag hold, tea/coffee, cozy, basic

Baggies Backpackers, 33 Oriental Place, Brighton, T:01273733740, *stay@ baggiesbackpackers.com/*; $24Bed, Kitchen:Y, B'fast:N, Pvt.room:Y, Locker:N, Recep:9a>9p; Note: laundry, luggage room, cash only, books, games

5 Hostels) BRISTOL is situated in the south of England, so a bit warmer than most towns. It has long been a major English port, second only to Liverpool. In the medieval era it was one of England's three most important cities until the rise of the Midlands during the Industrial Revolution. Landmarks include the cathedral church; St. Mark's; the Dominican priory of William Penn; the New Room in Broadmead; Broadmead Baptist Chapel; and the Theatre Royal, built in 1766.

YHA, 14 Narrow Quay, Bristol, Avon; T:08453719726, *bristol@ yha.org.uk/*; $28bed, Kitchen:Y, B'fast:$, Pvt.room:Y, Locker:Y, Recep:24/7; Note: 5 night max. stay, bar, c.c. ok, central, towel fee, member discount

Full Moon and Attic Bar, 1 North St., Stokes Croft, Bristol; *info@ fullmoonbristol. co.uk/*, T:01179245007; $24bed, Kitchen:Y, B'fast:N, Pvt.room:N, Locker:N, Recep.>11p, Note: resto/bar, wh/chair ok, parking, c.c. ok, near bus/ctr

007 Travellers Hostel, 150 West St, Bedminster, *Bristol*; *info@ 007hostel. net/*, T:+44/1179662936; $17bed, Kitchen:Y, B'fast:N, Pvt.room:N, Locker:Y, Recep:24/7; Note: weekly rate, luggage rm, c.c. ok, TV, coffee/tea, not central

Rock N Bowl Hostel, 22 Nelson St, Bristol, Avon; T:+44/1173251980, *bookings@ rocknbowlmotel.com/*, $25Bed, Kitchen:Y, B'fast:N, Pvt.room:Y, Locker:Y, Recep:24/7; Note: bar/club, billiards, laundry, luggage room, bowling below

Homestay Bristol, 68 Queen's Rd, Bristol, Avon; *homestaybristol.co.uk*; T:+44/7788836625, *homestaybristol@me.com*; $37Bed, Kitchen:Y, B'fast:Y, Pvt. room:Y, Locker:N, Recep:24/7; Note: laundry, luggage room

BUDE is a seaside town of 9000 in the far southwest of England where it juts into the sea, thus with a climate milder than most. Tourism is the main industry; fishing is second.

Bude Backpackers, 57 Killerton Rd, Bude, Cornwall; T:7970149486, *Info@ northshorebude.com/*; $28Bed, Kitchen:Y, B'fast:N, Pvt.room:Y, Locker:N, Recep:8:30a>10:30p; Note: luggage room, laundry, tour desk, parking, tour desk, beach

CAMBRIDGE is a city of 120,000 in east-central England and best known as one of England's premier university towns, home to the U. of Cambridge, one of the world's top schools. Today it is a center of high-tech and ethnic diversity.

YHA Cambridge, 97 Tenison Rd, Cambridge, Cambridgeshire; T:08453719728, *cambridge@ yha.org.uk/*;$30Bed, Kitchen:Y, B'fast:N, Pvt. room:Y, Locker:Y, Recep:24/7; Note: resto/bar, billiards, travel desk, laundry, bag hold, tours

2 Hostels) CANTERBURY is a cathedral city of 43,000 in the southeast of England, best known as the site of Thomas Beckett's 1170 murder, and subsequent pilgrimages, notably as described in Chaucer's *Canterbury Tales*. It is a UNESCO world heritage site today.

Kipps Hostel Canterbury, 40 Nunnery Fields, Canterbury; T:01227786121, *kipps-hostel.com/*; $25Bed, Kitchen:Y, B'fast:N, Pvt.room:Y, Locker:Y, Recep:8a>11p; Note: billiards, minimart, luggage room, tour desk, theme nights, central

YHA Canterbury, 54 New Dover Rd, Canterbury; T:08453719010, *canterbury@ yha.org.uk/*; $24Bed, Kitchen:Y, B'fast:N, Pvt.room:Y, Locker:Y, Recep:8a>11p; Note: resto, forex, luggage room, parking, c.c. ok

CARLISLE, a city of some 100,000 is known as the "Border City," and lies in the far northwest of England, on the border with Scotland. It dates from Roman times, as a *civitas* to service the forts of Hadrian's Wall, still visible in many nearby spots today.

Bunk Barn, Hillside farm, Boustead hill, Burgh by sands, Carlisle; T:01228576398, *hadrianswalkbnb.co.uk/*; $17Bed, Kitchen:Y, B'fast:$, Pvt.room:N, Locker:N, Recep:2p>9p; Note: cash only, working farm, need transport

CHESHUNT is a bedroom community on the London outskirts, only 13mi/21kg from Charing Cross by train. It is also a nice easy weekend getaway, with a lake and caving, climbing, cycling, and hiking.

YHA Lee Valley, Windmill Lane, Cheshunt, Hertfordshire, T:08453719057, *leevalley@yha.org.uk,*; $25Bed, Kitchen:Y, B'fast:N, Pvt.room:Y, Locker:Y, Recep:7a>11p; Note: pool, bikes, resto/bar, wh/chair ok, lift, luggage rm, tour desk

2 Hostels) CHESTER is a city of some 120,000 in north central England, along the Welsh border, and once a Roman fort. Today it is one of England's best-preserved walled cities.

The Bunkroom,106 Brook St, Chester, Cheshire, T:01244324524, *admin@ thebunkroom.co.uk/*; $28Bed, Kitchen:Y, B'fast:N, Pvt.room:Y, Locker:Y, Recep:ltd; Note: midday lockout, bikes, laundry, luggage room, maps, safe dep

Chester Backpackers, 67 Boughton, Chester; *sales@ chesterbackpackers. co.uk*, T:+44/1244400185; $22Bed, Kitchen:Y, B'fast:N, Pvt.room:Y, Locker:N, Recep:call; Note: laundry, luggage room, parking, tour desk

3 Hostels) CORNWALL is that 'Land's End' area of 500,000 people in southwestern-most England best described as a peninsula extending between the Celtic Sea and the English Channel. It still holds a remnant of the once vast

Celtic population whose language was once considered extinct, but whose 500 speakers now say, "not so fast…" Truro is the main city. With rural hostels, don't take WiFi for granted. Confirm if needed.

Innis Inn, Innis Moor, Penwithick, St Austell, *Info@ innisinn.com/*, T:01726851162; $30Bed, Kitchen:N, B'fast:$, Pvt.room:Y, Locker:N, Recep:2>11p; Note: resto/bar, billiards, luggage room, parking, c.c. ok

St Ives Backpackers, Town Centre, Cornwall, St Ives; T:+44(0)1736799444; *st.ives@ backpackers.co.uk/*; $26Bed, Kitchen:Y, B'fast:N, Pvt.room:N, Locker:N, Recep:10a//10p; Note: billiards, basic

Porthtowan Backpackers, Seamyst, Beach Rd, Porthtowan, Truro; *sicklamelazy.co.uk/*, T:+44/1209891697; *info@porthtowanbackpackers.co.uk*, $35Bed, Kitchen:Y, B'fast:Y, Pvt.room:Y, Locker:Y, Recep:ltd; Note: parking, cats

COTSWOLD is an area in south central England designated AONB, an AREA of Outstanding Natural Beauty, of rolling hills, farms and fields.

YHA Stow on the Wold, The Square, Stow-on-the-Wold, Gloucestershire; T:08453719540, *stow@ yha.org.uk/*; $27Bed, Kitchen:Y, B'fast:N, Pvt.room:Y, Locker:N, Recep:8a>10p; Note: resto/bar, historic village, parking, no WiFi

DARTMOOR is a national park area of southwestern England consisting of moorland and granite bedrock outcrops. There are many rivers, peat bogs, and stone circles.

YHA Dartmoor, Bellever, Postbridge, Devon; T:08453719622, *dartmoor@ yha.org.uk/*; $22Bed, Kitchen:Y, B'fast:N, Pvt.room:Y, Locker:N, Recep:8a//10:30p; Note: resto, laundry, parking

DERBY is a city of a quarter million in the north central Midlands region, and an early center of the Industrial Revolution. There is a historic cathedral, jail (with dungeon), and several museums.

YHA Hartington Hall, Hall Bank, Hartington, Buxton, Derbyshire; T:08453719740, *hartington@ yha.org.uk/*; $30Bed, Kitchen:Y, B'fast:N, Pvt.

room:Y, Locker:Y, Recep:8a>11p; Note: resto/bar, billiards, luggage room, parking, WiFi $

3 Hostels) DEVON is a county of a million people in southwestern England, with mild climate and two coasts. Attractions are the Dartmoor and Exmoor national parks, Jurassic Coast, North Devon's UNESCO Biosphere Reserve, and the 'English Riviera.'

Torquay Backpackers, 119 Abbey Rd, Torquay; *torquaybackpackers. co.uk/*, T:+44/1803299924; $28Bed, Kitchen:Y, B'fast:N, Pvt.room:Y, Locker:Y, Recep:12>9p; Note: parking, luggage room, tour desk, beer garden, tea/coffee

YHA Salcombe, Sharpitor, Salcombe, Devon; T:08453719341, *salcombe@ yha.org.uk/*; $23Bed, Kitchen:Y, B'fast:N, Pvt.room:Y, Locker:N, Recep:8a//10p; Note: resto/bar, coast, water sports, "fashionable Salcombe"

YHA Beer, Bovey Combe, Beer, Seaton, Devon; T:08453719502, *beer@ yha. org.uk/*; $23Bed, Kitchen:Y, B'fast:$, Pvt.room:Y, Locker:N, Recep:8a//10p; Note: resto, parking, steep drive, fossil hunting on Jurassic Coast

DORKING is a town of 17,000 in southeast England, some 21mi/34km south of London, a former staging post on the way to the English Channel. It has been restored nicely, and is well-known for its antiques.

YHA Holmbury St Mary, Radnor Lane, Dorking, Surrey; T:08453719323, *holmbury@ yha.org.uk/*; $23Bed, Kitchen:Y, B'fast:N, Pvt.room:Y, Locker:N, Recep:7a//11p; Note: resto, laundry, parking

DOVER is well known for its White Cliffs and as the closest point to the European continent, making it the natural ferry connection point.

Dover Backpackers, The Castle, Russell St, Dover; T:07776127592, *doverbackpackers.wordpress.com/*, $25Bed, *thecastleinndover@gmail.com*; Kitchen:Y, B'fast:N, Pvt.room:Y, Locker:N, Recep:ltd; Note: café/bar/club, very basic

EXETER is a city of 120,000 in the county of Devon, and once the farthest western extent of Roman administration. Once known for its architecture, it suffered heavily during WWII bombing. Among the best remains are: Exeter Cathedral Green, Exeter city wall, St Nicholas Priory, Medieval Exe Bridge, and St Catherine's Chapel.

Globe Backpackers, 71 Holloway St, Exeter; T:01392215521, *Info@ exeterbackpackers.co.uk;* $30Bed, Kitchen:Y, B'fast:N, Pvt.room:Y, Locker:Y, Recep:3>11p; Note: luggage room, laundry, TV, BYO towel, cash only, central

GLASTONBURY, a town of 9000 in the southwest, has long been a site of religious pilgrimage for its churches and abbeys, though lately the religion is more of the New Age style. The Glastonbury Festival of Performing Arts is the largest in the world.

Glastonbury Backpackers, 4 Market Pl, Glastonbury, Somerset; *Info@ glastonburybackpackers.com/*, T:+44/1458833353; $25Bed, Kitchen:Y, B'fast:$, Pvt. room:Y, Locker:N, Recep:ltd; Note: café/bar/club, billiards, bag hold, laundry

2 Hostels) GLOUCESTER is a city of 120,000 in near southwest England. Originally a Roman fort, today it is better known as a cultural center, with an R&B festival, Cajun & Zydeco Festival, several museums and historic architecture.

Longford Lodge, 68 Tewkesbury Rd, T:01452522243, *longfordlodge.co.uk/*

Centre Lodge Gloucester, 12 Arthur St, Gloucester; T:+44/1452526380, *centrelodgegloucester.co.uk/*, $36Bed, *jens_eberhardt_uk@hotmail.com*; Kitchen:Y, B'fast:Y, Pvt.room:Y, Locker:N, Recep:24/7; Note: TV, parking, laundry, central

HADRIAN'S WALL was built by Roman emperor Hadrian beginning in the year 122 and more or less parallels the English-Scottish border of today. It is a UNESCO world heritage site and the major tourist destination of north England.

Gibbs Hill Bunkhouse, Bardon Mill, Hexham; T:+44/1434344030, *val@ gibbshillfarm.co.uk/*; $26Bed, Kitchen:Y, B'fast:N, Pvt.room:N, Locker:Y, Recep:ltd: Note: billiards, games, parking, remote, no winter trans, Hadrian's Wall

HARLOW is a modern city of almost 80,000 and within the Greater London commute.

Harlow International Hostel, 13 School Ln, Harlow, Essex; *h-i-h. co.uk/*, T:+44/1279421702; $29Bed, Kitchen:Y, B'fast:$, Pvt.room:Y, Locker:N, Recep:8a>12m; Note: tour desk, bag hold, parking, meals $, a/c, @Stansted arpt

ILFRACOMBE is a town of almost 11,000 and a beach resort on the north Devon coast in southwest England. Once a center of maritime trade, it has experienced booms and busts as a tourist town, and currently not a bad budget option.

Ocean Backpackers, 29 St James Place, Ilfracombe, Devon; T:01271867835, *oceanbackpackers.co.uk/*; $20Bed, Kitchen:Y, B'fast:N, Pvt.room:Y, Locker:N, Recep:ltd; Note: parking, luggage room, sea views, surf, picturesque town

JERSEY is an island of 100,000 in the English Channel just off the coast of Normandy, France. It is a self-governing Crown Dependency like Guernsey and the Isle of Man.

Durrell Wildlife Hostel, La Profonde Rue, Trinity, Jersey; *durrell.org/ hostel/*, T:+44/1534860025, *hostelbookings@durrell.org*; $33Bed, Kitchen:Y, B'fast:Y, Pvt.room:Y, Locker:N, Recep:ltd; Note: wildlife park, bikes, prkng, laundry, luggage rm

JORDANS is a village of 700 in south-central England that is a center for Quakerism and the burial place of William Penn. The 'Mayflower Barn' supposedly is made from the timbers of a ship by that name.

YHA Jordans, Welders Lane, Jordans, Beaconsfield, Buckinghamshire, *jordans@ yha.org.uk*, T:08453719523; $28Bed, Kitchen:Y, B'fast:Y, Pvt.room:Y, Locker:N, Recep:9a//10:30p; Note: parking, 5mi/3kg>London Tube, nr Legoland

9 Hostels) THE 'LAKE DISTRICT' is a national park area of northwest England, known for its forests, mountains, lakes, and resident Romantic Poets Wordsworth, Coleridge, Byron, Shelley, Keats, etc.

Kendal Hostel, 118 Highgate Kendal, Cumbria, Lake Dist; T:01539724066, *Kristina@ kendalhostel.co.uk/*; $30Bed, Kitchen:Y, B'fast:N, Pvt.room:Y, Locker:Y, Recep:5>8p; Note: billiards, luggage rm, tour desk, maps, books, central

YHA Ambleside, Waterhead, Ambleside, Cumbria; *ambleside@ yha. org.uk/*, T:08453719620, $30Bed, Kitchen:Y, B'fast:N, Pvt.room:Y, Locker:N, Recep:7:30a>12m; Note: resto/bar, bikes, wh/chair ok, parking, laundry, games

Lake Dist. Backpackers, High St, Windermere, Cumbria; T:01539446374, *lakedistrictbackpackers.co.uk/*, $26Bed, *fletcher_recruitment@yahoo.co.uk/*, Kitchen:Y, B'fast:Y, Pvt.room:N, Locker:Y, Recep: ltd; Note: bikes, laundry, bag hold

Thorney How Grasmere, Thorney How, Grasmere, Ambleside, Cumbria; *enquiries@ thorneyhow.co.uk/*, T:01539435597; $16Bed, Kitchen:Y, B'fast:N, Pvt. room:N, Locker:Y, Recep:3:30>10:30p; Note: resto/bar, luggage room, parking

New Ing Lodge, Shap, (Lake District), Cumbria; *Info@ newinglodge.co.uk/*, T:01931716719; $28Bed, Kitchen:Y, B'fast:$, Pvt.room:Y, Locker:Y, Recep:>9p; Note: resto, laundry, luggage room, tour desk, parking, minimart, eco-friendly

YHA Grasmere Butharlyp Howe, Easedale Rd, Cumbria; *grasmere@ yha. org.uk/*, T:08453719319; $26Bed, Kitchen:Y, B'fast:$, Pvt.room:Y, Locker:Y, Recep:7a>11p; Note: WiFi $, resto/bar, billiards, parking, laundry, books, nature

YHA Hawkshead, Hawkshead, Ambleside, Cumbria, *hawkshead@ yha. org.uk/*, T:08453719321; $24Bed, Kitchen:Y, B'fast:$, Pvt.room:Y, Locker:Y, Recep: 7:30a>10:30p; Note: resto, billiards, laundry, parking, lake, TV, remote/ need car

Derwentwater Hostel, Barrow House, Borrowdale, Keswick, Lake District, *contact@ derwentwater.org/*, T:01768777246; $32Bed, Kitchen:Y, B'fast:$, Pvt.room:Y, Locker:N, Recep:12n>10:30p; Note: bar, remote, laundry, bag hold

YHA Keswick, Station Rd, Keswick, Cumbria, *keswick@ yha.org. uk/*, T:0843719746; $30Bed, Kitchen:Y, B'fast:$, Pvt.room:Y, Locker:N, Recep:7a>11p; Note: resto, bikes, books, laundry, luggage room, WiFi $$, central

LEWES is a town of 16,000 on the southeast coast known as a hub for tourism and transport. Pissed at the Pope? This is your place. The annual Lewes Bonfire usually burns an effigy of him in solidarity with the Protestant martyrs on Guy Fawkes Day 5 Nov.

YHA South Downs, Itford Farm, Beddingham, Lewes, East Sussex; *southdowns@ yha.org.uk/*, T:08453719574; $27Bed, Kitchen:Y, B'fast:$, Pvt. room:Y, Locker:N, Recep:5p>11p; Note: laundry, luggage room, TV, no Net

5 Hostels) LIVERPOOL can only mean one thing, of course, to anyone who lived during this side of the previous century, but there's a little more to it than just the Beatles. At one point 40% of the world's trade passed through the port of Liverpool. That brought in people from all over the world, including the UK's oldest Chinese and black African communities, and scads of Irish. Much of this trade was in the fruit of Manchester's looms, but much was also in slaves.

With the UK's decline in manufacturing prowess, Liverpool saw a sharp decline in prosperity and much unemployment. It is a long-term problem that defies easy solution. The Tate Liverpool, Merseyside County Museum and Library, the Walker Art Gallery, the Picton Library, and the University of Liverpool are among the cultural institutions. This is a point of embarkation for ferries to Ireland and the Isle of Man.

Hatters Liverpool, 56/60 Mount Pleasant, Liverpool; *hattersgroup.com/*, T:01517095570; $18bed, Kitchen:Y, B'fast:Y, Pvt.room:Y, Locker:N, Recep:24/7; Note: laundry, 2N min, billiards, wh/chair ok, lift, resto/bar, bag hold, tours, tea/coffee

Embassie Liverpool Backpackers, 1 Falkner Sq, Liverpool; T:01517071089, *reservations@ embassie.com/*; $26bed, Kitchen:Y, B'fast:Y, Pvt.room:N, Locker:$, Recep:24/7; Note: min. 2N, free Beatles tour, parking, billiards, luggage room

YHA Liverpool, 25 Tabley St, off Wapping, Merseyside, Liverpool; T:08453719527, *liverpool@ yha.org.uk/*; $21bed, Kitchen:Y, B'fast:$, Pvt. room:Y, Locker:N, Recep:24/7; Note: laundry, resto/bar, wh/chair ok, bag hold, parking

International Inn, 4 South Hunter St., Liverpool, Merseyside; T:01517098135, *info@ internationalinn.co.uk*; $28bed, Kitchen:Y, B'fast:Y, Pvt.

room:N, Locker:N, Recep:24/7; Note: nr train, billiards, café, lift, laundry, bag hold

Everton Hostel, 53 Everton Rd, Liverpool, Merseyside; *everton.hostel. com/*, T:07916495468; $11bed, Kitchen:Y, B'fast:Y, Pvt.room:N, Locker:Y, Recep:3p>10p; Note: bikes, billiards, bag hold, tours, tea/cof, cash, laundry

68 Hostels) LONDON is the capital and largest city of England, and one of the great cities in the history of the world. What can you say about London that hasn't already been said? It's huge, sprawling, magnificent, and once controlled about half the world. The Romans founded it in 43AD as Londinium on the River Thames, from which it grew to become the largest city in the world for almost a hundred years. To this day it's the best place from which to access the rest of the world, somewhat equidistant to all the rest, economically if not geographically.

You can easily spend a few days sight-seeing here. Major tourist attractions include the famous Houses of Parliament, Buckingham Palace, Big Ben and Westminster Abbey. That should keep you busy. If not, then check out the British Museum, the National Gallery, Madame Tussaud's wax museum, and the three major South Kensington museums (Victoria and Albert, Natural History, and Science).

Then there are the Tower Bridge, the Tower of London, the London Eye, St. Paul's Cathedral, Borough Market, Shakespeare's Globe Theatre and the Tate Modern Art Gallery. Tired yet? Trafalgar Square is more or less in the center of the cookie jar. Wear good shoes. Hostels are numerous and good, but be aware that many non-travelers use London hostels as a base for party weekends. There seems to be a lot of consolidation in the London market, too, chains now dominating the hostel scene, with ensuing price rises.

Generator Hostel, Compton Pl. off 37 Tavistock Pl., London; T:02073887655, *london@ generatorhostels.com/*; $26bed, Kitchen:N, B'fast:$, Pvt.room:Y, Locker:Y, Recep:24/7; Note: arpt trans, bar, café, wh/chair ok, lift, laundry

Monkeys in the Trees, 49 Becklow Rd, Shepherds Bush, London; T:02087499197, *info@ monkeysinthetrees.co.uk/*; $16bed, Kitchen:Y, B'fast:Y, Pvt.room:N, Locker:, Recep:>11p; Note: min. 2N, bag hold, bar, foosball, terrace, far

Equity Point, 100-102 Westbourne Terrace, London; *equity-point.com/*, T:02070878001; $33bed, Kitchen:Y, B'fast:Y, Pvt.room:Y, Locker:Y, Recep:24/7; Note: arpt trans, bar, café, lift, tours, towel fee, c.c. ok, WiFi $, maps

The Antigallican Hotel, 428 Woolwich Rd, Charlton; T:02088530143, *info@ antigallicanhotel.com/*; $22bed, Kitchen:Y, B'fast:N, Pvt.room:Y, Locker:Y, Recep:24/7; Note: close to O2 dome, bar, billiards, bag hold, laundry, parking, c.c. ok

Globe Trott Inns, 1 Barking Rd, London; *globetrott-inns.com/*, T:07723580911, *globetrottinns@gmail.com*; $20bed, Kitchen:N, B'fast:Y, Pvt. room:N, Locker:Y, Recep:>10p; Note: bar, luggage rm, laundry, tours, billiards, tea/coffee

Dover Castle Hostel, 6A Great Dover St, London; T:02074037773, *info@ dovercastlehostel.com/*; $18bed, Kitchen:Y, B'fast:Y, Pvt.room:N, Locker:$, Recep:24/7; Note: bar, tours, luggage rm, laundry, TV, forex, tea/coffee, billiards, maps

New Cross Inn, 323 New Cross Road, Greater London; *newcrossinn.co.uk/*, T:02083554976; $22bed, Kitchen:Y, B'fast:Y, Pvt. room:Y, Locker:$, Recep:24/7; Note: bar, parking, tour desk, luggage ok, laundry, a/c, c.c. ok, age 18-40

Arsenal Tavern Hostel, 175 Blackstock Rd, London; *arsenaltavern.com/*, T:02073596902, *arsenaltavern@gmail.com*; $19bed, Kitchen:N, B'fast:Y, Pvt. room:N, Locker:Y, Recep:24/7; Note: cash only, resto/bar, luggage room, billiards

Strand Continental, 143 Strand, London; *strand-continental.co.uk/*, T:02078364880, *strandcontinentalhotel@gmail.com*; $28bed, Kitchen:N, B'fast:Y, Pvt.room:Y, Locker:N, Recep:24/7; Note: 6 Fl no lift, resto/bar, safe dep, bag hold

Surprise Backpackers, 110 Vauxhall Bridge Rd, London; T:02078288620, *surprisebackpackers.com/*; $20bed, Kitchen:Y, B'fast:Y, Pvt.room:N, Locker:Y, Recep:8a>11p; Note: bar, billiards, TV, luggage rm, c.c. ok, nr Victoria stn

Court Hostel, 194 Earl's Court Rd, London; *nightsinn.co.uk/*, T:02073730027, *TheCourtHostel@hotmail.com*; $21bed, Kitchen:Y, B'fast:Y, Pvt.room:Y, Locker:Y, Recep:24/7; Note: cash only, tours, bag hold, coffee/tea

Royal Bayswater, 121 Bayswater Rd, London; T:02072298888, *bookings@ royalbayswater.com/*; $14bed, Kitchen:Y, B'fast:Y, Pvt.room:N, Locker:$, Recep:24/7; Note: restaurant, tour desk, forex, safe deposit, luggage $, lift, laundry

Brazen Backpackers, 69 Lisson St, London; *brazenbackpackers.com/*, T:02077235077; $16bed, Kitchen:Y, B'fast:Y, Pvt.room:N, Locker:Y, Recep:ltd; Note: resto/bar, luggage room, laundry, c.c. ok, ages 18-35

The Dictionary, Shoreditch, 10-20 Kingsland Rd, London, T:02076132784, *Info@ thedictionaryhostel.com/*; $20Bed, Kitchen:N, B'fast:Y, Pvt.room:Y, Locker:Y, Recep:24/7; Note: café/bar, luggage room, tour desk, books, tea/coffee

Safestay at Elephant & Castle, 144-152 Walworth Rd, T:02077038000 *reception@ safestay.co.uk/*, $20Bed, Kitchen:N, B'fast:Y, Pvt.room:Y, Locker:Y, Recep:24/7; Note: billiards, bar, bag hold, lift, laundry, meals $, manyy plugs

Walrus Hostel, 172 Westminster Bridge Rd, London, *walrussocial. com/*, T:+44/2079284368; $27Bed, Kitchen:Y, B'fast:Y, Pvt.room:Y, Locker:Y, Recep:8a>11:30p; Note: pub, luggage room, bikes, maps, books, @Waterloo

Meininger Hotel London Hyde Park, 65-67 Queen's Gate, T:02033181407; *welcome@ meininger-hotels.com/*; $23Bed, Kitchen:N, B'fast:$, Pvt.room:Y, Locker:Y, Recep:24/7; Note: bar, laundry, luggage room, tour desk, lift, wh/chair ok

Rest Up London, 172 New Kent Rd, T:+44(0)2036424549, *stay@ restup. co.uk/*; $38Bed, Kitchen:N, B'fast:$, Pvt.room:Y, Locker:Y, Recep:24/7; Note: TV, laundry, resto/bar, luggage room, tour desk, lift, wh/chair ok, maps

Saint James Backpackers, 21 Longridge Rd, *saint-james-backpackers.co.uk/*, T:+44/7450645573, *saintjamesbackpackers@outlook.com*; $31Bed, Kitchen:Y, B'fast:Y, Pvt.room:Y, Locker:Y, Recep:>11p; Note: luggage room, jobs board

Pride of Paddington, 1-3 Craven Rd, London; *Contactus@ theprideofpaddington.co.uk/*, T:+44/2074022156; $24Bed, Kitchen:N, B'fast:Y, Pvt.room:N, Locker:Y, Recep:8a>11p, Note: luggage room, meals $, pub

Central Hostel, 26 Princes Square, Bayswater, London; T:02077275807, *Info@ centralhostel.co.uk/*; $10Bed, Kitchen:Y, B'fast:N, Pvt.room:Y, Locker:N, Recep:24/7; Note: luggage room, bar, maps, tour desk, free tea/coffee, basic

London Backpackers, 8/10 Queens Parade, Queen's Rd, London; T:02082031319, *Info@ ukhostels.com*, $15Bed, Kitchen:Y, B'fast:Y, Pvt. room:Y, Locker:Y, Recep:ltd; Note: nr subway, laundry, luggage rm, tours, 18-35 only, far

Barmy Badger Backpackers, 17 Longridge Rd, London; *barmybadger. com/*, T:02073705213, *barmybadger@hotmail.com*; $36Bed, Kitchen:Y, B'fast:Y, Pvt.room:Y, Locker:Y, Recep:9a>8p; Note: laundry, luggage room, weekly rates, c.c.+%

London Eye Hostel, 73 Lambeth Walk, London; T:02075823088, *Info@ londoneyehostel.com*; $19Bed, Kitchen:Y, B'fast:Y, Pvt.room:Y, Locker:Y, Recep:24/7; Note: arpt trans, lobby bar, billiards, nr River Thames, luggage room, tours

23 Hostel, 23 Inverness Terrace, London; T:0207243211; *23hostel.com/*, $23Bed, Kitchen:N, B'fast:Y, Pvt.room:Y, Locker:Y, Recep:24/7; Note:18-35 y.o. only, billiards, tour desk, cozy

East London, 47 Shernhall St, Walthamstow, London; T :02072631683, *info@ eastlondonhostel.com/*; $23Bed, Kitchen:Y, B'fast:$, Pvt.room:N, Locker:N, Recep:2p>12m; Note: bar, parking, meals $, resto, laundry, c.c. ok

Curzon House Hotel, 58 Courtfield Gardens, London, *curzonhousehotel. co.uk/*, T:02075812116, $38Bed, Kitchen:Y, B'fast:Y, Pvt.room:Y, Locker:N, Recep:8a>10p; Note: weekly rates, age 18-30, bag hold, laundry, 4 fl no lift

Northfields Hostel, 264 Northfield Ave, London, T:02088403555, *Info@ northfieldshostel.com/*; $25Bed, Kitchen:Y, B'fast:N, Pvt.room:Y, Locker:N, Recep:24/7; Note: laundry, luggage room, parking, maps, basic

Acacia Hostel, 14 Queensberry Pl, London; T:+44/2078237103, *Info@ acaciahostel.co.uk/*; $24Bed, Kitchen:Y, B'fast:Y, Pvt.room:Y, Locker:N, Recep:24/7; Note: luggage room, maps, Sat TV

Hootananny Hostel, 95 Effra Rd, Brixton London, T:02077377273, *sophia@ hootananny.co.uk/*; $23Bed, Kitchen:Y, B'fast:Y, Pvt.room:N, Locker:Y, Recep:9a>12m, Note: hostel above club, no locals, resto, parking, billiards

Compton Guest House, 65 Compton Rd, Wimbledon, London; T:+44/2088793245, *comptonguesthouse.com/*; $38Bed, Kitchen:N, B'fast:Y, Pvt. room:Y, Locker:N, Recep:ltd; Note: cash only

The W14 Hotel & Bar, 16-22 Gunterstone Rd, London; *reservations@ thew14hotel.co.uk/*, T:+44/2076026600; $28Bed, Kitchen:Y, B'fast:Y, Pvt.room:Y, Locker:Y, Recep:24/7; Note: arpt trans, café/bar, billiards, luggage rm, tours

West 2 London, 22-23 Kensington Gardens Sq, London; T:+44/2079081963, *Info@ west2london.co.uk/*; $12Bed, Kitchen:Y, B'fast:N, Pvt.room:Y, Locker:Y, Recep:24/7; Note: luggage room, forex, parking, near major sites, basic

The Windmill, 50, Acton High St, Acton; T:02089695955, *Info@ windmillhotelnorthlondon.co.uk*; $31Bed, Kitchen:N, B'fast:$, Pvt.room:Y, Locker:N, Recep:ltd; Note: arpt trans, cash only, resto/bar, bikes, billiards, laundry, tours

Travel Joy Hostels Wimbledon, 89 Hartfield Rd; *info@*, T:02086171585

Travel Joy Hostels Chelsea, 111 Grosvenor Rd, Pimlico; T:02078349689, *info@ traveljoyhostels.com/*; $24bed, Kitchen:N, B'fast:Y, Pvt.room:Y, Locker:Y, Recep: 7:30a>12m; Note: Thai resto/bar, tours, bag hold, laundry, tea/coffee, parking

Palmer Lodge Hillspring, 233 Willesden Lane, T:+44(0)2070992435; $21bed

Palmer Lodge Swiss Cottage, 40 College Crescent, London; *palmerslodges. com*, T/F:020774838470/1; $21bed, Kitchen:N, B'fast:Y, Pvt.room:Y, Locker:Y, Recep:24/7; Note: bar, café, wh/chair ok, lift, tea/coffee, laundry, bag hold

Clink 78, 78 King's Cross Rd, T:+44/207183.9400, *info78@*, $24

Clink 261, 265 Gray's Inn Rd, London; T:02077137789, *info261@ clinkhostels. com/*, $21bed, Kitchen:Y, B'fast:Y, Pvt.room:N, Locker:N, Recep:24/7; Note: laundry, lift, luggage room, tours, maps, books, safe deposit

Journeys London Bridge, 204 Manor Pl; T:02077356581, *londonbridge@*

Journeys Greenwich West, 86 Tanner's Hill, 02086926219, *deptford@*

Journeys Kings Cross Hostel, 54-58 Caledonian Rd, London; T:0207833393, *kingscross@ visitjourneys.com/*; $27bed, Kitchen:Y, B'fast:Y, Pvt. room:Y, Locker:Y, Recep:24/7; Note: arpt trans, mart, laundry, tours, bag hold

Smart Camden Hostel, 55 Bayham, Camden, *sci.bookings@*, 02073888900

Smart Hyde Park Inn, 48 Inverness Terrace, *hpi.bookings@*, 02072290000

Smart Hyde Park View, 16 Leinster Terrace; *hpv.bookings@*, 02074024101

Smart Russell Square, 71 Guilford St, London, England; T:02078338818, *srs.bookings@ smartbackpackers.com/*; $16bed, Kitchen:Y, B'fast:Y, Pvt.room:Y, Locker:Y, Recep:24/7; Note: arpt trans, billiards, mart, bag hold, c.c.+5%, laundry

Astor Museum Inn, 27 Montague St, Bloomsbury, *museum@*, 02075805360

Astor Victoria, 71 Belgrave Rd, *victoria@*, T:02078343077

Astor Hyde Park, 191 Queen's Gate, *hydepark@*, T:02075810103

Astor Quest Hostel, 45 Queensborough Terrace, Bayswater, London; *astorhostels.co.uk/*, T:+44(0)2072297782, *quest@astorhostels.com/*; $23bed, Kitchen:Y, B'fast:Y, Pvt. room:N, Locker:Y, Recep:24/7; Note: age 18-35, laundry

Fresh@Crown, 102 Lavender Hill, Battersea; *crown@*, T:02077381122

Fresh@GreatEastern, Docklands, 1 Glenaffric Ave, *Greateastern@*, 02075316514

Fresh@White Ferry, Victoria, 1A Sutherland St; 02072336133, *whiteferry@*

Fresh@SteamEngine, Waterloo, 41 Cosser St; 02079280720, *steamengine@*

Fresh@GreenMan, Paddington, 308 Edgeware Rd, London; T:02077237980, *greenman@ bestplaceinns.com/*; $16bed, Kitchen:N, B'fast:Y, Pvt.room:N, Locker:Y, Recep:ltd; Note: 24 hr. pub, laundry, bag hold, tea/coffee, free tour, maps

St C's Shepherds Bush, 13 S. Bush Green, *Shepherdsbush@*, 02087350270

St C's London Village, 165 Borough High St, *Village@*, T:02079399710

St. C's London Bridge, 121 Borough High St, *Village@*, T:02079399710

St. C's Camden, 48-50 Camden High St, *Camden@*, T:0207.388.1012

St. C's Greenwich, 189 Greenwich High Rd, *Greenwich@*, T:02088583591

St. Christopher's Hammersmith, 28 Hammersmith Broadway; T:02087485285, *bookings@ st-christophers.co.uk/*; $26bed, Kitchen:N, B'fast:Y,

Pvt.room:Y, Locker:N, Recep:24/7; Note: party, bar, café, tours, no computers, min. 2N

YHA London Thameside, 20 Salter Rd, London; *hihostels.com/*, T:02072322114; *thameside@yha.org.uk*; $43bed, Kitchen:Y, B'fast:$, Pvt.room:Y, Locker:Y, Recep:24/7; Note: resto/bar, laundry, parking, tours

YHA London Central, 104-108 Bolsover St, Marylebone, London; T:08453719154, *londoncentral@ yha.org.uk/*; $28bed, Kitchen:Y, B'fast:$, Pvt. room:Y, Locker:Y, Recep:24/7; Note: laundry, bar, café, wh/chair ok, lift, bag hold

YHA London St. Pancras, 79-81 Euston Rd, London; T:08453719344, *stpancras@ yha.org.uk/*; $41bed, Kitchen:N, B'fast:$, Pvt.room:Y, Locker:Y, Recep:24/7; Note: bar, café, lift, laundry, bag hold, tours, nr Eurostar

YHA London Earls Court, 38 Bolton Gardens, Earl's Court, London; *earlscourt@ yha.org.uk/*, T:08453719114; $41Bed, Kitchen:Y, B'fast:$, Pvt.room:Y, Locker:Y, Recep:24/7; Note: café/bar, laundry, luggage room, WiFi $

YHA London Oxford Street, 14 Noel St, London; T:08453719133, *oxfordst@ yha.org.uk/*; $55Bed, Kitchen:Y, B'fast:N, Pvt.room:Y, Locker:Y, Recep:24/7; Note: West End, bar, laundry, no lift, luggage room, tour desk, WiFi $

YHA London St. Paul's, 36 Carter Lane, London; T:02072364965, *stpauls@ yha.org.uk/*; $37bed, Kitchen:N, B'fast:$, Pvt.room:Y, Locker:N, Recep:24/7; Note: bar, café, bikes, laundry, luggage room, tea/coffee, books, maps, TV

3 Hostels) MANCHESTER is the world's first industrialized city, maybe a dubious claim in a port-industrial Britain, but significant in world history. This industry was based on textile production and related support industries, including the cotton trade from ya'll-know-where. That also means chemicals, dyes, canals, railways, and machines, lots of them. It was also the scene of bread and labor riots. Marx met Engels here. The rest is history. The Royal Exchange now houses a freestanding theatre-in-the-round.

The old Central Station has been converted into an exhibition centre. A complex of buildings at Castlefield has been developed as a regional museum of science and industry. Other museums include the Whitworth Art Gallery, the Manchester City Art Gallery, the Manchester Museum, and the Museum of Science and Industry. Since a 1996 IRA bombing that injured two hundred people, Manchester has renovated and reinvented itself. Now its economy is largely service-oriented. It also has nightlife.

Hatters on Newton, 50 Newton St, Manchester; *hattersgroup.com/*, T:+44(0)1612369500; $20bed, Kitchen:Y, B'fast:Y, Pvt. room:N, Locker:Y, Recep:24/7; Note: near bus & train, coffee & tea, c.c. necessary, no lift, central

Hatters at Hilton Chambers, 15 Hilton St, Manchester; *hattersgroup.com/*, T:+44(0)1612364414; $25bed, Kitchen:Y, B'fast:Y, Pvt.room:N, Locker:N, Recep:24/7; Note: luggage room, safe dep, c.c. necessary, non-party, central

YHA Manchester, Potato Wharf, Castlefield, Manchester; *yha.org.uk/*, T:08453719647; $22bed, Kitchen:Y, B'fast:$, Pvt.room:Y, Locker:Y, Recep:24/7; Note: resto/bar, tour desk, parking, towel/luggage/membership fees, WiFi $

MILTON KEYNES is something of a purpose-built city of 230,000 composed of pre-existing villages in an area 45mi/72km northwest of London. Based entirely on theory and design, it features grid-square street layout, instead of the typical radial pattern. Duh.

YHA Milton Keynes, Vicarage Rd, Bradwell Village, Milton Keynes; T:08453719307, *miltonkeynes@ yha.org.uk*; $25Bed, Kitchen:Y, B'fast:$, Pvt. room:Y, Locker:N, Recep:8a//10p; Note: skiing, biking, resto, games

3 Hostels) NEWCASTLE is a city of 250,000 to 1,500,000 population (depending on how you count) in England's northeast, on the river Tyne and near the North Sea. Its name refers to the castle built by William the Conqueror's son in 1080. There is a notable Chinatown and the nightlife is legendary.

Backpackers Newcastle, 262 Westgate Rd, Newcastle upon Tyne; T:01913407334, *Info@ backpackersnewcastle.com/*; $25Bed, Kitchen:Y, B'fast:Y, Pvt. room:N, Locker:N, Recep:24/7; Note: laundry, luggage room, parking, maps

Albatross Backpackers In! 51 Grainger St, Newcastle; T:01912331330, *Info@ albatrossnewcastle.co.uk/*; $28Bed, Kitchen:Y, B'fast:N, Pvt.room:Y, Locker:N, Recep:24/7; Note: lift, wh/chair ok, tour desk, luggage rm, central, party wknds

Euro Hostel Newcastle, 17 Carliol Sq, Newcastle upon Tyne, *reservations@ euro-hostels.co.uk/*; T:+44/8454900371; $25Bed, Kitchen:Y, B'fast:Y, Pvt.room:Y, Locker:Y, Recep:24/7; Note: resto/bar, wh/chair ok, billiards, laundry, luggage rm

3 Hostels) NEWQUAY is a town of almost 20,000 in the far southwest county of Cornwall. There is nightlife and plenty of tourist activities, particularly surfing.

St. Christophers Inn Newquay, 35 Fore St, Newquay; T:01637859111, *newquay@ st-christophers.co.uk/*; $21Bed, Kitchen:N, B'fast:Y, Pvt.room:Y, Locker:Y, Recep:>11:30p; Note:resto/bar, billiards, luggage rm, loud, beach

Breakers Lodge, 12 Atlantic Rd, Newquay; *breakerslodge.co.uk/*, T:01637874198; $41Bed, Kitchen:Y, B'fast:N, Pvt.room:Y, Locker:N, Recep:2.10p; Note: bar, billiards, games, cash only

Driftwood Surf Lodge, 25 Grosvenor Ave, Newquay; *driftwoodsurflodge. co.uk/*, T:01637878109, *driftwoodsurflodge@talktalk.net*; $23Bed, Kitchen:Y, B'fast:N, Pvt.room:N, Locker:N, Recep:ltd; Note: surf lessons, laundry

2 Hostels) NORFOLK is England's easternmost county, largely rural, though with a population of over 850,000. Historically this is where the 'north folk' entered the area.

YHA Sheringham, 1 Cremer's Drift, Sheringham, Norfolk; T:08453719040, *Sheringham@ yha.org.uk/*; $22Bed, Kitchen:Y, B'fast:$, Pvt.room:Y, Locker:N, Recep:7a>10:30p; Note: resto, laundry, maps, parking, walk to sea front/shops

YHA Wells-next-the-Sea, Church Plain, Wells, Norfolk; T:08453719544, *wellsnorfolk@ yha.org.uk/*, $25Bed, Kitchen:Y, B'fast:N, Pvt.room:Y, Locker:N, Recep:8a>10p; Note: walk to village and beach. Laundry, parking

2 Hostels) NOTTINGHAM during the Industrial Revolution was known for its lace and its slums, but most visitors are attracted by the legend of Robinhood and Sherwood Forest, of which a remnant still remains. It used to be ruled by a Saxon chief named Snot. The old Saxon town is marked by a

castle on Standard Hill, which now houses a museum. The old market square dominates the center. There have been race riots.

Igloo Backpackers Hostel, 110 Mansfield Rd, Nottingham; T:01159475250, *info@ igloohostel.co.uk/*; $26bed, Kitchen:Y, B'fast:N, Pvt.room:Y, Locker:Y, Recep:>1a; Note: luggage room, laundry, tours, c.c. ok, long stay ok, central

Midtown Hostel, 5A Thurland St, Nottingham; T:01159410150, *book@ midtownhostel.co.uk/*; $28bed, Kitchen:Y, B'fast:N, Pvt.room:Y, Locker:N, Recep:24/7; Note: laundry, c.c. ok, tea & coffee, central

3 Hostels) OXFORD began its history in Saxon times as a ford for oxen (yep), long before it became famous as a university town in the 12th century. Radical clerics were burnt at the stake here in 1555. At only 50mi/80km from London, it's an easy day trip either way. Matthew Arnold called it "the city of dreaming spires." I like that. Most of them belong to the university, and were built in the 15th, 16th, and 17th centuries. Oxford is also famous for breweries. It has one of the highest rates of ethnic diversity in the UK.

Central Backpackers Oxford, 13 Park End St, Oxford UK; T:01865242288, *oxford@ centralbackpackers.co.uk/*; $28bed, Kitchen:Y, B'fast:Y, Pvt.room:N, Locker:Y, Recep:8a>11p; Note: luggage room, laundry, tours, c.c. ok, central

Oxford Backpackers, 9A Hythe Bridge Street, Oxford; T:01865721761, *oxford@ hostels.co.uk/*; $25, Kitchen:Y, B'fast:Y, Pvt.room:N, Locker:Y, Recep:8a>11p; Note: bar, printer, fax, lotsa sockets, tea/coffee, near bus/train

YHA Oxford, 2a Botley Rd, Oxford, Oxfordshire; T:08453719131, *oxford@ yha.org.uk/*, $27Bed, Kitchen:Y, B'fast:N, Pvt.room:Y, Locker:Y, Recep:24/7; Note: resto/bar, bikes, billiards, laundry, luggage room, nr center

3 Hostels) THE PEAK DISTRICT is an area in England's north consisting of a national park and covering 555sq.mi/1437sq.km. There are 22 million visitors per year.

YHA Ilam Hall, Ilam Hall, Ilam, Ashbourne, Derbyshire; T:08453719023, *ilam@ yha.org.uk*; $28Bed, Kitchen:Y, B'fast:N, Pvt.room:N, Locker:N, Recep:7a>11p; Note: resto/bar, pool, parking, luggage room

YHA Ravenstor, Millers Dale, Buxton, Derbyshire; T:08453719655, *Ravenstor@ yha.org.uk/*; $24Bed, Kitchen:Y, B'fast:N, Pvt.room:Y, Locker:N, Recep:7a/11p; Note: resto, luggage room, parking, national park

Roaches Bunkhouse Accommodation, Upperhulme Mill, Nr. Leek; *Info@ roachesbunkhouse.com/*, T:01538300308; $18Bed, Kitchen:Y, B'fast:N, Pvt. room:N, Locker:N, Recep:7a/11p; Note: resto, parking, games, tea/coffee

2 Hostels) PLYMOUTH is a city of 250,000 comprised of historical villages, one of which sent Pilgrims to America in the 1600's, and later, some slaves. It was rebuilt after WWII, but Union Street is still the entertainment strip. There are events and festivals in the summer.

Globe Backpackers Plymouth, 172 Citadel Rd, The Hoe, Plymouth; *exeterbackpackers.co.uk/*, T:01752225158, *Info@ plymouthbackpackers.co.uk/*; $28Bed, Kitchen:Y, B'fast:N, Pvt.room:Y, Locker:N, Recep:4-11p; Note: laundry

St Rita Hotel, 76-78 Alma Rd, Plymouth, Devon; *stritahotel.co.uk/*, T:+44/1752667024, *stritahotel@googlemail.com*; $25Bed, Kitchen:N, B'fast:$, Pvt. room:N, Locker:N, Recep:2>11p; Note: ages 18-35

SALISBURY is a city of 40,000 only 85mi/137km from London. The big attraction is the Neolithic ruins of Stonehenge only 8mi/13km away. The cathedral holds a copy of the Magna Carta and Britain's oldest mechanical clock. Tuesdays and Sundays are market days, as they have been since 1227.

YHA Salisbury, Milford Hill, Salisbury, Wiltshire; T:08453719537, *Salisbury@ yha.org.uk/*; $30Bed, Kitchen:Y, B'fast:N, Pvt.room:Y, Locker:Y, Recep:1>11p; Note: resto/bar, games, parking, WiFi $

SHEFFIELD is a city of over a half million in north-central England. An industrial city, it is famous for its steel. It is also famous for its green spaces, and partially overlaps the boundaries of the Peaks District National Park.

Russell Scott Hostels, 28 Brandreth Rd, Sheffield, South Yorkshire; *rshostels.co.uk/*, T:+44/1142334691; $28Bed, Kitchen:Y, B'fast:Y, Pvt.room:Y, Locker:N, Recep:24/7; Note: luggage room, parking

STRATFORD-upon-Avon is a pleasant town of 25,000 in central England on the river Avon, and best known as the birthplace and burial place of Will.I.Am Shakespeare. The town and its tourist industry are pretty much based on serving those 3M tourists per year.

YHA Stratford upon Avon, Hemmingford House, Alveston, Stratford, Warwickshire, *Stratford@ yha.org.uk/*; T:08453719661; $25Bed, Kitchen:Y, B'fast:$, Pvt.room:Y, Locker:N, Recep:7a>11:30p; Note: resto/bar, parking, WiFi $

STREATLEY is a village of almost 1000 between Oxford and Reading and located on the River Thames across from Goring. A bridge connects the two. The Bull's got brew.

YHA Streatley, Reading Rd, Streatley, Berkshire; T:08453719044, *streatley@ yha.org.uk/*; $25Bed, Kitchen:Y, B'fast:$, Pvt.room:Y, Locker:N, Recep:8a//11p; Note: resto, parking, TV, water sports

SUFFOLK County shares easternmost England with Norfolk, the northern and southern Angles who went on to rule this land. Today it is mostly rural.

YHA Blaxhall, Old School House, Blaxhall, Woodbridge, Suffolk; T:08453719305, *blaxhall@ yha.org.uk/*; $22Bed, Kitchen:Y, B'fast:$, Pvt. room:Y, Locker:N, Recep:8a//10p; Note: resto, laundry, parking, games, wh/chair ok

SWANAGE is a town of 10,000 located on the south coast of England, and the eastern limit of the Jurassic Coast, so-called because its cliffs span 180 million years of history. The population swells in the summer peak tourist season.

YHA Swanage, Cluny, Cluny Crescent, Swanage, Dorset; T:08453719316, *swanage@ yha.org.uk/*; $26Bed, Kitchen:Y, B'fast:$, Pvt.room:Y, Locker:Y, Recep:7:15a>10:30p; Note: resto/bar, bikes, luggage rm, school kids have priority

WEYMOUTH is a town of over 50,000 on England's south Jurassic Coast. Once important for fishing and maritime trade, tourism now rules, with nature, festivals and shopping the main attractions. The annual mid-August carnival attracts around 70,000.

Bunkhouse Plus, 47 Walpole St, Weymouth, Dorset County; *bunkhouseplus. co.uk/*, T:+44/1305775228; $27Bed, Kitchen:Y, B'fast:N, Pvt.room:Y, Locker:N, Recep:ltd; Note: tour desk, tea/coffee

WHITBY is a town of 13,000 on England's North Sea, famous for its (black) jet jewelry. The abbey dates back to AD 657, and produced Caedmon, the first Anglo-Saxon poet.

YHA Whitby, Abbey House, East Cliff, Whitby, North Yorkshire; T:08453719049, *whitby@ yha.org.uk/*; $28Bed, Kitchen:Y, B'fast:$, Pvt.room:Y, Locker:N, Recep:7:30a>10:30p; Note: resto/bar, bag hold, parking, c.c. ok, historic

WINDERMERE is a town of over 8000 in the South Lakeland district of Cumbria, located a kilometer (half mile) from the lake of the same name. There are mountains, museums, and boats to sail around the lake.

YHA Windermere, Bridge Lane, Troutbeck, Windermere, Cumbria; T:08453719352, *windermere@ yha.org.uk/*; $25Bed, Kitchen:Y, B'fast:$, Pvt.room:Y, Locker:Y, Recep:7:30a>11p; Note: laundry, bag hold, meals $, long walk

4 Hostels) YORK is a walled city of 200,000 in north England, and long a center of the railways and confectionery industries. There were once many monasteries, which were dissolved by Henry VIII, causing the city's decline, and inspiring local boy Guy Fawkes' Gunpowder Plot. The historic core is now a major tourist destination. There is a castle.

YHA York, Water End, Clifton, York, North Yorkshire; T:08453719051, *york@ yha.org.uk/*; $25Bed, Kitchen:Y, B'fast:N, Pvt.room:Y, Locker:N, Recep:24/7; Note: resto, billiards, luggage room, parking, 10 min. walk to town

Ace York, 88-90 Micklegate, York, North Yorkshire; *reception@ acehotelyork. co.uk/*, T:+44/1904627720; $27Bed, Kitchen:Y, B'fast:Y, Pvt.room:Y, Locker:Y, Recep:24/7; Note: café/bar, bikes, billiards, laundry, bag hold, maps

The Fort Boutique Hostel, 1 Stonegate, York; T:01904639573; *Info@ thefortyork.co.uk/*; $23Bed, Kitchen:Y, B'fast:$, Pvt.room:Y, Locker:N, Recep: 8a>11:30p; Note: resto/bar, laundry, luggage room, tea/coffee, maps, central

The Bivouac Hostel, Masham, Ripon, York; *hello@ thebivouac.co.uk/*, T:01765535020; $33Bed, Kitchen:N, B'fast:$, Pvt.room:N, Locker:Y, Recep: 3>6:30p; Note: hot tub, resto/bar, parking, luggage, games, c.c. ok, 'quirky café'

2) Ireland

Like Great Britain, Ireland was connected by land to the continent of Europe when sea levels were lower and ice covered the land. There is evidence of agriculture here from 4000 BC and Bronze and Iron Age artifacts that indicate trade with the other Celtic countries of Britain and the continent. By the time of the Roman Empire, Ireland was thoroughly settled by Gaelic Celts. The Roman presence itself here was not significant, except for the Christian missionaries that came in the last days of Empire, especially Saint Patrick in 432 AD.

Thus was established a nation and culture of monks and saints and Roman scholars far superior to what remained in the Europe of Dark Age turbulence and migrations. Roman culture persisted in Ireland hundreds of years after it had been rendered asunder elsewhere, because of its very isolation. So when Charlemagne and his regime wanted to revive the Roman Empire on the Continent, they needed the learned men of Ireland to help them.

Vikings caused havoc in the ninth century, but their cousins the Frenchified Normans came to conquer and stay. Ultimately they did more staying than conquering, assimilating into the population despite efforts to prevent it. I guess the girls were cute. The English didn't get serious about conquering until the 17th century, and within a couple hundred years it was complete. Ireland joined the UK in 1801 and almost immediately started trying to undo it. Where Scotland, already purged of Catholics, arguably benefited from that union, for Ireland it was the opposite. 'Plantations' of English were unjust, as were laws favoring Protestants, and 1840 famine.

By then many people just wanted to leave. So they did, decimating a population that hasn't risen to that level again as of this day. The Industrial Revolution didn't help much, either. That was elsewhere. The rise of nationalism gave freedom to Ireland by 1920, minus Ulster. At least it spared Ireland the Nazi bombings. It wasn't until toward the end of the 20th century as Ireland joined the EU that things started looking better. Membership has its privileges, they say. We're still awaiting final fallout from the Great Recession of 2008.

Ireland has had some of the greatest writers of the English language while being the last bastion of the Gaelic language. It also has one of the largest ratios of hostels in the world, maybe *the largest*. Because of that, and the rural nature of the country and its many hostels, I'll divide them by counties. Ireland has a tradition of county affiliation and loyalty. Euro is currency; phone code is +353.

21 Hostels) DUBLIN is Ireland's capital and largest city. It was originally a Viking settlement, Celts not being especially citified, apparently. Normans were largely assimilated, and the city grew rapidly until union with the UK in 1801, when it stagnated and declined. Dublin Castle was the English stronghold since 1204, but their dominion was gradually reduced in size until it included not much more than Dublin. English domination was defined by a wooden perimeter called the "Pale."

Beyond the Pale, the country was still Irish. 1801 changed all that, as innovation and trade largely shifted to English-dominated Belfast. Dublin Castle is the premier landmark of Dublin, with Norse, Norman, and Georgian influences. Near it are Christ Church and St. Patrick's, both allowed to run down before being rebuilt in the 1800's. Ironically some of the finest monuments stand on the north riverbank, as do the city's poorest parts. Ireland's national theatre, the Abbey, is just east of O'Connell Street.

Today Dublin is a "Celtic tiger" on a good day, its fate largely tied to Europe as a whole at this point. Literarily, it is unmatched in the world, with writers like Joyce, Swift, Yeats, Shaw, Beckett and Wilde in its history. Theatre and art aren't bad, either, including "underground" genres. Music is both traditional and modern, so that means string bands and U2. It is also one of the prime party centers of Europe. This is the center of the pub culture which has been spread throughout much of the world, along with its great beers: Guiness, Murphy's, Watney's, and all the rest. Hostels are generally good quality and tend to be in and around the Temple Bar area, Dublin's medieval district, the better for drinking, I reckon.

The Times Hostel-College St., 8 College St., Ranelagh, Dublin 2; T:016729028, *college@ timeshostels.com/*; $14bed, Kitchen:Y, B'fast:Y, Pvt. room:Y, Locker:N, Recep:24/7; Note: bag hold, pub crawl, laundry, by Temple Bar, tours

Times Hostels-Camden Place, 8 Camden Pl, Dublin 2; T:014758588, *camden@ timeshostels.com/*; $13bed, Kitchen:Y, B'fast:Y, Pvt. room:Y, Locker:N, Recep:24/7; Note: café, not ctr, laundry, arpt shuttle, luggage rm, hugs, tours, tea/cof

Generator Hostel-Dublin, Smithfield Square, Dublin 7; T:019010222, *dublin@ generatorhostels.com/*, $14bed, Kitchen:N, B'fast:Y, Pvt.room:Y, Locker:Y, Recep:24/7; Note: café, billiards, wh/chair, laundry, bag hold, bar, tours, "like a hotel"

Kinlay House-Dublin, 2-12 Lord Edward St, Temple Bar, Dublin 2; T:016796644, *info@ kinlaydublin.ie*; $17bed, Kitchen:Y, B'fast:Y, Pvt.room:Y, Locker:N, Recep:24/7; Note: bar, café, billiards, TV, tours, arpt trans, laundry

Abraham House, 83 Lower Gardiner St. I.F.S.C., Dublin 1; T:018550600, *stay@ abraham-house.ie/*; $14bed, Kitchen:Y, B'fast:Y, Pvt.room:Y, Locker:N, Recep:24/7; Note: arpt bus stop, big place, central, luggage room, tour desk, tea/coffee

Oliver St. John Gogarty, 21 Anglesea St, Ranelagh, D2, T:016711022, *info@ gogartys.ie/*; $17bed, Kitchen:Y, B'fast:Y, Pvt.room:Y, Locker:Y, Recep:24/7; Note: bar, café/club, wh/chair ok, lift, laundry, tour desk, parking, tea/coffee, luggage room

Abigail's Hostel, 7-9 Aston Quay, Dublin 2; T:016779007, *stay@ abigailshostel. com/*; $14bed, Kitchen:Y, B'fast:Y, Pvt.room:Y, Locker:N, Recep:24/7; Note: c.c. ok, Temple Bar area, lift, luggage room, tea/coffee, books, maps

Barnacles Temple Bar House, 19 Temple Lane S, Rathmines, Dublin 2; T:016716277, *templebar@ barnacles.ie/*; $21bed, Kitchen:Y, B'fast:Y, Pvt.room:Y, Locker:Y, Recep:24/7; Note: arpt trans, laundry, bag hold, tea/coffee, tour desk

Sky Backpackers-The Liffey, 2-4 Litton Lane, Dublin 1; *skybackpackers. com/*, T:018728389; $13bed, Kitchen:Y, B'fast:Y, Pvt.room:Y, Locker:N, Recep:24/7; Note: tours, c.c. ok, close to Temple Bar, bag hold, tea/coffee

Harrington House, 21 Harrington, Dublin; T:014754008, *harringtonhousedublin. weebly.com/*, $28Bed, *Harrington.house@gmail.com*; Kitchen:Y, B'fast:Y, Pvt. room:Y, Locker:N, Recep:ltd; Note: bikes, bag hold, basic

Jacobs Inn, 28 Talbot Pl, Dublin, *jacobsinn.com/*, T:018555660, *jacobs@ isaacs.ie*; $20Bed, Kitchen:Y, B'fast:Y, Pvt.room:Y, Locker:Y, Recep:24/7; Note: arpt trans, lift, wh/chair OK, billiards, bikes, laundry, bag hold

Ashfield House, 20 D'Olier St, Dublin 2, *ashfieldhouse.ie/*, T:016797734, *ashfield@indigo.ie*; $14Bed, Kitchen:Y, B'fast:Y, Pvt.room:Y, Locker:Y, Recep:24/7; Note: lift, luggage room, maps, books, coffee/tea, central

Avalon House, Aungier St, Dublin 2; T:+353/14750001, *Info@ avalon-house.ie/*; $20Bed, Kitchen:Y, B'fast:Y, Pvt.room:Y, Locker:Y, Recep:24/7; Note: arpt trans, luggage room, billiards, bikes, books, laundry, tour desk

Isaacs Hostel, 2-5 Frenchman's Ln, Dublin 1, T:018556215, *hostel@ isaacs. ie/*; $20Bed, Kitchen:Y, B'fast:Y, Pvt.room:Y, Locker:Y, Recep:24/7; Note: arpt trans, wh/chair ok, billiards, bikes, books, laundry, luggage room, tours, forex

Four Courts Hostel, 15-17 Merchant's Quay, Dublin 8; T:+353/16725839, *Info@ fourcourtshostel.com/*, $17Bed, Kitchen:Y, B'fast:Y, Pvt.room:Y, Locker:Y, Recep:24/7; Note: arpt trans, lift, central, pool, billiards, laundry, luggage rm, tours

Abbey Court, 29 Bachelors Walk, Dublin, *abbey-court.com/*; T:018780700, $14Bed, Kitchen:Y, B'fast:Y, Pvt.room:Y, Locker:Y, Recep:24/7; Note: arpt trans, café, billiards, tours bikes, parking, a/c, minimart, tea/coffee, nr Temple Bar

Paddy's Palace Dublin, 5 Beresford Place, Lower Gardiner St, Dublin 1; *paddyspalace.com/*, T:+353/18881756; $14Bed, Kitchen:Y, B'fast:Y, Pvt.room:Y, Locker:Y, Recep:24/7; Note: arpt trans, luggage room, tour desk, tea/coffee

Globetrotters/The Townhouse, 48 Gardiner St Lower, Dublin 1; T:018735893, *Info@ globetrottersdublin.com/*; $17Bed, Kitchen:Y, B'fast:$, Pvt. room:Y, Locker:Y, Recep:24/7; Note: lift, laundry, luggage room, tour desk, parking

Mount Eccles Court, 42 North Great George's St, Dublin 1, *reservations@ eccleshostel.com/*, T:+353/18730826; $13Bed, Kitchen:Y, B'fast:$, Pvt.room:Y, Locker:Y, Recep:24/7; Note:arpt trans, billiards, luggage rm, maps, prkng, central

Spire Hostel, 90-93 Marlborough St, Dublin, T:018734173, *reservations@ spirehostel.com/*; $17Bed, Kitchen:Y, B'fast:Y, Pvt.room:Y, Locker:Y, Recep:24/7; Note: arpt trans, billiards, books, bag hold, tour desk, central, long-stays

Marina House, 7 Old Dunleary Rd, Dublin, T:+353/12841524, *Info@ marinahostel.com/*; $22Bed, Kitchen:Y, B'fast:Y, Pvt.room:Y, Locker:Y, Recep:12n>10p; Note: maps, luggage room, tours, parking, nr ferry, not central

County Cavan

CAVAN is a town of 3600 in the far north near the Ulster border, built up around a 13th century castle.

Lakeside Hostel, Rosduff, Arvagh Rd, Aughnacliffe, Cavan; *lakesidehostel. com/*, T:0494335533, *lakesidehostel@hotmail.com*; $20Bed, Kitchen:Y, B'fast:Y,Pvt. room:Y, Locker:Y, Recep:12m>9p; Note: cash, laundry, gym, billiards

County Clare

10 Hostels) CLIFFS OF MOHER are a geological spectacle in Ireland's western County Clare and one of Ireland's most popular tourist attractions. KILFENORA is a village of 170, with ruined cathedral, just south of THE BURREN, a badlands-like karst landscape and national park. KILRUSH is a town of 2700 with a history that dates from the 16th century. ENNIS is a city of more than 20,000 in Ireland's western County Clare, on the River Fergus, only

12mi/19km from Shannon airport. It is a center of traditional music. Saturday is market day, including much that is organic. Computer use is promoted.

CLARE ISLAND lies off Ireland's west coast and has a population of 125. It is traditional home to the O'Malley family, including the pirate queen Grainne O'Malley. There is an abbey with medieval roof paintings. MILLTOWN MALBAY is one of the newer towns of the region, less than 200 years old, with a current population of 600. LAHINCH is a village of 600 best known for its golfing, though surfing is catching up. SHANNON is a new planned town, suburb of Limerick, best-known for its airport and foreign trade zone, current population almost ten thousand.

Jamaica Inn, Sixmilebridge, Co. Clare, Shannon; T:061369377; *Info@ jamaicainn.ie/*$28Bed, Kitchen:Y, B'fast:$, Pvt.room:Y, Locker:N, Recep:8:30a>10p; Note: cafe, tours, billiards, wh/chair, bag hold, parking, nr arpt

Clare's Rock Hostel, Carron, The Burren, Co. Clare; *info@ claresrock.com/*; T:+353/657089129; $28Bed, Kitchen:Y, B'fast:$, Pvt.room:Y, Locker:N, Recep:ltd; Note: bikes, billiards, wh/chair ok, laundry, tours, luggage rm, books, tea/cof

Lahinch Hostel, Church St, Clare, Lahinch; T:+353(0)657081040, *info@ lahinchhostel.ie/*; $21Bed, Kitchen:Y, B'fast:Y, Pvt.room:Y, Locker:N, Recep:4-10p; Note: bikes, laundry, luggage room, parking, tea/coffee, central, beach

West Coast Lodge, Station Road, Co Clare, Lahinch; T:0657082000, *lahinchaccommodation.com/*, $21Bed, *westcoastlodge@icloud.com*; Kitchen:N, B'fast:Y, Pvt.room:Y, Locker:N, Recep:8a>11p; Note: resto, bikes, tour desk

The Central Hostel, Main St, Milltown Malbay, Ennis, Co. Clare; *centralhostelclare.com/*, T:+353/657084754, *kellycentral@eircom.net*; $21Bed, Kitchen:N, B'fast:Y, Pvt.room:Y, Locker:Y, Recep:24/7; Note: resto/bar, central

Go Explore Hostel, Westport, Clare Island, T:+353/874108706, *stay@ goexplorehostel.ie/*; $25Bed, Kitchen:Y, B'fast:Y, Pvt.room:N, Locker:N, Recep:ltd; Note: resto/bar, billiards, tour desk, laundry, parking, tea/coffee, c.c. ok, trad music

Rowan Tree Hostel, Harmony Row, Ennis, Co. Clare, T:+353/656868687, *Info@ rowantreehostel.ie*; $20Bed, Kitchen:Y, B'fast:Y, Pvt.room:Y, Locker:Y,

Recep:24/7; Note:air trans, resto/bar, wh/chair ok, prkng, lift, laundry, luggage rm

Katie O Connors, 50 Frances St, Kilrush, Co. Clare, *katieshostel.com/*, T:+353/659051133; $28Bed, Kitchen:Y, B'fast:N, Pvt.room:Y, Locker:N, Recep:ltd; Note: local pubs w/ trad music, old bldg/old Eire

Kilfenora Hostel, Main St, Kilfenora, Co. Clare, T:+353/657088908, *enquiries@ kilfenorahostel.com/*; $28Bed, Kitchen:Y B'fast:Y Pvt.room:Y, Locker:Y Recep:ltd: Note: wh/chair ok, bag hold, tour desk, parking, trad music, eco-friendly

The Burren Hostel (Sleepzone), Lisdoonvarna, The Burren, Cliffs of Moher, T:+353/657074036, *Info@ sleepzone.ie/*, $21Bed, Kitchen:Y, B'fast:Y, Pvt.room:Y, Locker:N, Recep:9a//10p; Note: billiards, forex, tour desk, luggage rm, wh/chair ok

4 Hostels) DOOLIN is a village in the central west coast's County Clare that is a center for traditional music. There are also pubs, rock climbing, surfing, Doolin Cave, archeological sites, the Doolin Folk Music Festival, and ferries and boats to other spots.

Doolin Hostel, Fisher St, Doolin, Co. Clare, T:+353/872820587, *anthony@ doolinhostel.ie/*; $21Bed, Kitchen:Y, B'fast:Y, Pvt.room:Y, Locker:N, Recep:ltd; Note: resto, laundry, coffee/tea, luggage rm, tour desk, parking, forex, minimart, nr ferries

Aille River Hostel, Doolin, Co. Clare, *stay@ ailleriverhosteldoolin. ie/*; T:+353/657074260; $20Bed, Kitchen:Y, B'fast:$, Pvt.room:Y, Locker:Y, Recep:>8:30p; Note: luggage room, parking, laundry, tea, trad music

Rainbow Hostel Doolin, Doolin, Co. Clare, *rainbowhostel.net/*, T:0657074415, *rainbowhostel@eircom.net*; $20Bed, Kitchen:Y, B'fast:N, Pvt.room:Y, Locker:Y, Recep:>10p; Note: bikes, luggage rm, laundry, parking, tours

Flanagan's Village Hostel, Doolin, Co. Clare, *enquiries@ flanaganshostel. com/*, T:+353/657074564; $20Bed, Kitchen:Y, B'fast:Y, Pvt.room:Y, Locker:N, Recep:ltd; Note: laundry, parking, tea/coffee, cash only, trad. music

County Cork

4 Hostels) CORK is Ireland's SXSW county, a SW corner it shares with Kerry. BALTIMORE is a village of 377 at Ireland's southernmost tip. There are many summer homes and scuba diving is popular because of the many shipwrecks in the area. KINSALE is a fishing village of 2200 whose population increases substantially in the summer tourist season. There are water-based activities, antiquity, and a jazz festival, in addition to its status as a 'transition' town, discussing ways to deal with peak oil and climate change; sounds good. MIDLETON is twin city to Cork, with population 10,000.

An Stór Midleton Tourist Hostel, Drury's Ave, Midleton, Co. Cork; *stay@ anstor.ie/*, T:0214633106; $25Bed, Kitchen:Y, B'fast:N, Pvt.room:N, Locker:N, Recep:ltd; Note: resto, wh/chair, laundry, luggage room, parking, tea/coffee

Top of the Hill Hostel, 1 Freke Terrace, Baltimore, West Cork; *topofthehillhostel.com/*, T:0877431585, *topofthehillhostel@online.ms;* $25Bed, Kitchen:Y, B'fast:$, Pvt.room:Y, Locker:N, Recep:ltd; Note: tea/coffee, water sports

Joys Accommodation, 21 Cork St, Kinsale; *joysaccommodation.com/*, T:0879694792 *joyalwell@eircom.net*, $26Bed, Kitchen:Y, B'fast:$, Pvt.room:Y, Locker:N, Recep:ltd (advise ETA); Note: books, maps, luggage room, tea/coffee

Dempseys Hostel Kinsale, Eastern Rd, Kinsale, Co. Cork, *hostelkinsale. com/*, T:+353/214772124, *dandempseykinsale@gmail.com*; $21Bed, Kitchen:N, B'fast:$, Pvt.room:Y, Locker:N, Recep:ltd; Note: WiFi $, billiards, laundry

4 Hostels) CORK is in the far south of the island and is Ireland's second largest city. It is a city of culture and industry, considering itself as distinct from the rest of Ireland, the "Rebel County." Back in the early days of English aggression, it was one of their few outposts outside of Dublin, definitely "beyond the Pale." English residents in Cork used to pay "Black Rent" to the surrounding Gaels—for protection—from the surrounding Gaels. That sounds fair. Its famous products are Murphy's Irish Stout and Viagra.

Culture is to be found in the Crawford municipal art gallery, the Cork Opera House, the Triskel arts centre, the Cork Public Museum, and many art galleries. The city is also home to the long-established Guinness Jazz Festival.

Landmarks are the Protestant cathedral of St. Fin Barre and the Roman Catholic St. Mary's Cathedral. There is a covered market.

Bru Bar & Hostel, 57 MacCurtain St, Cork, Co. Cork; T:0214501074, *info@ bruhostel.com/*; $20bed, Kitchen:Y, B'fast:Y, Pvt.room:N, Locker:N, Recep:24/7; Note: bar, TV, tours, bag hold, laundry, c.c. ok, near bus/center

Sheilas Hostel, 4 Belgrave Place, Wellington Rd, Cork; **T:0214505562,** *info@ sheilashostel.ie/***;** $21bed, Kitchen:Y, B'fast:$, Pvt.room:Y, Locker:N, Recep:24/7; Note: restaurant, sauna, laundry, tour desk, forex, c.c. ok, near bus, uphill

Kinlay House Cork, Bob and Joan's Walk, Shandon, Cork City; T:0214508966, *info@ kinlayhousecork.ie/*; $20bed, Kitchen:Y, B'fast:Y, Pvt.room:Y, Locker:N, Recep:24/7; Note: luggage room, laundry, forex, c.c. ok

Cork International Hostel, 1 Red Cliff, Western Rd, Cork; T:0214543289, *info@ anoige.ie/*; $16bed, Kitchen:Y, B'fast:$, Pvt.room:Y, Locker:N, Recep:ltd; Note: member discount, restaurant, bag hold, c.c. ok, call after 5pm

County Donegal

LETTERKENNY, with almost 20,000 people, is the big city and market town of the county. They have hosted traditional music festivals and Pan-Celtic festivals. Market Square rocks every day. Main Street rocks every night.

Apple Hostel Letterkenny, Covehill, Port Rd, Letterkenny, Co. Donegal; T:0749113291, *Info@ letterkennyhostel.com/*; $21Bed, Kitchen:Y, B'fast:$, Pvt. room:Y, Locker:N, Recep:ltd; Note: lift, laundry, tea/coffee, central, Sky TV

5 Hostels) BUNDORAN is a town of 2140 on Ireland's far northwest coast. The boundaries of Ulster make access cumbersome. Surfing is popular these days.

Turfnsurf Lodge Bundoran, 6 W. End, Bundoran, Co. Donegal, T:+353/719841091, *Info@ turfnsurf.ie/*; $24Bed, Kitchen:Y, B'fast:Y, Pvt.room:Y, Locker:N, Recep:ltd; Note: parking, luggage room, seafront

Rougey Lodge, Bundoran Holiday Centre, Main St, Bundoran, Co. Donegal; T:0879959181, *Info@ rougeylodge.com/*; $21Bed, Kitchen:Y, B'fast:Y, Pvt.room:Y, Locker:N, Recep:8a>11p; Note: bikes, prkng, luggage rm, arpt trans

Donegal Bay Holiday Homes, Portbeg, Bundoran; T:0861739445; *Info@ donegalbayholidayhomes.com/*; $28Bed, Kitchen:Y, B'fast:$, Pvt.room:Y, Locker:N, Recep:2-7p; Note: parking, luggage room

Bundoran Surf Lodge, Main St, Bundoran, Co. Donegal, T:+353/719841968, *info@ bundoransurfco.com*; $28Bed, Kitchen:Y, B'fast:Y, Pvt.room:Y, Locker:N, Recep:ltd; Note: tea/coffee, parking, luggage room

Homefield Backpackers, Bayview Ave, Bundoran, T:0719829357, *Info@ homefieldbackpackers.com*, $28Bed, Kitchen:Y, B'fast:Y, Pvt.room:Y, Locker:N, Recep:24/7; Note: resto, tea/coffee, luggage rm, wh/chair OK, tours, music theme

7 Hostels) DONEGAL is a town of 2600 in that northern part of the Republic that is closer to Belfast than Dublin, and connected to the rest by only a thin strip of land along the coast. Fortunately the two states (and religions) cooperate now, so transport is not much of a problem. This is where St. Patrick made his first converts. Tweeds are woven here. There are beaches, and good surf. 'The Diamond' is the downtown hub for entertainment.

Donegal Town Independent Hostel, Doonan, Donegal Town, Co. Donegal; T:0749722805, *Info@ donegaltownhostel.com/*; $22Bed, Kitchen:Y, B'fast:$, Pvt. room:Y, Locker:N, Recep:ltd; Note: luggage rm, coffee/tea, parking, books

Tra Na Rossan, Co Donegal YHA, Downings; T:0749155374, $22bed

Errigal, Co Donegal YHA, Errigal, Dunlewy, Gweedore, Co Donegal; *hihostels.com/*, T:353/749531180, *info@anoige.ie*; $26Bed, Kitchen:Y, B'fast:$, Pvt. room:Y, Locker:Y, Recep:24/7; Note: wh/chair OK, lift, tour desk, prkng, bag hold

Corcreggan Mill, Dunfanaghy, Co. Donegal, *millhouse@ corcreggan.com/* T:0749136409, $25Bed, Kitchen:Y, B'fast:Y, Pvt.room:Y, Locker:N, Recep:ltd; Note: closed winter, bar, luggage room, tour desk, parking, beautiful countryside

Tullyarvan Mill Hostel Buncrana, Mill Lane, Buncrana, Inishowen, Donegal, T:+353(0)749361613, *Info@ tullyarvanmill.com/*, $21Bed, Kitchen:Y, B'fast:$, Pvt.room:Y, Locker:Y, Recep:>10p; Note: wh/chair OK, tours, prkng, bag hold

Sandrock Holiday Hostel, Port Ronan Pier, Malin Head, Co. Donegal; *Info@ sandrockhostel.com/*, T:0749370289; $17Bed, Kitchen:Y, B'fast:$, Pvt. room:N, Locker:N, Recep:>10p; Note: bikes, cash only, laundry, parking, wh/chair ok, tours

Fin McCool Surf Lodge, Main St, Rossnowlagh, Co. Donegal, *finmccoolsurfschool.com/*, T:0868049909, *finmccools@gmail.com*; $26Bed, Kitchen:Y, B'fast:N, Pvt.room:Y, Locker:N, Recep:ltd; Note: parking, luggage rm, beach

County Galway

4 Hostels) CONNEMARA is a loosely defined region in Ireland's western end of its western County Galway, and has the greatest concentration of Gaelic speakers in the country, maybe 75% of the 32,000 population. CLIFDEN is the main town. There is a national park.

Clifden Town Hostel, Market St, Connemara, Clifden; *clifdentownhostel. com/*, T:353/9521076, *seancth@eir.com*; $24Bed, Kitchen:Y, B'fast:N, Pvt. room:N, Locker:Y, Recep:ltd; Note: tour desk, luggage room, parking

The Connemara Hostel (Sleepzone), Leenane, Connemara, *Info@ sleepzone.ie/*, T/F:091566999; $21Bed, Kitchen:Y, B'fast:Y, Pvt.room:Y, Locker:Y, Recep:ltd; Note: bar, bikes, books, billiards, lift, laundry, parking, tour desk

Letterfrack Lodge, Letterfrack, Connemara, Co. Galway, *letterfracklodge. com/*, T:09541222, *letterfracklodge@iol.ie*; $24Bed, Kitchen:Y, B'fast:$, Pvt.room:Y, Locker:N, Recep:ltd; Note: wh/chair ok, laundry, luggage rm, natl park

The Bards Den, Letterfrack, Connemara, Co. Galway, T:+353/9541042; *Info@ bardsden.com/*; $21Bed, Kitchen:Y, B'fast:Y, Pvt.room:Y, Locker:N, Recep:ltd; Note: resto/bar, wh/chair, tour desk, parking, billiards, forex

9 Hostels) GALWAY is on the west coast of Ireland and has a reputation as its cultural heart. As such its percentage of Irish-language speakers is higher than elsewhere, around ten percent. Traditional music is big here, too. There are many festivals, Galway Arts Festival in July first and foremost among them. Portions of the old city walls remain. Historical architecture includes the remains of a Franciscan friary and St. Nicholas's Church, which dates from 1320.

Sleepzone, Bothar na mBan, Galway; T:091566999, *info@ sleepzone. ie/*; $20bed13, Kitchen:Y, B'fast:N, Pvt.room:Y, Locker:Y, Recep:24/7; Note: wheelchairs ok, lift, tour desk, luggage ok, forex, c.c. ok, central

Woodquay Hostel, 23/24 Woodquay, Galway; *woodquayhostel.ie/*, T:091562618; $20bed, Kitchen:Y, B'fast:N, Pvt.room:Y, Locker:N, Recep:24/7; Note: cash only, laundry, luggage room, parking, central, tea & coffee

Kinlay Eyre Square Hostel, Merchants Rd, Eyre Square, Galway, *info@ kinlaygalway.ie/*; T:091565244; $17Bed, Kitchen:Y, B'fast:Y, Pvt.room:Y, Locker:Y, Recep:24/7; Note: bikes, books, lift, luggage ok, tour desk, central

Barnacles Quay St Galway City, 10 Quay St, Latin Quarter, Galway; T:091568644; *galway@ barnacles.ie/*; $14Bed, Kitchen:Y, B'fast:Y, Pvt.room:Y, Locker:N, Recep:24/7; Note: maps, books, laundry, luggage room, tours, party dist.

Snoozles Hostel Galway, Forster St, Galway, *snoozleshostelgalway.ie/*, T:+353/91530064, *Info@snoozleshostel.ie/*; $14Bed, Kitchen:Y, B'fast:Y, Pvt. room:Y, Locker:Y, Recep:24/7; Note: arpt trans, lift, bikes, luggage rm, laundry

The Galway City Hostel, Eyre Square, Galway; *Info@ galwaycityhostel. com/*, T:+353/91566959; $14Bed, Kitchen:Y, B'fast:Y, Pvt.room:N, Locker:Y, Recep:24/7; Note: luggage room, books, tour desk, parking, central, long-stays

Salmon Weir Hostel, 3 St. Vincent Ave, Woodquay, Galway; *Info@ salmonweirhostel.com/*, T:+353/91561133; $17Bed, Kitchen:Y, B'fast:N, Pvt. room:Y, Locker:Y, Recep:>3a; Note: 3am curfew, bikes, luggage room, tours, parking

Oughterard Holiday Hostel/Angling Cntr, Station Rd, Oughterard, Co Galway; *oughterardhostel.com/*, T:091552388, *canrawer@indigo.ie/*; $25Bed, Kitchen:Y, B'fast:$, Pvt.room:Y, Locker:N, Recep:>11p; Note: luggage room, laundry

Nimmos Hostel, 1 Upper Dominick St, Galway; T:+353/91586661; *booking@ nimmoshostel.com/*; $14Bed, Kitchen:Y, B'fast:$, Pvt.room:N, Locker:N, Recep:ltd; Note: maps, books, luggage room, tea/coffee, basic

County Kerry

8 Hostels) COUNTY KERRY lies in Ireland's far southwest, known for its beauty and 'Ring of Kerry,' with lakes, beaches, walks, and legends.

KENMARE is a town of almost 2200 at the head of Kenmare Bay, and is the county's traditional market town and now holiday-home center. GLENBEIGH is a village of 1000 and the far southwest county's 'jewel' in fact, with the still-standing-castle, 'Wynne's Folly.' Check out Rossbeigh Beach, Glenbeigh Tower, and Coomasharn Lake. BALLINSKELLIGS is a Gaelic-speaking village of 350. CAHERSIVEEN is a town of 1400. WATERVILLE is a village of over 500 residents, and was a favorite of Charlie Chaplin. There is now a celebration here in his honor.

Silver Sands Hostel, Main St, Waterville, Co. Kerry, *silversandshostel.com/*, T:0863692283, *silversandshostel@gmail.com*; $24Bed, Kitchen:Y, B'fast:Y, Pvt. room:Y, Locker:N, Recep:24/7; Note: resto, laundry, tours, parking, tea/coffee

Bru na Dromoda (Dromid Hostel), Cillin Liath, Mastergeehy nr Waterville); *hosteldromidwaterville.com/*, T:+353(0)669474782; $21Bed, Kitchen:Y, B'fast:$, Pvt.room:Y, Locker:N, Recep:ltd; Note: cash only, noon checkout, parking, far

Caitin's, Gleesk, Cahersiveen, T:+353(0)669477614; *Info@ caitins.com/*, $21Bed, Kitchen:Y, B'fast:$, Pvt.room:Y, Locker:N, Recep:ltd; Note: bar, TV, forex, parking, view of bay, remote/need car, biscuits, entertainment

Sive Hostel, 15 E End, Cahersiveen, Co. Kerry; T:+353/669472717, *sivehostel.ie/*; $21Bed, Kitchen:Y, B'fast:Y, Pvt.room:Y, Locker:N, Recep:ltd; Note: luggage room

Skellig Hostel, Ballinskelligs, Ring of Kerry, Co. Kerry; T:0669479942, *Info@ skellighostel.com/*; $17Bed, Kitchen:Y, B'fast:$, Pvt.room:Y, Locker:N, Recep:ltd; Note: wh/chair ok, luggage room, tour desk, water sports

The Sleepy Camel, Glenbeigh, Co. Kerry; T:0669768660, *info@ thesleepycamel.com*; $31Bed, Kitchen:Y, B'fast:$, Pvt.room:Y, Locker:N, Recep:24/7; Note: bikes, wh/chair OK, lift, luggage room, tour desk, parking, central

Greenwood Hostel, Templenoe, Kenmare, *greenwoodhostel.com/*, T:0646689247, *greenwoodhostel@eircom.net/*; $25Bed, Kitchen:Y, B'fast:$, Pvt. room:Y, Locker:N, Recep:ltd; Note: luggage room, parking, hard find/need car

Kenmare Failte Hostel, Shelbourne St, Kenmare, Co. Kerry; *Info@ kenmarehostel.com/*, T:+353/646642333; $25Bed, Kitchen:Y, B'fast:$, Pvt.room:Y, Locker:N, Recep:2-7p; Note: 1:30a curfew, bikes, laundry, parking, coffee/tea

HI Black Valley Hostel, Nr Beaufort, Gap of Dunloe, Kerry; T:06434712

HI Dun Chaoin Hostel, Dunquin, Kerry, Ballyferriter, Tralee, Co Kerry *hihostels.com/*, T:+353/669156121, *info@anoige.ie*; $22Bed, Kitchen:Y, B'fast:N, Pvt.room:Y, Locker:N, Recep:9a//10p; Note: lockout, laundry, luggage rm, parking

7 Hostels) DINGLE is a town of 1920 in the far southwest Gaelic region. It is historically a port town, though tourism is now important. There is a neo-Gothic church and much Irish music to be had with beers. There is also an Oceanworld Aquarium. There are also linguistic duals (pun) over which language for them (and the tourists) to use.

The Hideout Hostel, Dykegate St, Dingle, Co. Kerry, T:0669150559, *info@ thehideouthostel.com/*; $22Bed, Kitchen:Y, B'fast:Y, Pvt.room:Y, Locker:Y, Recep:ltd; Note: arpt trans, resto, tour desk, parking, tea/coffee, luggage rm, central

Dingle Gate Hostel, The Mall, Annascaul, Dingle, T:0669157150, *info@ dinglegatehostel.com/*; $17Bed, Kitchen:Y, B'fast:Y, Pvt.room:Y, Locker:N, Recep:24/7; Note: billiards, tours, laundry, prkng, wh/chair ok, luggage rm

Rainbow Hostel Dingle, Dingle, Co. Kerry; T:+353(0)669151044, *Info@ rainbowhosteldingle.com/*; $22Bed, Kitchen:Y, B'fast:$, Pvt.room:Y, Locker:Y, Recep:ltd; Note: farm, no parties, wh/chair ok, tours, laundry, prkng, luggage rm

Lovett's Hostel, Cooleen, Dingle, *dingle-region.com/dinglehostel.htm/*; T:+353(0)669151903, *dinglehostel@hotmail.com*; $20Bed, Kitchen:Y, B'fast:$, Pvt. room:Y, Locker:N, Recep:ltd; Note: central, bikes, parking

Muiris Dan's Pub & Accommodation, John St, Dingle, *muirisdansdingle. com/*, T:0860785575, *muirisdans@gmail.com*; $25Bed, Kitchen:Y, B'fast:$, Pvt. room:N, Locker:N, Recep:ltd; Note: bar, billiards, bag hold, tea/coffee

Dingle Esk Tower View Hostel, Mail Road, Dingle, T:0667199026, *kerryhostels.ie/dingle-esk-view/*; $28Bed, Kitchen:Y, B'fast:$, Pvt.room:Y, Locker:N, Recep:12m>9p; Note: billiards, laundry, tour desk, parking, tea/coffee

Paddy's Palace - Dingle Peninsula, Main Street, Annascaul; T:08230822, *paddyspalace.com/annascaulhostel.php/*; $14Bed, Kitchen:N, B'fast:Y, Pvt.room:N, Locker:N, Recep:4>8p; Note:resto/bar, pool, billiards, wh/chair OK, parking

7 Hostels) KILLARNEY is a town of 14,000 and one of the oldest tourist destinations in Ireland, dating to 1750. The "ring of Kerry" is the main attraction, a 100-plus mile tour of local scenery, which has several variations on the basic theme of a pretty place that can be driven, biked, or hiked. Its first settlement was a monastery mid-first millennium at nearby Aghadoe, and the Normans built Parkavonear Castle there, also. Killarney was strongly Republican in the Irish War of Independence, and atrocities occurred nearby. It's better now. The town rocks in summer. Killarney Summerfest is especially nice, with major musical acts.

Neptune's Town Hostel, New St., Killarney; *neptuneshostel.com/*, T:0646635255, *neptunes@eircom.net*; $14bed, Kitchen:Y, B'fast:Y, Pvt.room:Y, Locker:Y, Recep:ltd; Note: wh/chair OK, luggage rm, laundry, tour desk

Paddy's Palace Killarney, 31 New St, Killarney, *paddyspalace.com*; T:06435382; $11bed, Kitchen:Y, B'fast:Y, Pvt.room:Y, Locker:N, Recep:>8p; Note: central, street parking free, close to Natl. Park

Railway Hostel, Dennehy's Rd, Fair Hill, Killarney, Co. Kerry; T:064635299, *info@ killarneyhostel.com/*; $14bed, Kitchen:Y, B'fast:Y, Pvt. room:Y, Locker:N, Recep:24/7; Note: nr train/bus, wheelchairs ok, bag hold, laundry, tours, prkng

Killarney Intl. An Oige, Aghadoe House, Fossa, Killarney; T:0646631240, *info@anoige.ie*; $14bed, Kitchen:Y, B'fast:$, Pvt.room:Y, Locker:N, Recep:8a>9p; Note: resto, laundry, tour desk, bikes, not central, big park

Killarney Sugan Hostel, Michael Collins Place, Lewis Rd, Killarney, *info@ suganhostelkillarney.com/*, T:0646633104; $21Bed, Kitchen:Y, B'fast:Y, Pvt. room:Y, Locker:N, Recep:9a>9p; Note: bikes, luggage room, tour desk, central

Fossa Holiday Hostel, Fossa, Killarney, Co. Kerry, T:+353(0)646631497, *fossacampingkillarney.com/*, $14Bed, *fossaholidays@eircom.net*; Kitchen:Y, B'fast:$, Pvt.room:N, Locker:N, Recep:ltd; Note: rural park w/ camping, hiking, horses

Dunloe View Hostel, Gortacollopa, Fossa, Killarney, Co. Kerry; *Info@ dunloeviewhostel.ie/*, T:0646644187; $24Bed, Kitchen:Y, B'fast:Y, Pvt.room:Y, Locker:N, Recep:3:30p>8p; Note: bikes, laundry, tour desk, luggage rm, animals

4 Hostels) TRALEE is a city of almost 24,000 and an all-weather tourist destination, with museum, aquadome, and folk theater.

Bibis Hostel, Boherbee, Tralee, *Info@ bibishostel.com/*, T:0667122674; $20Bed, Kitchen:Y, B'fast:Y, Pvt.room:Y, Locker:N, Recep: ltd; Note: bikes, luggage room, tour desk, parking

Castle Hostel, 27 Upper Castle St Tralee, Co. Kerry, T:+353/667125167, *reception@ castlehostel.ie/*; $17Bed, Kitchen:Y, B'fast:Y, Pvt.room:Y, Locker:Y, Recep: 24/7; Note: arpt trans, bikes, minimart, luggage rm, tours, parking, central

The White House Accommodation, Boherbee, Tralee; T:+353/667102780, *welcome@ whitehousetralee.com/*; $21Bed, Kitchen:Y, B'fast:N, Pvt.room:Y, Locker:N, Recep:ltd; Note: pub w/music, maps, tea/coffee, central

Tralee Holiday Lodge, Mary Street, Tralee, Co Kerry; T:0667180081, *Info@ traleeholidaylodge.com/*, $24Bed, Kitchen:N, B'fast:Y, Pvt.room:Y, Locker:Y, Recep:ltd; Note: pool, bikes, luggage room, parking

County Kilkenny
4 Hostels) KILKENNY is only 60mi/100km south of Dublin, so an easy getaway to experience Ireland's more traditional culture. With Norman and monastic roots, these days Irish music and pub culture are main attractions. Arts and crafts are abundant and there are many festivals, such as the Rhythm and Roots Festival in May and the Arts festival in August. Kilkenny Castle is refurbished and open to view. Other historical landmarks are St. Canice's Cathedral, the Roman Catholic Cathedral of St. Mary, the churches of St. Mary and St. John, The Tholsel, Shee's Almshouse, and Grace's Old Castle. Kilkenny Ale is brewed here.

Kilkenny Tourist Hostel, 35 Parliament St, Kilkenny; T:0567763541, *info@ kilkennyhostel.ie*; $20bed, Kitchen:Y, B'fast:N, Pvt.room:N, Locker:Y, Recep:ltd; Note: laundry, luggage room, safe deposit, central

Lanigan's Hostel, Rose Inn St, Kilkenny; T:(0)567721718, *info@ hostelkilkenny.ie/*; $22bed, Kitchen:Y, B'fast:$, Pvt.room:Y, Locker:Y, Recep:24/7; Note: resto/bar, wheelchairs ok, luggage room, laundry, a/c, c.c. ok

The Metropole, High St, Kilkenny; *Info@ themetropolekilkenny.com/,* T:+353/567763778; $20Bed, Kitchen:N, B'fast:Y, Pvt.room:Y, Locker:N, Recep:2-10p; Note: café/bar, maps, central, basic

Macgabhainns Backpackers Hostel, 24 Vicar St, Kilkenny; T:0567770970, *macgabhainnsbackpackers.com,* $21Bed, *hostelvicarstreet@live.ie*; Kitchen:Y, B'fast:Y, Pvt.room:Y, Locker:Y, Recep:10a>10p; Note: bikes, gym, laundry, luggage rm, prkng

County Louth

CARLINGFORD is a town of 1000 in the northeast, and the site of previous Norman penetration. Today it is one of the few towns with medieval characteristics, including the original King John's Castle, Taaffe's Castle, the town gate, the mint, the town wall, Church of the Holy Trinity, and market square. There is an oyster festival in August.

Carlingford Adventure Centre, Tholsel St, Carlingford, Co. Louth, T:+353(0)429373100, *info@ carlingfordadventure.com*; $21Bed, Kitchen:N, B'fast:N, Pvt.room:Y, Locker:N, Recep:24/7; Note: luggage room, central

County Mayo

6 Hostels) ACHILL is an island off Ireland's west coast, population 2700, and attached to the mainland by bridge. People have apparently been here 4-5000 years. It is mostly peat bog. There is a Deserted Village of houses abandoned during the 1845 famine. BELMULLET is a village of over 1000 people in the Gaelic-speaking northwest. There are notable festivals in the summer including the Gaesala Festival in August. CONG is a village of a few hundred surrounded by streams. KNOCK is a village of 600 whose shrine to the Virgin Mary is a major Catholic pilgrimage site. WESTPORT is a heritage town of over 5500, unique in that it was planned, by James Wyatt, in the 18th century. For its charm and lively entertainment, it is one of Ireland's

most popular tourist destinations. Events include Westport Arts Festival the first week of October, Westport music festival in July and Westport Bluegrass Festival in June.

The Oldmill Holiday Hostel, Barrack Yard, James St, Westport, Co. Mayo; *oldmillhostel.com/*, T:+353/9827045, *oldmillhostel@gmail.com*; $21Bed, Kitchen:Y, B'fast:Y, Pvt.room:N, Locker:N, Recep:ltd; Note: wh/chair OK, laundry

Abbeywood Hostel, Abbeywood, Newport Rd, County Mayo, Westport; *Info@ abbeywoodhouse.com*, T:+353/9825496; $28Bed, Kitchen:Y, B'fast:Y, Pvt. room:Y, Locker:Y, Recep:ltd; Note: parking, central, ex-monastery

Valleylodge Farm Hostel, Facefield, Claremorris, Knock, Co. Mayo; *valleylodgeaccommodation.com/*, T:+353/949365180, *valleylodge@eircom.net*; $21Bed, Kitchen:Y, B'fast:Y, Pvt.room:Y, Locker:N, Recep:24/7; Note: wh/chair ok

Cong, Co Mayo YHA, Lisoughrey, Quay Rd, Cong, Co Mayo; *hihostels. com/*, T:+353/18822577, *info@anoige.ie*; $24Bed, Kitchen:N, B'fast:N, Pvt. room:Y, Locker:Y, Recep:ltd; Note: bikes, wh/chair, forex, laundry

Kilcommon Lodge, Pullathomas, Belmullet, Co. Mayo; T:+353/9784621, *Info@ kilcommonlodge.ie/*, $24Bed, Kitchen:Y, B'fast:$, Pvt.room:Y. Locker:N, Recep:ltd; Note: billiards, laundry, parking, tea/coffee, quiet, nature

Valley House, Achill Island, Co. Mayo, *info@ valley-house.com/*, T:+353/9847204; $22Bed, Kitchen:Y, B'fast:Y, Pvt.room:Y, Locker:N, Recep:ltd; Note: bar, bikes, billiards, luggage room, parking, remote: car helps, island

County Meath

NEWGRANGE is a UNESCO world heritage and archeological site known for its rock art and dating from the Neolithic Age, about 3200 BC, so older than Stonehenge or the Egyptian pyramids.

Newgrange Lodge, Donore, Newgrange; T:353/419882478, *Info@ newgrangelodge.com/*; $22Bed, Kitchen:Y, B'fast:Y, Pvt.room:Y, Locker:N, Recep:24/7; Note: bikes, wh/chair OK, tour desk, luggage room, parking

County Sligo

4 Hostels) SLIGO is a city of almost 20,000 in the county of the same name, on the west coast and Ulster's border. Sligo Live happens every October. Nightlife is good.

Harbour House, Finisklin Rd, Sligo, *harbourhousehostel.com/* T:+353/719171547, *harbourhouse@eircom.net;* $21Bed, Kitchen:Y, B'fast:Y, Pvt.room:Y, Locker:N, Recep:2-9p; Note: luggage room, parking, tour desk, cof/tea

ArrowRock Lodge, Ballynary, nr Castlebaldwin, Lough Arrow, Co. Sligo, T:353/719666073, *info@ arrowrocklodge.com/;* $21Bed, Kitchen:Y, B'fast:$, Pvt. room:Y, Locker:N, Recep:ltd; Note: billiards, bikes, laundry, parking, views

Benwiskin Centre, Ballintrillick, Co. Sligo; T/F:0719176721, *info@ benwiskincentre.com/;* $21Bed, Kitchen:Y, B'fast:N, Pvt.room:Y, Locker:Y, Recep:9-5; Note: bikes, wh/chair ok, laundry, eco-friendly, remote/need car, near sea

Gyreum, Corlisheen, Castlebaldwin, Co Sligo; T:+353/871388945, *info@ gyreum.com/;* $21Bed, Kitchen:N, B'fast:$, Pvt.room:Y, Locker:N, Recep:>9p; Note: wh/chair ok, tour desk, parking, hard find/remote/need car, cat, basic

County Tipperary

2 Hostels) TIPPERARY is a town of 4400 and county of the same name in south-central Ireland, a historical center of agriculture and markets. This is the heartland of the country. CASHEL is a town of almost 3000. The main attraction is the Rock of Cashel, the first millernnium castle itself, whose oldest structure dates from 1100. There is also a folk village.

Cashel Hostel, 6 John St, Cashel, Co. Tipperary; T:+353/6262330, *Info@ cashelhostel.com/;* $17Bed, Kitchen:Y, B'fast:N, Pvt.room:Y, Locker:Y, Recep:ltd; Note: bikes, laundry, luggage room, parking, books, maps

Fairy Fort Farm, O'Donnell's Farm, Summerhill, Borrisoleigh, Tipperary, *Info@ fairyfortfarm.com/,* T:+353/864021659; $21Bed, Kitchen:Y, B'fast:N, Pvt. room:Y, Locker:N, Recep:ltd; Note: pool, parking, remote, farm animals

County Waterford

TRAMORE is a city of more than 10,000, originally a southeast coast fishing village turned seaside resort, now gaining popularity as a surfers' strand.

Beach Haven Hostel, Tivoli Terrace, Tramore; T:+353/51390208, *Info@ beachhavenhouse.com/*; $24Bed, Kitchen:Y, B'fast:$, Pvt.room:Y, Locker:Y, Recep:ltd; Note: luggage room, parking, water sports

3 Hostels) WATERFORD is a city of 47,000 — one of Ireland's largest — and originally established by the Vikings, vestiges of which still remain. Notable edifices include the Viking Triangle of museums, Reginald's Tower, Waterford Municipal Art Gallery, The Theatre Royal, and Garter Lane Arts Centre. Events include the Waterford Music Fest, the Spraoi festival of theater, Waterford Festival of Light Opera, Waterford Harvest Food Festival, a St. Patrick's Day Parade, two Arts Festivals, and Waterford Winterval. Enjoy.

Portree Hostel, 10 Mary St, Waterford, T:+353/51874574, *Info@ portreehostel. ie/*; $32Bed, Kitchen:Y, B'fast:$, Pvt.room:N, Locker:Y, Recep:>7:30p; Note: pool, luggage room, parking, nr bus/train

Comeragh Hostel, Fews, Kilnagrange, Kilmacthomas, Waterford; *comeraghhostel.com/* T:+353/51294147; $25Bed, Kitchen:Y, B'fast:$, Pvt. room:Y, Locker:N, Recep:ltd; Note: bikes, luggage room, parking, working farm, hard find

Tom's Hostel Ireland, Rathkieran, Mooncoin, Waterford; T:353/868241124, *tomshostelireland.com*, $20Bed, *tomshostelireland@gmail.com*; Kitchen:N, B'fast:$, Pvt.room:Y, Locker:N, Recep:10a>11:30p; Note: bikes, shuttle, laundry, luggage rm

County Wexford

WEXFORD is a city of 20,000 and county of the same name in the country's southeast. Founded in 800AD by Vikings, they ruled for 300 years. The antique Yola dialect was spoken until recently.

Beaches Youth Hostel, Sandylane, Seamount, Gorey, Co Wexford; T:+353(0)877994214, *marie@ beachesyouthhostel.com/*; $22Bed, Kitchen:Y,

B'fast:$, Pvt.room:N, Locker:N, Recep:4-10p; Note: cash only, hot tub, laundry, tea/cof

County Wicklow
4 Hostels) WICKLOW is a city of over 10,000 and county of the same name on Ireland's east coast, therefore fair game for the Vikings of the Middle Ages. An important port, it is also increasingly a commuter town in the Dublin orbit.

Captain Halpins Bunkhouse, Bachelors Walk, Wicklow, Co. Wicklow; T:+353/40469126, *info@ wicklowtownhostel.ie/*; $17Bed, Kitchen:Y, B'fast:$, Pvt. room:Y, Locker:Y, Recep:ltd; Note: tour desk, tea/coffee, books, maps

The Old Presbytery, 43 Cork St, Kinsale, Co. Cork; T:+353/214772027, *Info@ oldpres.com/*; $21Bed, Kitchen:Y, B'fast:$, Pvt.room:Y, Locker:N, Recep:ltd; Note: wh/chair ok, luggage room, parking

Glendalough Intl YHA, The Lodge, Glendalough, Co Wicklow; *hihostels. com/*, T:+353/40445342, *info@anoige.ie*; $22Bed, Kitchen:Y, B'fast:Y, Pvt. room:Y, Locker:Y, Recep:5-10p; Note: resto, wh/chair ok, laundry, luggage room, parking

HI Knockree YH, Lackan, Lackandarragh, Enniskerry, Wicklow; *hihostels. com/*, T:+353/12767981, *info@anoige.ie*; $25Bed, Kitchen:Y, B'fast:$, Pvt.room:Y, Locker:N, Recep:8a>9p; Note: bikes, billiards, wh/chair ok, lift, hard find

3) Northern Ireland

Not really an independent country properly speaking, Northern Ireland "opted out" of Irish independence and decided to stay with the UK when the rest of Ireland was granted independence in 1921. Ostensibly this was to protect the rights of the Protestant majority in the north, so the upshot was that the minority Catholics were disadvantaged instead. The problem has yet to yield a long-term solution, and is perhaps unsolvable considering that during the "Plantation of Ulster" in the early 1600's, land was confiscated and reserved for Scottish and English colonists who were required to be English-speaking and Protestant, not much different from Chinese transmigration to Tibet today.

The "Troubles" that began on Bloody Sunday 1972 ended home rule for Northern Ireland and lasted until an agreement was finally reached in 1998. The fact that in some areas—Agriculture, Education, Environment, Health, Tourism, and Transport—issues will be handled on an all-island basis, gives hope that old animosities and outdated religious issues will fade in the light of a new era and new modes of cooperation. For the foreseeable future at least, the war is over, and Northern Ireland is wide open for tourism. Currency is the pound, phone code is +44, and languages are English, Irish, and Scots.

2 Hostels) BALLYCASTLE is a small town of almost 5100 on Northern Ireland's far north shore, where you can see Fairhead rock in the sea and the isles of Scotland farther away. The 400-year-old Lammas Fair is held every August. There is a bike path to Cushendun. The Holy Trinity Church, Bonamargy Friary, and Kinbane Castle are prominent fixtures.

Sheep Island View, 42A Main St, Ballintoy, Ballycastle, County Antrim; T:+44/2820769391, *Info@ sheepislandview.com/*; $24Bed, Kitchen:Y, B'fast:$, Pvt.room:Y, Locker:N, Recep:4>8p; Note: wh/chair ok, parking

Castle Hostel, 38 Quay Rd, Ballycastle, *claireewhite@btinternet.com*, T:+44/2820762845, *castlehostel.co.uk/*; $24Bed, Kitchen:Y, B'fast:$, Pvt.room:N, Locker:N, Recep:ltd; Note: laundry, parking, central

8 Hostels) BELFAST is the major city in Northern Ireland, of course, and an industrial one in the English fashion that it so admires. Shipbuilding is historically one of its specialties, and the *Titanic* was built here. It's a place with a recent history of political "troubles," but that's mostly forgotten these days, and Belfast is open for business, with connections to both the rest of the UK and the Republic of Ireland, too. Still there are neighborhoods segregated between republicans and unionists, so much work yet to do. But it's cheaper over here, so not a bad place to linger, if you have the urge. Not unlike other secondary markets, hostels here try harder, so high marks for many.

Global Village, 87 University St, Belfast, UK; T:+44(0)2890313533, *globalvillagebelfast.com/*; $23bed, Kitchen:Y, B'fast:Y, Pvt.room:Y, Locker:N, Recep:24/7; Note: towel fee, laundry, bit of a walk

Vagabonds Belfast, 9 University Rd, Belfast, UK; T:02890233017, *info@ vagabondsbelfast.com/*; $21bed, Kitchen:Y, B'fast:Y, Pvt.room:N, Locker:Y, Recep:ltd; Note: laundry, lounge

Lagan Backpackers, 121 Fitzroy Ave, Belfast, UK; *laganbackpackers. com/*, T:+44(0)2895140049; $16bed, Kitchen:Y, B'fast:Y, Pvt.room:Y, Locker:N, Recep:>11p; Note: English breakfast, 30min walk>center

Linen House Hostel, 18-20 Kent St, Belfast UK; T:+44(0)2890586400, *info@ belfasthostel.com*; $10bed, Kitchen:Y, B'fast:N, Pvt.room:Y, Locker:N, Recep:24/7; Note: $5 pizza, late night party in basement

Paddy's Palace, 68 Lisburn Road, Belfast, UK; *paddyspalace.com/*, T:+44(0)2890333367; $10bed, Kitchen:Y, B'fast:Y, Pvt.room:Y, Locker:N, Recep:24/7; Note: Free Giants' Causeway tour, central

Belfast City Backpacker, 53-55 Malone Ave, Belfast; T:+44/2890660030, *Info@ ibackpacker.co.uk/*; $23Bed, Kitchen:Y, B'fast:Y, Pvt.room:Y, Locker:Y, Recep:ltd; Note: luggage room, laundry, tour desk, parking, books, maps

Belfast International YH, 22-32 Donegall Rd, Belfast, *hihostels.com/*, T:+44/2890315435, *info@hini.org.uk*; $15Bed, Kitchen:Y, B'fast:$, Pvt.room:Y, Locker:Y, Recep:24/7; Note: max 7N, lift, wh/chair OK, laundry, luggage room

Arnies Backpackers, 63 Fitzwilliam St, Belfast; T:+44/2890242867 *Info@ arniesbackpackers.co.uk/*; $22Bed, Kitchen:Y, B'fast:Y, Pvt.room:Y, Locker:N, Recep:9a>9p; Note: laundry, luggage room, tour desk, prkng, tea/coffee, central

BUSHMILLS is a village of more than 1300 on the north coast, 57mi/95km from Belfast and only 6mi/10km from Ballycastle. Giant's Causeway is nearby and there's a distillery.

Mill Rest Hostel, 49 Main St, Bushmills; *hihostels.com/*, T:02820731222, *bushmills@hini.org.uk*; $21Bed, Kitchen:Y, B'fast:$, Pvt.room:Y, Locker:N, Recep:8a//10p; Note: wh/chair, laundry, luggage ok, c.c. ok, nr distillery

CASTLEROCK is another village of 1300+ on the north shore. Attractions are the 18th century Bishop of Derry's ruined palace, the Mussenden Temple, and the Black Glen.

Downhill Hostel, Glenhassan Hall, 12 Mussenden Rd, Downhill, Castlerock; T:02870849077; *Info@ downhillhostel.com/*; $23Bed, Kitchen:Y, B'fast:$, Pvt.room:Y, Locker:N, Recep:3>8p; Note: wh/chair ok, laundry, parking, nr sea

CUSHENDALL is yet another village on the north coast of around 1300. The Antrim coast route is renowned for its beauty. Attractions are Oisin's Grave, the ruins of Layde church, Red Bay Castle, and Glenariff Forest Park. There is a golf club.

Ballyeamon Barn Tourist Hostel, 127 Ballyemon Rd, Cushendall; *ballyeamonbarn.com/*, T:02821758451; $23Bed, Kitchen:Y, B'fast:$, Pvt. room:N, Locker:N, Recep:1:30p>10p; Note: cash, nature, laundry, luggage room, tea/coffee

3 Hostels) DERRY, aka Londonderry, is Northern Ireland's second city, and best known as the site of resistance to the Unionist government. It dates back to at least the sixth century as a monastic settlement. The old city was walled, the remains of which are one of Europe's finest—and final—examples of such, and Derry's most famous tourist attraction, complete with four gates. That's because it was planned as one of the "Plantations of Ulster" by which British Protestants were "planted" in Ireland to develop it along British lines.

It used to be so well-known for shirt-making that Karl Marx mentioned it in *Das Kapital*. Then there was partition, which put Derry right on the new borderline. The Catholics were unhappy and oppressed. They organized to air their grievances. On January 30, 1972, thirteen unarmed protesters were gunned down by British paratroopers in an event known as Bloody Sunday, which was the start of years of "troubles." It's better now, and Ireland will soon be reunited. You can bank on it, at Lloyd's of London.

Derry City Independent Hostel, 44 Great James St, Derry; *derryhostel. com/*, T:02871280542, *derryhostel@hotmail.com;* $23bed, Kitchen:Y, B'fast:Y,

Pvt.room:N, Locker:N, Recep:>10p; Note: $5 BBQ, pub crawls, tours, tour desk, parking

Paddy's Palace, 1 Woodleigh Terrace, Asylum Rd, Londonderry; *paddyspalace.com/*; T:02871309051; $16bed, Kitchen:Y, B'fast:Y, Pvt.room:Y, Locker:N, Recep:ltd; Note: parking, TV, tour desk, luggage room, laundry

Fairman House, 2 Fairman Pl, Londonderry; *fairmanhouse.co.uk/*, T:02871308000, *fairmanhouse@hotmail.co.uk*; $18Bed, Kitchen:N, B'fast:Y, Pvt. room:Y, Locker:N, Recep:ltd; Note: arpt trans, parking, luggage rm, not ctr

LARNE is a city of more than 18,000 on Northern Ireland's east coast, and has been a seaport for over 1000 years. Ferries run to Scotland from here, only 25 miles and one hour away by fast boat. The city has many parks and there are waterfalls and forest nearby. Diving tours are popular and colonies of seals, otters, whales, and birds are near.

Humphrey's at Rathmore, Rathmore House, Glenarm Rd 126, Larne; *humphreysatrathmore.com/*, T:+44/2828276556, *tandrhumphrey@gmail.com* $26Bed, Kitchen:Y, B'fast:$, Pvt.room:Y, Locker:Y, Recep:ltd; Note: laundry

MOURNE MOUNTAINS are the highest in Ulster, topping out at 2790ft/850mt, and feature many granite outcrop *tors*. Popular with hikers, it has been proposed as a national park. There is railway access at Newry.

The Mourne Lodge, Bog Rd, Atticall, Kilkeel, Co Down, Mourne Mts; T:02841765859, *Info@ themournelodge.com/*; $32Bed, Kitchen:Y, B'fast:Y, Pvt. room:Y, Locker:Y, Recep:ltd; Note: café, wh/chair ok, luggage room, parking

2 Hostels) PORTRUSH is a town of almost 6400 on the north coast, lined up along a mile-long peninsula — Ramone Head — that houses tourists in the summer and university students during the school season. There are beaches, nightclubs, a fun park, and golf.

Portrush Holiday Hostel, 24 Princess St, Portrush, County Antrim; T:+44/2870821288, *Info@ portrushholidayhostel.co.uk/*; $24Bed, Kitchen:Y,

B'fast:Y, Pvt.room:Y, Locker:Y, Recep:8:30a>9:30p; Note: bikes, laundry, luggage room, parking

Portrush Townhouse, 118 Parker Ave, Portrush, Antrim; T:07713272940, *Info@ causewaycoastself-catering.co.uk*; $26Bed, Kitchen:Y, B'fast:N, Pvt. room:Y, Locker:Y, Recep:3-10p; Note: 'surf 'n stay', laundry, bag hold, tea/coffee, parking

PORTSTEWART is Portrush's companion seaside town, home to 7800, and the quiet one of the two. It features 2mi/3km of beach, and is popular with surfers. There is a Dominican Convent and College.

Rick's Causeway Coastal Hostel, 4 Victoria Terrace, Portstewart; T:02870833789, *rickscausewaycoast.hostel.com/*; $23Bed, Kitchen:Y, B'fast:$, Pvt. room:Y, Locker:N, Recep:2>8p; Note: coast, bus stop, wh/chair ok, bag hold

4) Scotland

Scotland occupies the northern third of the island of Great Britain in addition to some 790 islands that come with the territory. The Picts, an earlier Celtic Brythonic-speaking group presumably related to the Welsh, were here first. Gaels emigrated from Ireland to form the western province of Dal Riata mid-first-millennium and eventually form a united Pictish Kingdom that was increasingly Gaelic. After the Norman conquest of England in 1066, though, English speakers steadily filtered into the lowlands, relegating the Gaelic cultures to the highlands. An era of peace and stability ended in 1296 with the Scottish wars of independence (from England) and an alliance with France that included participation in the 100 Years War against England.

England and Protestantism ultimately prevailed and after a famine that killed twenty percent of its populace, Scotland entered into an act of union with England in 1707. Great prosperity followed for Scotland as a full member of the British Empire and Industrial Revolution. The Scottish Enlightenment that followed was second to none and gave Scotland a great reputation for its ideas, its science, and its arts. They were not peripheral to Britain's success around the world; there were instrumental to it, and much the same holds true for the two countries today. If they hit a rough patch for a while there, it's mostly forgotten as Scotland's fortunes grow along with North Sea oil, and a partial return to self-government has quelled calls for complete secession.

"Scottishness" has lost little over the years. The widely-spoken Scots dialect is a form of old English that developed independently of the English standard in the days of French rule there, becoming mutually unintelligible at some point. Gaelic speakers are few and far between, gradually diminishing until relegated to highland enclaves and the far west coast. The phone code is +44. The currency is the pound. Scottish pounds may be hard to pass in England; vice versa is no problem. And no, the Firth of Forth is not a fraction.

ABERDEEN is Scotland's third largest city after Glasgow and Edinburgh. It is the center of the North Sea oil industry, which has largely replaced the traditional fishing and paper-making industries. The climate is mild for such a northern latitude. Ironically some of the oldest landmarks survive in New Aberdeen, near the Castlegate, which still contains an old Market (City) Cross and two ancient houses, Provost Skene's House and Provost Ross's House. Others are the Music Hall and Marischal College on Broad Street.

Aberdeen SYHA Hostel, 8 Queen's Road, Aberdeen, Scotland, UK; T:01224646988, *Aberdeen@ syha.org.uk/*; $35bed, Kitchen:Y, B'fast:N, Pvt. room:Y, Locker:N, Recep:7a//11p; Note: luggage room, laundry, parking, c.c. ok

3 Hostels) AVIEMORE is a town of some 2500 within the Cairngorns National Park of the Scottish Highlands. Popular for skiing and winter sports the town itself has a brewery and a variety of pubs and clubs. CARRBRIDGE is a nearby village of 700. There is an antique stone bridge.

Carrbridge - Slochd Mhor Lodge, Inverness-shire, Carrbridge; *hihostels. com/, T:01479841666; Slochd666@aol.com*; $30Bed, Kitchen:Y, B'fast:$, Pvt.

room:Y, Locker:N, Recep:ltd; Note: laundry, bikes, wh/chair ok, parking, luggage room

Aviemore SYHA, 25 Grampian Rd, Aviemore, *hihostels.com/*, T:01479810345, *aviemore@syha.org.uk*; $27Bed, Kitchen:N, B'fast:$, Pvt.room:N, Locker:N, Recep:ltd; Note:w/chair OK, billiards, laundry, luggage rm, prkng

Cairngorm Lodge SYHA, Glenmore, Cairngorm, Aviemore; *hihostels. com/*, T:01479861238; *cairngorm.lodge@syha.org.uk*; $28Bed, Kitchen:Y, B'fast:$, Pvt.room:N, Locker:N, Recep: 7:30a//10:30p, Note: mountains, walk>beach, laundry

BALLATER is a town of 1500 in the east, known for spring water and center for hiking. There are mountains and Balmoral Castle nearby. There is a Walking Festival in May.

Habitat @Ballater, Bridge Sq, Ballater, Aberdeenshire UK, T:01339753752 *Info@ habitat-at-ballater.com/*; $34Bed, Kitchen:Y, B'fast:$, Pvt.room:Y, Locker:Y, Recep:3>10p; Note: wh/chair, laundry, luggage room, coffee/tea, parking

BRAEMAR is another village in the east, population over 800. There is a Highland Games Gathering in September. The local dialect of Gaelic went extinct a few years ago.

Braemar SYHA, 21 Glenshee Rd, Corrie Feragie, Braemar; *hihostels.com/*, T:01339741659; *braemar@syha.org.uk*; $29Bed, Kitchen:Y, B'fast:N, Pvt.room:Y, Locker:N, Recep:8a//9:30p; Note: laundry, bikes, forex, TV, c.c. ok, forest

CRIANLARICH is a village of a couple hundred in the south, "gateway to the highlands." It is at the cross roads of A82 and A85.

Crianlarich SYHA, Station Rd, Crianlarich; *hihostels.com/*, *T:01838300260*, *crianlarich@syha.org.uk*; $26Bed, Kitchen:Y, B'fast:N, Pvt.room:N, Locker:Y, Recep:7a>11p; Note: laundry, wh/chair ok, c.c.ok, store, WiFi$

COMRIE is a town of 1800 in the southern highlands, and a haven for retirees. The town itself is a historic village, and is located in a national Scenic Area. It sits at the confluence of the rivers Ruchill, Lednock, and Earn. It sits smack on the Highland Boundary Fault.

Comrie Croft, Braincroft, Crieff; *hihostels.com/, T:+44(0)1764670140, info@ comriecroft.com*, $32Bed, Kitchen:N, B'fast:$, Pvt.room:Y, Locker:N, Recep:24/7; Note: bikes, wh/chair OK, tour desk, luggage room, parking, laundry, Nature

DUNDEE is a city of over 150,000, Scotland's fourth-largest, on the Firth of Tay, just off the North Sea, on the country's east shore. Once a medieval burg of note, it came to fame in the textile trade, which has since disappeared. It is now a center of high-tech. There are castles, though mostly of the Early Modern Era, as the city's medieval architecture was mostly destroyed in the fights over Queen Mary. There is no shortage of entertainment.

Dundee Backpackers Hostel, 71 High St, Dundee, Angus UK; *Info@ hoppo. com/*, T:+44/1382224646; $23Bed, Kitchen:Y, B'fast:N, Pvt.room:Y, Locker:N, Recep: 8a>12m; Note: c.c.+2%, lift, wh/chair ok, bag hold, laundry, billiards

17 Hostels) EDINBURGH is the historic heart of Scotland — intellectually, economically and culturally. It is also the capital and second-largest city. This was one of Europe's prime centers of the Enlightenment a few centuries ago and one of the UK's prime tourist attractions now. The Old Town and New Town are both UNESCO World Heritage sites. The Edinburgh Festival held through the entire month of August is a collection of individual festivals that includes the top-rated Fringe festival. The castle is the city's top tourist draw. The old town contains the cathedral of St. Giles, the Parliament House, the City Chambers, and the Market Cross, hub of the old city. The new town, approved in 1767, was intended for people "of a certain rank and fortune." Yeah, right, sounds boring. The railway changed all that. Hostel quality and locations are generally good.

Castle Rock Hostel, 15 Johnston Terrace, Edinburgh; T:01312259666, *castlerockedinburgh.com/*, $21bed, *castlerock@macbackpackerstours.com*; Kitchen:Y, B'fast:$, Pvt.room:Y, Locker:Y, Recep:24/7; Note: billiards, laundry

Caledonian Backpackers, 3 Queensferry St, Edinburgh; T:01314767224, *caledonianbackpackers.com/*; $24bed, Kitchen:Y, B'fast:Y, Pvt.room:N, Locker:Y, Recep:24/7; Note: bar, café, free tour/info, c.c. ok, laundry, billiards, bag hold

Budget Backpackers, 39 Cowgate, Grassmarket, Edinburgh, Scotland UK; T:01312266351, *hi@ budgetbackpackers.com/*; $19bed, Kitchen:Y, B'fast:N, Pvt. room:Y, Locker:Y, Recep:24/7; Note: bar/café, laundry, bag hold, tours, billiards

St. Cristopher's Edinburgh, 9-13 Market St, Edinburgh; T:01312261446, *feedback@ st-christophers.co.uk/*; $16bed, Kitchen:N, B'fast:Y, Pvt.room:N, Locker:N, Recep:24/7; Note: min. 2N, central, bar, café, laundry, tea/cof, lift, bag hold

Royal Mile Backpackers, 105 High St, Edingurgh; T:01315576120, *royalmilebackpackers.com/*, $19bed, *royalmile@scotlandstophostels.com*; Kitchen:Y, B'fast:$, Pvt.room:N, Locker:Y, Recep:ltd; Note: laundry, bag hold, tours, coffee/tea

Westend Hotel, 35 Palmerston Place, Edinburgh; T:01312253656, *info@ thewestendhotel.co.uk/*; $15bed, Kitchen:Y, B'fast:$, Pvt. room:N, Locker:N, Recep:>11p; Note: resto/bar, laundry, luggage room, tea/coffee, historic bldg

Argyle Backpackers, 14 Argyle Place, Edinburgh; T:01316679991, *reception@ argyle-backpackers.co.uk/*; $18bed, Kitchen:Y, B'fast:$, Pvt.room:Y, Locker:Y, Recep:9a>10p; Note: free coffee/tea, c.c. ok, laundry, bikes, bag hold

High St. Hostel, 8 Blackfriars St, Old Town, Edinburgh; T:01315573984, *highstreethostel.com/*; $21bed, Kitchen:Y, B'fast:$, Pvt.room:N, Locker:Y, Recep:24/7; Note: stairs, bikes, billiards, laundry, bag hold, tea/coffee, tours

Edinburgh Central Hostel, 9 Haddington Pl, Edinburgh; T:08701553255, *reservations@ syha.org.uk/*; $33bed, Kitchen:Y, B'fast:$, Pvt.room:Y, Locker:Y, Recep:24/7; Note: laundry, bar, arpt trans, café, wh/chair ok, lift, prkng, bag hold

Brodies Hostel, Royal Mile 93 High St, Edinburgh; T:01315562223, *bookings@ brodieshostels.co.uk/*; $14bed, Kitchen:Y, B'fast:N, Pvt.room:N, Locker:$, Recep:ltd; Note:coffee/tea, laundry, hard find, good view, WiFi $, tours, maps

Hoppo Edinburgh Backpackers 65 Cockburn St, E'burgh, T:01312201717

Hoppo Belford Hostel, 6/8 Douglas Gardens, Edinburgh; T:01312202200, *Info@ hoppo.com/*; $14Bed, Kitchen:Y, B'fast:$, Pvt.room:Y, Locker:Y, Recep:ltd; Note: bar, billiards, books, tours, maps, tea/coffee, West End, old church remodel

Cowgate Tourist Hostel, Cowgate, Edinburgh; T:01312262153, *Info@ cowgatehostel.com/*; $15Bed, Kitchen:Y, B'fast:$, Pvt.room:Y, Locker:N, Recep:8a>11p; Note: luggage rm, tours, tea/cof, central, nr pub, old house

The Hostel, 3 Clifton Terrace, Edinburgh; T:01312026107; *reservations@ hosteledinburgh.co.uk/*; $12Bed, Kitchen:Y, B'fast:$, Pvt.room:Y, Locker:Y, Recep:ltd; Note: billiards, laundry, luggage room, tour desk, maps, basic

Smartcityhostels, 50 Blackfriars St, Edinburgh; T:01315241989, *reception@ reservations@ smartcityhostels.com/*; $21Bed, Kitchen:Y, B'fast:$, Pvt.room:Y, Locker:Y, Recep:24/7; Note: resto/bar, billiards, lift, wh/chair, laundry, ctr

Princes Street Backpackers East, 5 West Register St, Edinburgh; *bookings@ edinburghbackpackers.com/*, T:01315566894; $18Bed, Kitchen:Y, B'fast:$, Pvt. room:Y, Locker:Y, Recep:24/7; Note:77steps/no lift, minimart, laundry, luggage rm

Haggis Hostels, 5/3 West Register St, Edinburgh; T:01315570036, *Info@ haggishostels.co.uk/*; $22Bed, Kitchen:Y, B'fast:Y, Pvt.room:Y, Locker:Y, Recep:24/7; Note: arpt trans, laundry, bag hold, tours, maps, safe dep, tea/ coffee, central

7 Hostels) FORT WILLIAM is the largest town in the Scottish Highlands, second only to the city of Inverness. It is also a major tourist center, due to its proximity to Ben Nevis (that's a peak), the highest point in the UK at 4409ft/1344m (no snickering). With Fort William at sea level, though, along the Great Glen strike/slip fault that dissects northernmost Scotland, 4409 feet is plenty. There are still Gaelic speakers here. "Rob Roy," "Highlander" and "Braveheart" were filmed here.

Fort William Backpackers, Alma Rd, Fort William; T:01397700711, *fortwilliambackpackers.com/*; $27bed, Kitchen:Y, B'fast:$, Pvt.room:N, Locker:N, Recep:8a>10p; Note: midday lockout, tours, parking, c.c. ok, living room/ fireplace

Bank Street Lodge, Bank St, Fort William, Scotland UK; T:01397700070, *bankstreetlodge.co.uk/*, $27bed, *bankstreetlodge@btconnect.com*; Kitchen:Y, B'fast:N, Pvt.room:Y, Locker:N, Recep:24/7; Note: resto, parking, laundry, @ train, central

Glen Nevis SYHA, Glen Nevis, Fort William; *hihostels.com/*, T:01397702336, *glen.nevis@syha.org.uk*; $33bed, Kitchen:Y, B'fast:N, Pvt.room:Y, Locker:N, Recep:7a>11p; Note: resto, parking, laundry, c.c. ok, not central, WiFi:$

Farr Cottage Lodge, Farr Cottage, Corpach, Fort William; T:01397772315, *mail@ farrcottage.com/*; $24bed, Kitchen:Y, B'fast:$, Pvt.room:Y, Locker:N, Recep:4:30>10p; Note: bar, prkng, luggage rm, laundry, bus>center

Chase the Wild Goose Hostel, Banavie by Fort William; T:01397748044, *enquiries@ great-glen-hostel.com/*; $21bed, Kitchen:Y, B'fast:$, Pvt.room:N, Locker:N, Recep:>11p; Note: TV, parking, laundry, luggage room

Calluna, Heathercroft, Fort William; *Info@ fortwilliamholiday.co.uk/*, T:44/139770045; $26Bed, Kitchen:Y, B'fast:$, Pvt.room:Y, Locker:N, Recep:24/7; Note: bikes, shuttle wh/chair ok, laundry, luggage room, parking, hiking, not central

Aite Cruinnichidh, 1 Achluachrach, By Roy Bridge, Fort William; *gavin@ highland-hostel.co.uk/*, T:01397712315, $27Bed, Kitchen:Y, B'fast:$, Pvt.room:Y, Locker:N, Recep:ltd; Note: mountains, rivers, bag hold, parking, remote (take food)

GAIRLOCH is a village of a few hundred, and parish of almost 1000, on Scotland's east coast. There is tourist trade in the summer, with golf, a museum, and more.

Gairloch Carn Dearg SYHA, Gairloch, Carn Dearg; *hihostels.com/*, T:+44(0)1445712219, *carn.dearg@syha.org.uk*; $29Bed, Kitchen:Y, B'fast:$, Pvt. room:Y, Locker:N, Recep:5.11p; Note: loch, parking, laundry, c.c. ok

6 Hostels) GLASGOW is Scotland's largest city and the UK's third. If Edinburgh is the cultural and intellectual heart of Scotland, Glasgow is the industrial heart. It came to prominence with the Industrial Revolution and

the British Empire for its shipbuilding and engineering. Prior to that, it was a trading city with an annual fair. The tobacco trade was very important at one time. The slums were reportedly horrific.

Today it is being reinvented as a green city with culture, with many previously rundown areas gone upscale to lure back the upper classes that fled to the suburbs. Merchant City is now a "culture quarter." Ancient buildings are few, just the cathedral and the oldest house of Provand's Lordship, but the historic district of Glasgow Cross has buildings from the 17th and 18th centuries. Museums include Kelvingrove Art Gallery and Museum, The Burrell Collection, the Gallery of Modern Art and the Lighthouse. Then there's the Glasgow Science Center. West End is the bohemian district. The music scene is lively.

Glasgow Youth Hostel, 8 Park Terrace, Glasgow, Lanarkshire UK; *syha. org.uk/*, T:01413323004; $27bed, Kitchen:Y, B'fast:$, Pvt.room:N, Locker:Y, Recep:24/7; Note:Victorian house, hard find, stairs, resto/bar, billiards, bag hold

Queen's Park Budget Hotel, 10 Balvicar Dr., Glasgow, Scotland UK; *info@ budgethotelsglasgow.co.uk/*, T:01414231123; $18bed, Kitchen:Y, B'fast:Y, Pvt. room:Y, Locker:N, Recep:24/7; Note: not central, luggage rm, tea/coffee

Bunkum Hostel, 26 Hillhead St., Glasgow; *bunkumglasgow.co.uk,* T:01415814481, *BunkumGlasgow@hotmail.com;* $25bed, Kitchen:Y, B'fast:N, Pvt.room:N, Locker:Y, Recep:>10p; Note: univ. area, bit of a hike, stairs, tea/cof

Alba Hostel, 6 Fifth Ave, Anniesland, Glasgow, Scotland UK; T:01413322588, *info@ albalodge.co.uk/*; $24bed, Kitchen:Y, B'fast:$, Pvt.room:N, Locker:Y, Recep:4>11p; Note: luggage room, parking, not central, c.c. +3%

Bluesky Hostel, 65 Berkeley St, Glasgow, Scotland UK; *blueskyhostel.com/* T:01412211710, *blueskyhostel@btconnect.com;* $18bed, Kitchen:Y, B'fast:N, Pvt. room:Y, Locker:Y, Recep:8a>12m; Note: age 18-35, tea/coffee, central, dog

Euro Hostel Glasgow, 318 Clyde St, Glasgow; T:+44/1412222828 *reservations@ euro-hostels.co.uk/*; $19Bed, Kitchen:Y, B'fast:$, Pvt.room:N, Locker:Y, Recep:24/7; Note: bar, billiards, lift, wh/chair ok, laundry, luggage rm, tours

2 Hostels) GLENCOE is a village located at the glen itself, in the west of Scotland, one of the most beautiful places in Scotland, wild and woolly, high and hilly, perfect for hiking and biking, with no shortage of amenities.

Glencoe Independent Hostel, Glencoe, Ballachulish, Argyll; T:01855811906 *Info@ glencoehostel.co.uk/*; $21Bed, Kitchen:Y, B'fast:$, Pvt.room:N, Locker:Y, Recep:ltd; Note: luggage room, coffee/tea, parking, mid-forest, remote

Glencoe SYHA, Ballachulish, Glencoe; T:+44/1855811219, *glencoe@ syha. org.uk/*; $26Bed, Kitchen:Y, B'fast:$, Pvt.room:N, Locker:N, Recep:7a>11p; Note: laundry, parking, c.c. ok, scenery

HUNTLY is a town of 4500 in the east of Scotland. This is where the Gordon Highlanders regiment is from. There is a cultural center and a castle; good fishing, too...

Highlander Bunkhouse, Gordon Arms Hotel, The Square, Huntly; *info@ highlanderbunkhouse.com/*, T:01466792288; $27Bed, Kitchen:Y, B'fast:$, Pvt. room:N, Locker:N, Recep:ltd; Note: no WiFi, resto/bar, wh/chair ok

8 Hostels) INVERNESS is the unofficial capital of the Scottish Highlands. It's also one of Europe's fastest-growing cities. Now you're getting into some true north country, up around fifty-five degrees north latitude, farther north than Moscow or Copenhagen. In the summer, you can get transportation even farther north, to the Orkney Islands or the Shetlands, if you're truly motivated. For most travelers, though, it's the jumping-off point to Loch Ness; Inver-NESS, get it? It's a former Pict stronghold. It's a university town. There are music festivals. It's a center of Scots traditional culture. It's beautiful country; beware of monsters. Hostel quality is good. And, oh yeah, there's a castle.

Bazpackers Hostel, 4 Culduthel Rd, Inverness; T:+44(0)1463717663, *bazpackershostel.co.uk/*; $23bed, Kitchen:Y, B'fast:N, Pvt.room:Y, Locker:Y, Recep:8a>11p; Note: near castle, free coffee/tea, laundry, c.c. ok

Inverness Student Hostel, 8 Culduthel Rd, Inverness, UK; *invernessstudenthotel.com/*, T:+44(0)1463236556; $24bed, Kitchen:Y, B'fast:$, Pvt.room:N, Locker:N, Recep:ltd; Note: coffee/tea, WiFi $, laundry, parking, tours

Inverness Tourist Hostel, 24 Rose St, Inverness, UK; T:01463241962, *info@ invernesshostel.com/*; $15bed, Kitchen:Y, B'fast:N, Pvt.room:N, Locker:Y, Recep:>11p; Note: free coffee/tea, loud club, luggage room, parking, games, maps

Inverness Youth Hostel, Victoria Drive, Inverness; *hihostels.com/*, T:01463231771, *inverness@syha.org.uk;* $28bed, Kitchen:Y, B'fast:$, Pvt.room:Y, Locker:N, recep:ltd; Note: not central, midday lockout, member SYHA, WiFi $

Eastgate Backpackers Hostel, 38 Eastgate, Inverness, Scotland UK; *eastgatebackpackers.com/*, T:+44(0)1463718756; $23bed, Kitchen:Y, B'fast:N, Pvt. room:Y, Locker:Y, Recep:ltd; Note: stairs, midday lockout

Inverness - Hillview House, 26 Merlewood Rd, Inverness; *hihostels.com/*, T:+44/7581111200, *info@invernesshostel.co.uk;*$24Bed, Kitchen:Y, B'fast:Y, Pvt. room:Y, Locker:N, Recep:4>10p; Note: laundry, luggage rm, tea/cof, not ctr

Struy Guesthouse, 109 Ballifeary Rd, Inverness; *struyguesthouse.co.uk/*, T:+44/1463240622, *struyguesthouse@gmail.com*; $19Bed, Kitchen:N, B'fast:$, Pvt. room:Y, Locker:N, Recep:ltd; Note: bikes, parking, luggage room, tea/coffee

Highlander Hostel, 23a High St Inverness, Highland; T:+44/1463221225, *highlanderhostel@ highlanderhostel.com/*; $16Bed, Kitchen:Y, B'fast:$, Pvt. room:N, Locker:Y, Recep:9a>11p; Note: resto, billiards, laundry, luggage rm, tours

2 Hostels) ISLE OF ARRAN lies off the west coast in the Firth of Clyde, with a population over 5000. With its highland and lowland areas, it is sometimes referred to as "Scotland in miniature." The last speaker of Gaelic Arran died in the 1970's; r.i.p.

Lochranza SYHA, Lochranza, Isle of Arran, , *T:+44(0)1770830631, lochranza@ syha.org.uk/*; $27Bed, Kitchen:Y, B'fast:N, Pvt.room:N, Locker:Y, Recep:ltd; Note: laundry, c.c. ok, WiFi $

Corrie Croft Bunkhouse, North High Corrie, Corrie, Isle of Arran; T:+44/1770810288, *Claire@ corriecroftbunkhouse.co.uk/*; $19Bed, Kitchen:Y, B'fast:$, Pvt.room:Y, Locker:N, Recep:4p>7:30p; Note:luggage room, parking, tea/cof

ISLE OF LEWIS (and Harris) is the largest of the Outer Hebrides, with a population of about 18,500. The flora and fauna include eagles, deer, and seals. The Callanish Standing Stones are a local mini-Stonehenge. Gaelic talk still rules here, though all are bilingual.

Heb Hostel, 25 Kenneth St, Stornoway, Isle of Lewis, UK; T:01851709889, *Christine@ hebhostel.com/*; $26Bed, Kitchen:Y, B'fast:Y, Pvt.room:Y, Locker:Y, Recep:ltd; Note: laundry, near bus & ferry, central

6 Hostels) ISLE OF SKYE is the largest and most northern of the Inner Hebrides, though you might not even know it's an island if you haven't been there or looked at the map carefully. It's even connected to the mainland by bridge now. More importantly, this is one of the last bastions of Gaelic language and culture. Portree, the largest town, has less than 2000 people. There are Mesolothic and Neolothic remains, but little evidence of the long Norse and Viking presence of the Middle Ages. The Highland Clearances of the mainland occurred here, too, and tenant farmers were dispossessed of their land to allow wealthy landowners to raise sheep. Things are calmer now; tourism is healthy, and the island is experiencing a renewal. There is a lively music and arts scene. Single malt whiskey is made here.

Skye Backpackers, Kyleakin, Isle of Skye; *skyebackpackers.com*, T:01599534510; $26bed, Kitchen:Y, B'fast:$, Pvt.room:N, Locker:N, Recep:8a>10p; Note: checkin 5pm, noon lockout, parking, c.c. ok, day tours, tea/cof

Isle of Skye – Broadford SYHA, Broadford, Isle of Skye, Scotland UK; *hihostels.com/*, T:01471822442, *broadford@syha.org.uk;* $28bed, Kitchen:Y, B'fast:N, Pvt.room:Y, Locker:N, Recep:8a>10p; Note: store, garden, laundry, c.c. ok, prkng

Broadford Backpackers, High Rd, B'ford; *broadfordbackpackers.co.uk/*, T:01471820333, *broadfordbackpackers@gmail.com;* $24bed, Kitchen:Y, B'fast:N, Pvt.room:Y, Locker:N, Recep:9a>11p; Note: wh/chair ok, bag hold, laundry

Saucy Mary's Lodge, Main St, Kyleakin, Isle of Skye; *saucymarys.com/*, T:01599534845, *saucymarys1@btconnect.com;* $30bed, Kitchen:Y, B'fast:$, Pvt.room:Y, Locker:N, Recep:ltd; Note:resto/bar, wh/chair ok, prkng, tours, views

Skyewalker Hostel, The Old School, Portnalong, Isle of Skye; T:01478640250, *enquiries@ skyewalkerhostel.com/*; $26Bed, Kitchen:Y, B'fast:N, Pvt.room:Y, Locker:N, Recep:ltd; Note: music, instruments, parking, coffee/tea

Broadford SYHA, Broadford, *hihostels.com/*, *T:+44(0)1471822442, broadford@syha.org.uk*; $27Bed, Kitchen:Y, B'fast:$, Pvt.room:N, Locker:N, Recep:7:30a>10:30p; Note: laundry, meals $, parking, Nature, few buses, Net $$

2 Hostels) KYLE OF LOCHALSH is a village of over 700 on the northwest coast, 63mi/100km from Inverness and connected by bridge to Kyleakin on the Isle of Skye. There is a railway to Inverness. Life is slow and easy. RATAGAN is a small village on the southwest shore of the sea loch, Loch Duich in Lochalsh.

Ratagan SYHA, Glenshiel, Kyle, Ratagan; *hihostels.com/*, *T:01599511243, ratagan@syha.org.uk*; $27Bed, Kitchen:Y, B'fast:$, Pvt.room:N, Locker:Y, Recep:7:30a>10:30p; Note: minimart, laundry, luggage room, parking, views

Stationmasters Hostel, Stromeferry Near Kyle of Lochalsh, T:01599577212, *beds@ stationmastershostel.co.uk/*; $29Bed, Kitchen:Y, B'fast:Y, Pvt.room:Y, Locker:N, Recep:3>8p; Note: rural, shops>10m/16k, billiards, wh/chair ok

5 Hostels) LOCH NESS is a large lake in Northern Scotland and home to the cryptozoological (I like that word) Loch Ness monster, whose existence is about as likely as the aliens that have visited this planet repeatedly over the millennia. It lies along the Great Glen Fault and with its great depth is the largest lake by volume in the UK.

Morag's Lodge, Fort Augustus, Loch Ness, UK; T:01320366289, *info@ moragslodge.com*; $34bed, Kitchen:Y, B'fast:$, Pvt.room:Y, Locker:Y, Recep:ltd; Note: bar w/fire & live music, meals, parking, laundry, c.c. ok, tea/coffee

Loch Ness Hostel, Glenmoriston, Loch Ness, UK; *hihostels.com/*, T:01320351274, *loch.ness@syha.org.uk*; $32bed, Kitchen:Y, B'fast:$, Pvt.room:Y, Locker:N, Recep:8a//10p; Note: laundry, parking, c.c. ok

Loch Ness Backpackers, Coiltie Farmhouse, E. Lewiston, Drumnadrochit; T:+44/1456450807, *Info@ lochness-backpackers.com/*; $29Bed, Kitchen:N, B'fast:$, Pvt.room:Y, Locker:N, Recep:24/7; Note: bikes, wh/chair ok, luggage rm, tours

Invergarry Lodge, Mandally Rd, Invergarry, Inverness-Shire; *mail@ invergarrylodge.co.uk/*, T:01809501412; $27Bed, Kitchen:N, B'fast:$, Pvt.room:Y, Locker:N, Recep:4>10:30p; Note: bikes, wh/chair ok, luggage ok, parking, c.c.+3%

Great Glen Hostel, South Laggan, Spean Bridge, Inverness-Shire; T:01809501430, *bookings@ greatglenhostel.com/*; $27Bed, Kitchen:Y, B'fast:N, Pvt.room:Y, Locker:N, Recep:ltd; Note: minimart, laundry, far, "hikers' hostel"

3 Hostels) OBAN is a picturesque west coast seaside town of some 8000 people that can swell to over 25,000 at the height of the tourist season. It occupies a beautiful location on a bay in the Firth of Lom. It grew up around a distillery.

Oban Backpackers, Breadalbane St, Oban, Scotland; *obanbackpackers. com/*, T:1631567189, *info@ backpackersplus.com*; $24bed, Kitchen:Y, B'fast:Y, Pvt. room:N, Locker:N, Recep:ltd; Note: luggage room, laundry, tour desk, c.c. ok

Oban Hostel, Esplanade, Oban, Scotland UK; *hihostels.com/*, T:01631562025, *oban@syha.org.uk*; $32bed, Kitchen:Y, B'fast:$, Pvt.room:Y, Locker:N, Recep:24/7; Note: laundry, parking, c.c. ok, good views

Backpackers Plus, Dunollie Halls, Breadalbane St, Oban; T:+44/1631567189, *Info@ backpackersplus.com/*; $29Bed, Kitchen:Y, B'fast:Y, Pvt.room:Y, Locker:N, Recep:4>10:30p; Note: billiards, luggage room, laundry, parking, books, maps

2 Hostels) PITLOCHRY is a Victorian tourist town of over 2500 in the center of the country, the main attraction being the scenery. There are also two distilleries. In the summer the Pitlochry Festival Theatre has six different plays in six days. The Winter Words Festival does it with books over ten days in the winter. There are pipe bands. Railway comes here.

Pitlochry Backpackers, 134 Atholl Rd, Pitlochry, Perthshire; T:01796470044, *pitlochrybackpackershotel.com/*; $27Bed, Kitchen:Y, B'fast:$, Pvt.room:Y, Locker:N, Recep:7a>10p; Note: billiards, laundry, bag hold, tours, tea/cof

Pitlochry SYHA, Knockard Rd, Pitlochry; *hihostels.com/*, T:01796472308, *pitlochry@syha.org.uk*; $29Bed, Kitchen:Y, B'fast:$, Pvt.room:N, Locker:N, Recep:7a//11p; Note: closed 2345>0700, brewery, laundry, bikes, meals

2 Hostels) STIRLING was once the capital of Scotland, and is still a center of local government, with a population pushing 34,000 on a busy day. On the River Forth, it straddles the boundary between highland and lowland. There is a medieval old town, castle, Church of the Holy Rude, and prehistoric Randolphfield Standing Stones.

Willy Wallace Hostel, 77 Murray Pl, Stirling; *willywallacehostel.com/*, T:+44/1786446773, *willywallacehostel@gmail.com*; $24Bed, Kitchen:Y, B'fast:$, Pvt.room:Y, Locker:Y, Recep:9a>9p; Note: bikes, books, laundry, bag hold, tea/cof

Stirling SYHA, St John St, Stirling; *hihostels.com/*, T:+44/1786473442; *stirling@syha.org.uk*; $27Bed, Kitchen:Y, B'fast:$, Pvt.room:N, Locker:Y, Recep:24/7; Note: bikes, laundry, bag hold, wh/chair ok, Wifi$, old town, @castle

THURSO is the northernmost point on the British mainland, at 59 deegrees N, with a population of 9000. As such, it was the Norse point of entry into Great Britain, and was long a port for the rest of Europe, too. You can see the Orkneys. The railway comes here.

Sandra's Backpackers Hostel, 24 Princes St, Caithness, Thurso; *Info@ sandras-backpackers.co.uk/*, T:01847894575, $26Bed, Kitchen:Y, B'fast:Y, Pvt. room:Y, Locker:Y, Recep:ltd; Note: resto, bikes, hard find, cntr, basic, luggage rm

TOBERMORY is a village of 700 on the Isle of Mull off the southwest coast of Ireland. There is a traditional music festival in April, a local Mod (Gaelic fest) in September, and Highland Games in the summer. There is ferry service.

Tobermory SYHA, Main St, Tobermory; *hihostels.com/*, T:+44/1688302481, *tobermory@syha.org.uk*; $29Bed, Kitchen:Y, B'fast:N, Pvt.room:N, Locker:N, Recep:7:30a>10p; Note: laundry, c.c. ok, WiFi $, waterfront

2 Hostels) ULLAPOOL is a town of 1300 on the far northwest mainland, with an impact greater than its size, since it is the largest town in the area…with major tourism. In addition to the original fishing port, there is a yacht marina,

and ferries to the Outer Hebrides. It is also an arts center, with book festival in May, Guitar Festival in September, and Loopallu Music Festival, in addition to the many events in the local bars. TORRIDON is a village on the shore of Loch Torridon, and surrounded by hills.

Torridon SYHA, by Achnasheen, Torridon; *hihostels.com/, T:01445791284, torridon@syha.org.uk*; $29Bed, Kitchen:Y, B'fast:$, Pvt.room:N, Locker:N, Recep:7:30a>11p; Note: parking, laundry, c.c. ok, loch view

Ullapool SYHA, Shore St, Ullapool; *hihostels.com/, T:01854612254; ullapool@syha.org.uk*; $29Bed, Kitchen:Y, B'fast:$, Pvt.room:Y, Locker:N, Recep:7:30//10:30; Note: midnight curfew, lockout, laundry, meals, books

5) Wales

Wales is the other country comprising the United Kingdom — besides England, Scotland and Northern Ireland — and is arguably the most traditional of the lot. It is more or less defined by its non-Anglo roots, and is the remnant of a once-large area of original non-Germanic peoples in post-Roman Britain. You can hear radio programs in Celtic here; you'll be hard pressed to find that in Scotland. The Romans ruled for several hundred years, but Anglo-Saxons made little impact until after the Norman Conquest in 1066.

Shortly thereafter the Cardiff Castle was built and English settlers began trickling in. Wales was soon absorbed into England's affairs, and made official partner with an Act of Union in 1536. Since then, Wales was been most closely identified with coal mining, an activity in sharp decline these days. Now a post-industrial economy, tourism in Wales is on the rise. Blaenavon, an early coal-mining and ironworks center, is now a UNESCO site. Pound sterling is currency, phone code is +44; languages are English and Welsh.

BWLCH ('pass') is a village strung out along A40 in southern Wales, 1mi/2km north of the River Usk, and with some nice views of the valley. Nearby are Tretower Castle and Court, the ruins of a Norman castle, and a couple of prehistoric 'standing stones.'

Beacons Backpackers, Bwlch, Brecon; T:01874730215, *Info@ beaconsbackpackers.co.uk/*; $32Bed, Kitchen:N, B'fast:Y, Pvt.room:N, Locker:N, Recep:ltd; Note: bar, luggage room, parking, mounntains, walkers, natl park

BRIDGEND is a city of 40,000 only 22mi/35km west of Cardiff, with historic bridge. With roots in the Roman Era, coal transformed the landscape, literally, with numerous quarries. It produced munitions in WWII, attracting bombers. Now it attracts shoppers. The pubs have music of all types and genres.

Betws Ecolodge, Heol Dewi Sant, Bettws, Bridgend; *betwsecolodge.co.uk/*, T:01656729569, *ecolodge@btinternet.com*; $29Bed, Kitchen:Y, B'fast:$, Pvt. room:Y, Locker:Y, Recep:4>8p; Note: wh/chair OK, billiards, luggage rm, prkng, cof/tea, new

4 Hostels) CAERNARFON is a town of almost 10,000 in the northwest of Wales. The Romans ruled here for a few hundred years, and so did the Normans, before the English moved in to build a castle and set up housekeeping. Still the area has the greatest number of Celtic-speakers in the region. The ancient Market Hall is on Hole-in-the-Wall Street. PORTHMADOG is a nearby coastal town of 4800, wide open for tourism, terminus of the Ffestiniog tourist railway, and with easy access to Snowdonia National Park.

Once a prominent port for trade, now it is a prominent shopping center for trade, serving the region with three railway stations, many buses and several highways. TRAWSFYNYDD is a village with population under 1000 near Blaenau Ffestiniog, the historic mining town on the Ffestiniog Railway. It is close to Lake Llyn Trawsfynydd, a manmade reservoir near the nuclear power station.

Llys Ednowain Heritage Centre/Hostel, Trawsfynydd; *llysednowain. co.uk/*, T:01766770324, *llysednowain@btconnect.com*; $30Bed, Kitchen:Y, B'fast:N,

Pvt. room:N, Locker:Y, Recep:ltd; Note: wh/chair ok, lift, luggage rm, laundry, quiet, far

Cwm Pennant Hostel, Garndolbenmaen, Gwynedd, Porthmadog; T:01766530888, *Info@ cwm-pennant.co.uk/*; $28Bed, Kitchen:Y, B'fast:$, Pvt. room:Y, Locker:N, Recep:ltd; Note: wh/chair ok, bag hold, parking, tea/cof, far

Totters, Plas Porth Yr Aur, 2 High St, Caernarfon, Gwynedd; *totters. co.uk/*, T:+44/1286672963, *totters.hostel@googlemail.com*; $27Bed, Kitchen:Y, B'fast:Y, Pvt.room:Y, Locker:Y, Recep:ltd; Note: cash only, luggage rm, sea/castle/old town

YHA Llanberis, Llwyn Celyn, Llanberis, Caernarfon; *hihostels.com/*, T:01286870280, *llanberis@yha.org.uk*; $21Bed, Kitchen:Y, B'fast:$, Pvt.room:Y, Locker:Y, Recep:24/7; Note: cash, resto, laundry, bag hold, parking, not center

5 Hostels) CARDIFF is the largest city and commercial center of Wales, and formerly the largest coal port in the world. Services and tourism are big today, with Cardiff Castle being one of the major attractions. There are also other castles, hence its claim to have more castles than anywhere else in the world. Other historic buildings include Llandaff Cathedral and the medieval parish church of St. John. Also worth visitng are the Welsh National Museum and Gallery; Techniquest, an interactive science museum; and the Museum of Welsh Life, at St. Fagan's Castle, 4.5 miles (7 km) west of the city centre. There are ruins of burial chambers near Cardiff that pre-date Stonehenge. With its status as a port, Cardiff is ethnically diverse. There is a huge free festival called Cardiff Big Weekend held every summer. There is an active nightlife. Hostels are generally good here, divided between party and non-party ones.

Riverhouse B'packers, 59 Fitzhamon Embankment, Cardiff, S. Wales; *riverhousebackpackers.com/*; T:02920399810; $24bed, Kitchen:Y, B'fast:Y, Pvt. room:Y, Locker:Y, Recep:24/7; Note:wh/chair ok, laundry, prkng, tea/cof, tours, cntr

Nomad Hostel, 11-15 Howard Grdns, Roath, Cardiff, S. Glamorgan; T:02920256826, *info@ nomadcardiff.co.uk/*; $16bed, Kitchen:Y, B'fast:Y, Pvt. room:Y, Locker:Y, Recep:24/7; Note: bar, games, parking, bag hold $, central, billiards

NosDa Studio Hostel, 53-59 Despenser St, Riverside, Cardiff; T:02920378866, *info@ nosda.co.uk/*; $22bed, Kitchen:Y, B'fast:Y, Pvt.room:Y, Locker:Y, Recep:24/7; Note: bar, billiards, laundry, bag hold, c.c. ok, gym, min. 2N

Bunkhouse Hostel, 94 Saint Mary St, S. Glamorgan; T:02920228587, *info@ bunkhousecardiff.co.uk/*; $16bed, Kitchen:N, B'fast:Y, Pvt.room:N, Locker:Y, Recep:24/7; Note: bar, club, central, wh/chair ok, laundry, bag hold, tea/ coffee

YHA Cardiff, 2 Wedal Rd, Roath Park, Cardiff; *hihostels.com/*, T:08453719311, *cardiff@ yha.org.uk/*; $24bed, Kitchen:Y, B'fast:$, Pvt.room:N, Locker:Y, Recep:7a>11p; Note: membership fee, distant, WiFi:$, bar, café, bag hold

CARMARTHEN is a city of 15,000 in south Wales, 8mi/13km up the River Rowy from Carmarthen Bay. It was at one time the country's capital and claims to be the oldest city, with several Roman ruins. Merlin the Magician is from here. So is St. Peter's Church.

Pant-yr-Athro Intl Hostel, Carmarthen; *backpackershostelwales.co.uk/*, T:+44/01267241014, *kenknuckles@hotmail.com*; $24Bed, Kitchen:Y, B'fast:$, Pvt. room:Y, Locker:N, Recep:ltd; Note: need car

CONWY is a town of over 14,000 on Wales' far north shore, with many tourist attractions. There is a castle, town walls, a parish church, suspension bridge, tubular railway bridge, 14th century Aberconwy (merchant's) House, and the Elizabethan Plas Mlawr. Then there's the smallest house in the world, at 3x1.8 meters. Sounds fun.

YHA Conwy, Sychnant Pass Rd, Larkhill, Conwy; *hihostels.com/*, T:+44/1492593571, *conwy@yha.org.uk*; $23Bed, Kitchen:Y, B'fast:$, Pvt.room:Y, Locker:Y, Recep:8a/10:30p; Note: resto/bar, pool, billiards, wh/chair

FISHGUARD is a town of 5000 in the far southwest. There is a ferry to Ireland. It is a typical fishing village and has a Thursday market.

Hamilton Backpacker Lodge, 21 Hamilton St, Fishguard; T:01348874797, *hamiltonbackpackers.co.uk/*, $27Bed, *hamiltonbackpackers@yahoo.co.uk*; Kitchen:Y, B'fast:Y, Pvt.room:Y, Locker:N, Recep:>8p; Note: parking, central, friendly natives

LLANDUDNO is "Queen of the Welsh Resorts," with a population of 20,000. If that makes it a bit more commercial than the rest, with such attractions as the Victorian Carnival and Mostyn Street funfair, Marine Drive carriage way, 2300ft/700mt long pier, Happy Valley gardens and fake ski run, then so be it. Take the kids.

Llandudno Hostel, 14 Charlton St, Llandudno, Gwynedd; T:01492877430, *Info@ llandudnohostel.co.uk/*, $29Bed, Kitchen:N, B'fast:Y, Pvt.room:Y, Locker:N, Recep:ltd; Note: near train/beach/center, microwave, luggage room

PART II: Central Europe

You wouldn't believe how many times the cities of Central Europe have changed hands between nations. It has been a battlefield for most of the history of civilization, Celts once widespread, only to be replaced by Germans, and Slavs, among others. Then when Jews attempted to carve out a niche for themselves, well, you know... Things are calmer now, with borders fairly well established, and hopefully superseded by the gradual unification of Europe.

Countries that once fought each tooth and nail a few short years ago are now partners in something bigger and hopefully better than any one of them individually. Though Germanic people pretty much occupy the west and Slavic people the east, the reality is never that simple, of course. If ancient settlement patterns scrambled the boundaries before, then economic inequalities scramble them now, as people from poorer countries like Poland flood into the west to work for higher wages.

Aside from economics, the countries of Central Europe are fairly similar, full of history and plenty of hidden architectural gems. And fully integrated bus, rail, and air services have woven them all together tightly. The distances are not that great anyway. You can easily leave London in the evening and wake up in Poland. That's only a one-hour flight BTW, and the flights have never been cheaper, what with the proliferation of discount airlines over the last ten years.

Languages range from Netherlandic and German in the west (and a little bit of Belgian French for spice), to the Slavic Polish in the east, the former closely related to English, the latter to Russian, though they are all mutually unintelligible...unless maybe if you're a local. Anyway your modern Standard English should suffice in these areas of wide-scale tourism. There certainly shouldn't be any language problem in the hostels. That's one reason they exist.

The countries farther east will be cheaper, of course, and the people are as friendly as the architecture is stunning. Poland is not a bad hub to the East in fact, not bad at all, and something like Germany's Slavic twin by size. It is cheap, well-connected in all directions by bus, rail and discount planes, and the hostels are of good quality. Kitchens are sometimes hard to find, but breakfast is fairly common. Only Russia and Belarus are 'old-school,' in that they require visas (for Westerners), letters of introduction, and all that nonsense. Though likely cheaper, except maybe in Russia, hostels in the East may also be better. Poorer countries try harder. They party, too, sometimes non-stop.

6) Belgium

Belgium exists as part of the historical uncertainty as to where the line is drawn between northern and southern Europe and what exactly that means. Part and parcel of that historical occurrence is the emergence of Belgium as continental Europe's first focus of the Industrial Revolution in the early 1800's. When Belgium seceded from the Netherlands in 1830, French speakers immediately formed the elite class, a situation which still causes problems to this day. French and Dutch (local dialects of the two) plus German, to a lesser extent, are the languages. Euro is currency. Phone code is +32.

4 Hostels) ANTWERP has been a port of trade since time immemorial, a role it still fulfills today. As such, it has always been very much an international city. It inherited much of the trade that Bruges lost after its river silted up, and expanded on that with a banking industry very advanced for its time. Antwerp is also a center for Orthodox Jews, many involved in the diamond trade. Cultural amenities include the Royal Museum of Fine Arts, the National Maritime Museum, the Mayer van den Bergh Museum, the Museum of Contemporary Art, and the Middelheim Open-Air Museum of Sculpture.

The performing arts are led by the Royal Flemish Opera House and Royal Dutch Theatre.

Abhostel, Kattenberg 110, Antwerpen; *abhostel.com/*, T:0473570166, *abhostel@ hotmail.com/*; $28Bed, Kitchen:Y, B'fast:Y, Pvt. room:Y, Locker:Y, Recep:12n/8p; Note: under 50 y.o. only, bar, books, maps, games, luggage room

Alias YH, Provinciestraat 256, Antwerpen; *info@youthhotel.be*, T:032300522, *wix.com/aliasyouthhostel/home*; $25bed, Kitchen:N, B'fast:Y, Pvt.room:Y, Locker:Y, Recep:8a>5p; Note: not central, long-stays, luggage room, cash

HI Antwerp Central Hostel, Bogaardeplein 1, Antwerp; *hihostels.com/*, T:+32(0)32340314, *antwerpen@vjh.be*; $33Bed, Kitchen:N, B'fast:Y, Pvt.room:Y, Locker:Y, Recep:>11p; Note: resto/bar, lift, luggage room, central, wh/chair ok

Boomerang Hostel, Lange Leemstraat 95, Antwerpen; *boomeranghostel.be/*, T:032384782, *boomeranghostel@hotmail.com*; $17Bed, Kitchen:Y, B'fast:N, Pvt. room:N, Locker:N, Recep:24/7; Note: bar, smoking, cash only, basic, parties

BOUILLON is a town of 5500 in the southeast portion of the country, the French-speaking part. The castle, high above the town center, is the main attraction.

Les Auberges de Jeunesse de Bouillon, Rte du Christ 16, Bouillon; *info@ lesaubergesdejeunesse.be/*, T:061468137; $23Bed, Kitchen:Y, B'fast:Y, Pvt. room:Y, Locker:Y, Recep:ltd; Note: resto/bar, laundry, luggage room, tours, parking, maps

6 Hostels) BRUGES (Brugge) lies in a propitious site for trade, one it took full advantage of in the late Middle Ages. At the southern end of the Hanseatic routes and the northern end of the Genoese and Venetian ones, Bruges was the perfect conduit to funnel exotic Asian merchandise into the rapidly developing pre-Renaissance countries and economies of northern Europe. But Bruges couldn't maintain its advantage, or a silt-free channel, and by the late 1800's was being referred to as a "city of the dead."

Thus was born the Bruges tourist industry, finding glory in a well-preserved past. Fortunately its medieval architecture survived the WWII nightmare relatively intact and today is a UNESCO world heritage site. It can be visited on a day-trip from Brussels. Medieval remains in the city include the old Market Hall and the Town Hall. Notable churches include the Cathedral of St. Salvator, the Church of Notre Dame, and the Church of Jerusalem. Museums include the Memling Museum in the 12th C. Hospital of St. John, the Groeninge Museum, and the 15th C. Gruuthuse mansion.

St. Christopher's Inn-Bauhaus, Langestraat 135, Brugge; T:050341093, *info@ bauhaus.be/*; $24bed, Kitchen:N, B'fast:Y, Pvt.room:Y, Locker:Y, Recep:24/7; Note: bar, café, wh/chair ok, a/c, bikes, laundry, bunk curtains, bag hold, tours

Charlie Rockets, Hoogstraat 19, Brugge; *info@ charlierockets.com/*, T:050330660; $24bed, Kitchen:N, B'fast:$, Pvt.room:N, Locker:N, Recep:24/7; Note: bar, café luggage, parking, tours, laundry, c.c. ok, billiards, minimart

Hostel Lybeer, Korte Vuldersstraat 31, Brugge, *info@ hostellybeer.com*, T:050334355; $22Bed, Kitchen:Y, B'fast:N, Pvt.room:Y, Locker:N, Recep:ltd; Note: bar, laundry, luggage room, tours, maps, historic city, central, nr train

Snuffel Backpacker Hostel, Ezelstraat 47-49, Brugge; *info@ snuffel.be/*, T:050333133; $22Bed, Kitchen:Y, B'fast:Y, Pvt.room:N, Locker:Y, Recep:ltd; Note: café/bar, bikes, books, terrace, tour desk, parking, luggage room, minimart

HI Bruges Europa, Baron Ruzettelaan 143, Brugge; *hihostels.com*, T:+32/50352679; *brugge@vjh.be*; $27Bed, Kitchen:N, B'fast:Y, Pvt.room:Y, Locker:Y, Recep:8a>10p; Note: bar, wh/chair Ok, luggage room, parking

HI Brugge Dudzele Herdersbrug, Louis Coiseaukaai 46, Brugge, Dudzele, *hihostels.com/*, T:050599321, *brugge.dudzele@vjh.be*; $32Bed, Kitchen:N, B'fast:Y, Pvt.room:Y, Locker:Y, Recep:8a/10p; Note: b'fast buffet, laundry, bikes

9 Hostels) BRUSSELS (Bruxelles) is Belgium's main city and largely a French-speaking enclave in Dutch-speaking Flanders. Maybe best known now as the capital of a now at-least-partially-united Europe, perhaps Brussels can accomplish for Europe what it has yet to accomplish for Belgium; perhaps. Cultural life includes the National Archive, the Albert I Royal Library, many museums and the Palace of Fine Arts. There is a red-light district that

resembles Amsterdam without the canals. That's how you know it's a Dutch area, I guess. This is next to the largest Muslim area north of Tangier. Go figure.

Grand Place, Haringstraat 6-8, Brussels, T:+32(2)2193019

2GO4 Quality Hostel, Blvd Emile Jacqmain 99, Brussels; T:022193019, *info@ 2go4.be/*; $34bed, Kitchen:Y, B'fast:N, Pvt.room:Y, Locker:Y, Recep:8a>11p; Note: dorm age limit 35, check-in 4p, lift, bag hold, maps, real beds!

Sleep Well, Rue du Damier 23, Brussels, *info@ sleepwell.be/*, T:022185050; $32Bed, Kitchen:N, B'fast:Y, Pvt.room:Y, Locker:Y, Recep:24/7; Note: bikes, resto/bar, laundry, billiards, wh/chair, lift, bag hold, parking, WiFi $, maps

Sleep Here, Rue de la Source 82, Saint-Gilles; *sleephere-la-source.com/*, T:0496599379; $39Bed, Kitchen:Y, B'fast:Y, Pvt.room:Y, Locker:N, Recep:ltd; Note: reception closed 1p>6:30p, homey, central, luggage room, tea/ coffee, maps

Hello Hostel, Rue de l'Armistice 1, Koekelberg, *reception@ hello-hostel.eu/*, T:0471935927; $24Bed, Kitchen:Y, B'fast:Y, Pvt.room:Y, Locker:Y, Recep:24/7; Note: café/bar, laundry, luggage room, minimart, books, ATM, nr metro far>ctr

Centre Vincent Van Gogh/chab, Rue Traversière 8, Brussels; T:022170158, *info@ chab.be/*; $30Bed, Kitchen:Y, B'fast:Y, Pvt.room:Y, Locker:N, Recep:24/7; Note: 2N min, bar, billiards, laundry, luggage rm, age>35y.o.

Generation Europe YH, Rue de l'Eléphant 4; T:+32/24103858

YH Jacques Brel, Rue de la Sablonnière 30, Brussels; T:+32(0)2180187, *Brussels.brel@ lesaubergesdejeunesse.be/*; $35Bed, Kitchen:Y, B'fast:Y, Pvt.room:Y, Locker:Y, Recep:8a>1a; Note: wh/chair OK, lift, café/bar, laundry, bag hold

Auberge de 3 Fontaines, Chaussée de Wavre 2057, Brussels; *contact@ auberge3fontaines.be/*, T:+32(0)2663.2432; $28Bed, Kitchen:N, B'fast:N, Pvt.room:Y, Locker:Y, Recep:9a>10p; Note: resto, lift, wh/chair ok, >35 y.o. dorm age

3 Hostels) GHENT is a city of almost 300,000 in the northwest Flemish (Dutch) part of Belgium, with almost twice that population in the metropolitan area. Originally settled by Celts and lated occupied by Germanic Franks, the city

was one of Europe's largest and richest in the Middle Ages, thanks to its wool and its cloth. There were continuous political problems with the Holy Roman Empire and Habsburgs, the Spanish and Austrians, until finally forming a part of independent Belgium in 1830 after a stint with the Netherlands.

The Germans occupied Ghent in both World Wars, but its architecture largely remained intact. They in general and the UNESCO-recognized beguinages in particular are the main tourist attractions. There are also museums of Fine Arts, Design, Contemporary Art, Textiles, and the City Museum. Festivals include "Gentse Feesten,"

"I Love Techno," and "10 Days Off" musical festivals, Flanders International Film Festival Ghent, and The Festival of Flanders.

HI Gent Hostel De Draecke, St Widostraat 11, Gent; *hihostels.com/*, T:+32/92337050, *gent@vjh.be;* $30Bed, Kitchen:N, B'fast:Y, Pvt.room:Y, Locker:Y, Recep:7a>11p; Note: café/bar, parking, buffet brekkie

Ecohostel Andromeda, Bargiekaai 35, Gent; T:+32/486678033, *Andromeda@ ecohostel.be/*; $31Bed, Kitchen:Y, B'fast:Y, Pvt.room:Y, Locker:Y, Recep:ltd; Note: luggage room, tour desk, maps, books, house boat

Hostel Uppelink, Sint-Michielsplein 21, Gent, T:092794477; *Info@ hosteluppelink.com/*; $35Bed, Kitchen:N, B'fast:Y, Pvt.room:Y, Locker:Y, Recep:>10p; Note: non-party, max stay 6N, bar, luggage rm, books, maps, central

3 Hostels) LEUVEN is a city of almost 100,000 in the center of the country and Dutch-speaking. This is corporate headquarters for Anheuser-Busch InBev and its flagship brew Stella Artois (ha! gotcha!). There is a Lemmings Institute of music therapy, and a Marktrock summer rock festival; different kind of therapy, I guess. Landmarks include the Town Hall, the Linen Hall, St. Anthony's Chapel, 'Totem' and 'Fonske' statues, Large Bequinage, and churches of St. Peters, St. Michael, and St. Quentin.

Leuven City Hostel, Ravenstraat 37, Leuven; T:+32/16843033, *Info@ leuvencityhostel.com*; $32Bed, Kitchen:N, B'fast:Y, Pvt.room:Y, Locker:Y, Recep:9a//8p; Note: bar, wh/chair ok, luggage room, central

HI De Blauwput, Martelarenlaan 11A, Leuven, *leuven-hostel.com/*, T:016639062, *leuven@vjh.be*, $30Bed, Kitchen:N, B'fast:Y, Pvt.room:Y, Locker:Y, Recep:3p>10p; Note: resto/bar, lift, wh/chair ok, bag hold, near train

St. Jacob, Brusselsestraat 125, Leuven; T:016893759, *Info@ stjacob.be/*; $46Bed, Kitchen:Y, B'fast:Y, Pvt.room:Y, Locker:N, Recep:ltd; Note: resto, luggage room, parking, laundry, safe dep, maps, WiFi$, central

2 Hostels) LIEGE is a French-speaking city of almost 200,000 in the eastern part of the country. The metropolitan area has a population several times over, and is the economic capital of Wallonia, the French-speaking region. OVIFAT is a nearby village of 500.

Gite d'etape d'Ovifat, Rue des Charmilles, Ovifat; T:080444677, *gite. ovifat@ gitesdetape.be/*; $28Bed, Kitchen:N, B'fast:Y, Pvt.room:Y, Locker:N, Recep:ltd; Note: pool, resto/bar, bikes, wh/chair ok, parking

Liege YH, Rue Georges Simenon 2, Liege; T:+32/43445689, *liege@ lesaubergesdejeunesse.be/*; $28Bed, Kitchen:Y, B'fast:Y, Pvt.room:Y, Locker:Y, Recep:>1a; Note: central, waffles, bar, lift, wh/chair, laundry, luggage room

MALMEDY is a German-speaking city of 12,000 in the far eastern part off the country, which it shares with French speakers. The borders with Germany have fluctuated often.

Malmedy YH, Route D'Eupen 36, Malmedy; T:080338386, *malmedy@ lesaubergesdejeunesse.be/*; $26Bed, Kitchen:Y, B'fast:Y, Pvt.room:Y, Locker:N, Recep:ltd; Note: café/bar, wh/chair ok, laundry, luggage room, parking

MECHELEN is a city of over 80,000 in the Flemish part off the country, and known for historical art, tapestries and lace, woodcarving and furniture. Landmarks include St. Rumboldt's cathedral, Brusselpoort city gate, Church of St. John the evangelist, palaces of Margaret of York and Margaret of Austria, the Lakenhall of woolen cloth merchants, large and small beguinages, Toy Museum, and Jewish Museum.

HI Mechelen De Zandpoort, Zandpoortvest 70, Mechelen; *hihostels. com/*, T:+32/15278539, *mechelen@vjh.be*; $30Bed, Kitchen:N, B'fast:Y, Pvt. room:Y, Locker:Y, Recep:8a//11p; Note: resto/bar, lift, wh/chair, parking, bag hold, big

MONS is a city of 93,000 in the French-speaking Wallonia region. Attractions include the *Grand Place*, centre of the historic town; the City Hall, which dates from the 15ᵗʰ century; the collegiate church of Sainte-Waudru; the Baroque-style belfry, a World Heritage Site, from the 17th century; the *Spanish House* from the 16ᵗʰ century, and the Museum François Duesberg.

Auberge du Beffroi, Rampe du Château 2, Mons; T:065875570, *mons@ lesaubergesdejeunesse.be/*; $28Bed, Kitchen:Y, B'fast:Y, Pvt.room:Y, Locker:Y, Recep:ltd; Note: resto/bar, laundry, bag hold, central, meals $, heritage site

NAMUR is a city of 110,000 in the French-speaking province of Wallonia, and is its capital. There is a citadel and 8ᵗʰ century cathedral dedicated to St. Aubainand, a UNESCO belfry, the Couvent des Soeurs de Notre-Dame of Mosan art by Hugo d'Oignies, and an archeological museum and a museum dedicated to Félicien Rops.

YH Félicien Rops, Ave. Félicien Rops 8, Namur; T:081223688, *Namur@ lesaubergesdejeunesse.be/*; $28Bed, Kitchen:Y, B'fast:Y, Pvt.room:Y, Locker:Y, Recep:ltd; Note: bar, wh/chair ok, laundry, bag hold, prkng, meals $, lockout 10-4

OSTEND is a Flemish city of 70,000 on the North Sea. Attractions include the casino, Fort Napoleon, the James Ensor museum, the *Mercator* sailing ship, St. Petrus and St. Paulus churches, the Hippodrome Wellington horse races, and Mu Zee museum of modern art.

HI Oostende De Ploate, Langestraat 82, Oostende; *hihostels.com/*, T:+32(0)59805297, *oostende@vjh.be*; $30Bed, Kitchen:N, B'fast:Y, Pvt.room:Y, Locker:N, Recep:ltd; Note: buffet brek, bar, parking, meals $, c.c. ok

2 Hostels) ROCHEFORT is a town of 12,500 in the eastern Walloon province of Namur. Dark sweet beers are brewed here in the Rochefore Brewery. HAN-SUR-LESSE is a nearby village, famous for its caves.

Gîte d'Etape, Rue du Gîte d'Etape 10, Han-sur-Lesse; *gitesdetape.be/*, T:022090300; $28Bed, Kitchen:n, B'fast:Y, Pvt.room:Y, Locker:N, Recep:ltd; Note: pool, bar, parking

Gite d'etape Rochefort, Rue du Hableau 25, Rochefort; *giterochefort.be/*, T:+32/84214604, *giterochefort@skynet.be*; $28Bed, Kitchen:N, B'fast:Y, Pvt. room:Y, Locker:N, Recep:5-10p; Note: resto/bar, pool, bikes

TOURNAI is a city of 70,000 in the French-speaking Walloon half of Belgium. It dates back to the Roman era as a stopover on the old Roman road from Cologne to Boulogne. It then played a role in the early French kingdoms of Clovis and Charles the Bald. Today that ancient architecture is a UNESCO world heritage site. The Grand Place is the center of social life. Tapestries, Mosan and 'Primitive' art of the Flemish school are notable.

YH Tournai, Rue Saint-Martin, 64, Tournai; T:+32(0)69216136, *tournai@ lesaubergesdejeunesse.be*; $Bed, Kitchen:Y, B'fast:Y, Pvt.room:Y, Locker:N, Recep:5-8p; Note: bar, wh/chair ok, laundry, luggage room, meals $

7) Czech Republic

The Czech Republic is the other Eastern European nation — besides Poland and Hungary — most intertwined with the West historically, and long a constituent part of the Habsburg Empire and its successor Austria-Hungary. Before that, as Bohemia, it was part of the Great Moravian Empire, then the Holy Roman Empire. Upon integration into the Habsburg monarchy it was subjected to forced "Germanization" and eventual industrialization. After WWI it became one-half of Czechoslovakia and after WWII became a Communist-ruled part of the Warsaw Pact. It always chafed at the bit, though, and the Prague Spring of 1968 fired the first (okay, second after Hungary) shot across the bow of the Soviet hulk to signal that all was not right in the Empire. That was crushed brutally but twenty years later it was more like velvet crush in the Velvet Revolution of 1989 that brought down the Communists and eventually separated the Czechs and Slovaks back into their constituent republics.

Today the Czech Republic is a fully developed country, democratic and healthy and tourist central. Interestingly, for such a small country, rivers from the Czech Republic drain into three different seas. The country itself is entirely landlocked, except for a lot on the Hamburg docks awarded to it by the Treaty of Versailles. I bet the Reeperbahn is close by. Did I mention that this is ancient Bohemia? Yes, the beer is good. Yes, you can get one for breakfast. No, you won't be alone. There are also castles and spas. Czech music and literature are among the best. Czech is the language; *koruna* (CZK) is currency, and the calling code is +420.

2 Hostels) BRNO is the Czech Republic's second city and an important university town. It is in the eastern Moravian part of the country, so not quite so Bohemian. Its history extends back to a Middle Age fortified settlement in an area where Celtic and Germanic tribes had lived previously. It soon would become one of the major cities of Moravia. Like the rest of central Europe, the main historical drama was the struggle between Germans, Slavs, and Jews. WWII settled all that, with the loss of Brno's 12,000 Jews and the expulsion of Germans. Today it is an important exhibition and trade center.

Brno has historical sites, festivals, and nature to enjoy, first among them Spilberk Castle, the Cathedral of Saints Peter and Paul, and the Moravian Karst formations. Since the fall of Communism, it has undergone a cultural rebirth, including the revival of old traditions. Some of the finest surviving buildings include the churches of St. Thomas and St. James, the Augustinian monastery, and Tugendhat House, a World Heritage Site.

Hostel Mitte, Panská 11, Brno; T:+420/734622340, *info@ hostelmitte.com/*; $26bed, Kitchen:Y, B'fast:Y, Pvt.room:Y, Locker:Y, Recep:ltd; Note: bar, luggage room, c.c. ok, central, close to train

Hostel Fleda, Štefánikova 24, Brno, Czech Republic; T:+420/533433638, *info@ hostelfleda.com/*; $16bed, Kitchen:Y, B'fast:$, Pvt. room:Y, Locker:Y, Recep:ltd; Note: laundry, downstairs bar/club, c.c. ok, old house

CESKE BUDEJOVICE is also known as Budweis, with all that name represents, mostly beer. The American and Czech brands are not the same. There is also historic architecture if you need something to look at while getting happy, including an arcaded town square and the Baroque Samson's Fountain. There's a Museum of South Bohemia.

Cuba Bar & Hostel, Nová 2024/18, České Budějovice 3; T:777723803, *info@ cuba-bar.cz/*; $15bed, Kitchen:Y, B'fast:N, Pvt. room:Y, Locker:Y, Recep:5p>; Note: check-in at bar, laundry, parking

5 Hostels) CESKY KRUMLOV is a medieval town complete with a castle of the same name that is second in size only to Hradcany (Prague Castle) complex in Prague, unusual for such a small town. The Castle Theatre is especially nice. It has historically been a part of the German-speaking Sudetenland, and therefore subject to frequent political drama. There are cultural festivals. On summer solstice the entire town dresses in medieval costume.

Hostel Krumlov House, Rooseveltova 68, Cesky Krumlov; T:+420/380711935, *info@ krumlovhostel.com/*; $18bed, Kitchen:Y, B'fast:N, Pvt. room:Y, Locker:Y, Recep:ltd; Note: luggage room, laundry, parking

Hostel 99, Věžní 99, Český Krumlov; T:380712812, *hostel99@ hostel99.cz/*; $15bed, Kitchen:Y, B'fast:N, Pvt.room:N, Locker:Y, Recep:9a>9p; Note: resto/ bar, parking, laundry, coffee & tea

Hostel Merlin, Kájovská 59, Český Krumlov; *info@ hostelmerlin.com/*; T:606256145, $13bed, Kitchen:Y, B'fast:N, Pvt.room:Y, Locker:N, Recep:11a>8p; Note: parking, coffee & tea

Travellers Hostel Soukenicka, Soukenická 43, Český Krumlov; T:380711345, *krumlov@ travellers.cz/*; $14bed, Kitchen:Y, B'fast:$, Pvt.room:Y, Locker:Y, Recep:ltd; Note: resto/ bar, laundry, c.c. ok

Hostel Havana, U Svateho Ducha 135, Cesky Krumlov; T:+420/777723244, *info@ havanahostels.cz/*; $13bed, Kitchen:Y, B'fast:N, Pvt. room:Y, Locker:Y, Recep:ltd; Note: travel desk, parking, quiet, garden

OLOMOUC is the historic capital of Moravia and sixth largest city in the Czech Republic today. Aside from the usual jockeying for position between locals, Germans, and Jews, Olomouc has also played the fall guy for Swedes during their empire and the Prussians during theirs. Being the capital is dangerous. There are several historical ecclesiastical monuments and a torture rack. Historic buildings include the 14th C. Gothic St. Wenceslas' Cathedral, and the town hall, with an astronomical clock. Notable fountains are Triton and Caesar's. Holy Trinity Column, a UNESCO World Heritage site, is an example of the Olomouc Baroque style.

Poets Corner Hostel, Sokolská 1, Olomouc, Czech Republic; *hostelolomouc. com/*, T:777570730; $15bed, Kitchen:Y, B'fast:N, Pvt. room:Y, Locker:Y, Recep:ltd; Note: luggage room, laundry, tour desk, central

PILSEN is the Czech Republic's fourth city and is located in the western Bohemian part of the country, only 55mi/90 km west of Prague. It is a trade and industrial center and once had large populations of Germans and Jews. There are important cathedrals and synagogues and lots of beer, the ones that made it famous. Landmarks are St. Bartholomew's church, the Franciscan Church of the Virgin Mary, and the Renaissance town hall.

Euro Hostel Pilsen, Na Roudne 13, Pilsen; T:+420/377259926, *info@ eurohostel.cz/*; $20bed, Kitchen:N, B'fast:$, Pvt. room:Y, Locker:Y, Recep:24/7; Note: restaurant, parking, laundry, luggage room, travel desk

27 Hostels) PRAGUE sits on a prime piece of Vitava River real estate that was occupied by Celtic tribes, then Germanic, before Slavic ones came in during the great migrations that followed the post-Roman era in Europe. Merchants would settle here just to trade, and by the ninth century were in place the beginnings of Prague Castle, then bridges, then cathedrals. Germans had their neighborhoods, as did Jews, and this created tensions, especially when the Industrial Revolution increased wealth and defined social classes.

When Hitler entered Czechoslovakia in 1939 (and the West did nothing), Prague's fate was sealed, for a while at least. At war's end, Prague was the capital of a Soviet-occupied tank-filled Czechoslovakia that not even "Prague Spring" could change. Today it is the main tourist destination in the Czech Republic, it being one of the first cities behind the former "Iron Curtain" that Western tourists, mostly young, flocked to and started *ad hoc* colonies for the purposes of low-budget partying.

The city is friendly and the architecture is stunning. The entire historic center is a UNESCO world heritage site, and there are some 2000 recognized monuments. Some of the highlights are Charles Bridge, the castle of Hradčany (Prague Castle), Old Town, Wenceslas Square, the Jewish Quarter, the Church of St. George, St. Vitus' Cathedral, the Týn Church on Staroměstské ("Old Town") Square, Powder Tower, Bethlehem Chapel, St. Agnes Convent, the Old-New Synagogue, the Old Jewish Cemetery, Valdštejn and Clam-Gallas palaces, St. Nicholas Church, the Antonín Dvořák Museum, the Golz-Kinský Palace, the Bedřich Smetana Museum, the Belvedere Palace, the National Museum, the National Theatre... and of course Lennon Wall, devoted to John, testament to Prague's long flirtation with Lennonism even in the darkest days of Stalinism.

Hostel Lipa, Tachovské náměstí 288/6, Prague 3-Žižkov; T:602211182, *info@ hostellipa.com/*; $13bed, Kitchen:Y, B'fast:N, Pvt.room:Y, Locker:Y, Recep:ltd; Note: restaurant, wheelchair ok, prkng, Jacuzzi, not central, microbrew

Art Hole Hostel, Soukenická 1756/34, Prague 1-Nové Město; T:222314028, *info@ artholehostel.com/*; $23bed, Kitchen:Y, B'fast:Y, Pvt.room:N, Locker:Y, Recep:24/7; Note: close to old town, age restrictions

Hostel One Prague, Cimburkova 916/8, Prague 3-Žižkov; *hosteloneprague. com/*, T:222221423, *hostelprague@gmail.com*; $15bed, Kitchen:Y, B'fast:N, Pvt. room:Y, Locker:Y, Recep:>12m; Note: lift, café, bikes, laundry, bag hold

Czech Inn, Francouzská 76, Prague, T:+420/267267612, *info@ czech-inn. com*; $15bed, Kitchen:N, B'fast:$, Pvt.room:Y, Locker:Y, Recep:24/7; Note: c.c. +4%, bar/café, lift, ATM, luggage room, laundry, not central

Miss Sophie's, Melounova 3, Prague; T:296303530, *info@ miss-sophies. com/*; $20bed, Kitchen:Y, B'fast:$, Pvt.room:Y, Locker:Y, Recep:24/7; Note: c.c. +4%, luggage room, safe deposit, central

Hostel Miles, Vodičkova 38, Praha, T:+420/773800732, *robert@ hostelmiles. com/*; $20bed, Kitchen:Y, B'fast:N, Pvt.room:Y, Locker:Y, Recep:24/7; Note: lift, forex, tours, a/c, c.c. ok, luggage room, laundry, central

Hostel Orange, Vaclavske namesti 20, Prague; *hostelorange.com/*, T:223018557, *Hostelorange20@gmail.com*; $13bed, Kitchen:Y, B'fast:$, Pvt. room:Y, Locker:Y, Recep:>11p; Note:resto/bar/club, prkng, free tour/info, forex, c.c.

Little Town, Malostranské náměstí 260/11, Prague 1; T:242406965, *info@ littletownhotel.cz/*; $20bed, Kitchen:Y, B'fast:$, Pvt.room:Y, Locker: Y, Recep:24/7; Note: resto/bar/club, free tour, travel desk, close to castle, laundry, c.c. ok

Hostel Mango, Míšeňská 68/8, Prague 1-Malá Strana; *hostelmango.com/en/*, T:776238563, *hostelmango@gmail.com*; $14bed, Kitchen:Y, B'fast:$, Pvt.room:Y, Locker:Y, Recep:ltd; Note: café/resto/bar/club, tours, bag hold, central

Sir Toby's Hostel, Dělnická 1155/24, Praha 7-Holešovice; *sirtobys.com/*, T:246032611; $11bed, Kitchen:Y, B'fast:$, Pvt.room:Y, Locker:N, Recep:24/7; Note: bar, parking, free tour, luggage room, laundry, c.c. ok, un-central

St. Christopher's at Mosaic House, Odboru 4, Prague, T:246008324, *info@ mosaichouse.com/*; $16bed, Kitchen:N, B'fast:N, Pvt.room:Y, Locker:Y, Recep:24/7; Note: wheelchair ok, resto/bar, travel desk, bag hold, forex, c.c. ok

Hostel Rosemary, Růžová 971/5, Prague 1-Nové Město; T:222211124, *info@ praguecityhostel.cz/*; $13bed, Kitchen:Y, B'fast:N, Pvt.room:Y, Locker:N, Recep:>7p; Note: lift, laundry, bag hold, free tour, travel desk, c.c. ok, central

Little Quarter Hostel, Nerudova 246/21, Prague 1-Malá Strana; *littlequarter.com/*, T:257212029, *LQ@avehotels.cz*; $26bed, Kitchen:Y, B'fast:$, Pvt.room:Y, Locker:Y, Recep:24/7; Note: no bunks, luggage rm, tour desk, forex, c.c. ok,

Plus Prague Hostel, Přívozní 1562/1, Praha-Holešovice; *plushostels.com*, T:220510046; $12bed, Kitchen:N, B'fast:$, Pvt.room:Y, Locker:Y, Recep:24/7; Note: resto/bar/club, prkng, luggage ok, forex, c.c. ok, pool, sauna

Prague Sqare Hostel, Melantrichova 471/10, Prague 1-Old Town; T:224240859, *info@ praguesquarehostel.com/*; $14bed, Kitchen:Y, B'fast:Y, Pvt.

room:Y, Locker:Y, Recep:24/7; Note: resto/bar/club, luggage room, travel desk, central

Hostel Marabou, Koněvova 738/55, Žižkov, Prague; T:222581182, *info@ hostelmarabou.com/*; $16bed, Kitchen:Y, B'fast:Y, Pvt.room:Y, Locker:Y, Recep:24/7; Note: bar, free tour, forex, c.c. ok, 2.5mi/4km from old town, smoking

Advantage Hostel, Sokolská 11, Prague; *advantagehostel.cz/*, T:739343864, *advantage@jsc.cz*; $20bed, Kitchen:Y, B'fast:Y, Pvt.room:Y, Locker:Y, Recep:24/7; Note: resto/bar, free tour/info, bikes, luggage ok, laundry, c.c. ok, TV

Riverbank Hostel, Masarykovo nábřeží 2016/6, Praha 4 NewTown; *riverbank.cz/*, T:724879687, *info.riverbank@yahoo.com*; $15bed, Kitchen:Y, B'fast:N, Pvt.room:Y, Locker:Y, Recep:ltd; Note: luggage room, river view, central

Travellers Hostel Dlouha, Dlouhá 33, Prague 1; T:224826663, *hostel@ travellers.cz/*; $21bed, Kitchen:Y, B'fast:Y, Pvt.room:Y, Locker:Y, Recep:24/7; Note: wheelchair ok, bar, luggage room, laundry, c.c. ok, central

Hostel Clown & Bard, Bořivojova 102, Praha 3; T:222716453, *horek@ clownandbard.com/*; $12bed, Kitchen:Y, B'fast:$, Pvt.room:Y, Locker:Y, Recep:24/7; Note: cash, smoking in bar, free tour/info, luggage room, forex, not central

Hostel Marrakesh, Biskupská 1139/4, Prague 1-Nové Město; T:734373425, *info@ hostelmarrakesh.com/*; $15bed, Kitchen:Y, B'fast:Y, Pvt. room:N, Locker:N, Recep:ltd; Note: tours, forex, ATM, luggage rm, a/c, c.c. ok, staff few

Hostel Aplus Hotel, Na Florenci 1413/33, Praha 1; *info@ aplus-hostel.cz/*, T:222314272; $15bed, Kitchen:Y, B'fast:Y, Pvt.room:N, Locker:Y, Recep:24/7; Note: resto/bar/club, tours, bag hold, laundry, cc ok, 10-min walk>ctr

Emma Hostel, Na Zderaze 267/10, Prague-New Town; *hostel-emma.com/*, T:222521269, *emmahostel@yahoo.com*; $8bed, Kitchen:Y, B'fast:N, Pvt.room: Y, Locker:N, Recep:24/7; Note: tours, prkng, luggage rm, pets ok, central

Pension Tara, Havelska 15, Praha 1, Prague; T:+420/224228083, *info@ pensiontara.net/*; $18bed, Kitchen:N, B'fast:$, Pvt.room:Y, Locker:Y, Recep:ltd; Note: restaurant, free tour/info, historical, c.c. ok, stairs no lift, central

Euro Guesthouse, Krakovska 3, Praha 1, Prague; *euroguesthouse.eu/*, T:+420/608414422; $24bed, Kitchen:Y, B'fast:N, Pvt.room:Y, Locker:N, Recep:9a>9p; Note: arpt pickup, resto/bar, free tour, overbooks to Hostel 123, center

Sokolska Youth Hostel, 52 Sokolska str., Prague; *hostel52.com/*, T:+420/252546181, *hostel52@gmail.com*; $14bed, Kitchen:Y, B'fast:$, Pvt.room:Y, Locker:N, Recep:24/7; Note: resto, parking, tours, bag hold, c.c. ok, central

Hostel City Center, Ječná 509/12, Prague 4-Nové Město; T:420/266315266, *info@ hostel-citycenter.cz/*; $16bed, Kitchen:N, B'fast:$, Pvt.room:Y, Locker:N, Recep:24/7; Note: tour desk, bag hold, parking, c.c. ok, central

8) Germany

At the beginning of the last millennium, the Holy Roman Empire was largely comprised of German territories, and their kings became Holy Roman emperors. There was always competition between Prussia and Austria, though, so no real political unity, and the religious unity was fractured with the German-based Protestant Reformation initiated by Martin Luther, from which it would never recover. Napoleon's conquests put a definitive end to the Holy Roman Empire (finally) and a German state was able to coalesce — minus Austria — in 1871 under the leadership of Otto von Bismarck. By this time Germany was a hotbed of ideas and science and literature and art and was anxious to make a name for iself. It was also landlocked and overpopulated and largely surrounded by Slavic peoples that it had little sympathy with. The results of two World Wars were disastrous.

Today Germany is the industrial heart of Europe, the engine that keeps the rest of it running and competitive, and one of the world's major export economies. It's also a major moral force, having been divided into opposite political poles and reunited successfully. The division of the country into Communist and Democratic halves set it back a hundred years, until reunification finally came in 1990. Still this is a nation that likes its R&R, and hostelling is strong. 'ß' is equivalent to 'ss' btw, and pronounced as such, frequently seen in the German word "Straße"=strasse=street. Many German cities rank high in world "livability" ratings. German is the language, Euro is the currency, and the telephone country code is +49.

BAYREUTH is a city of 72,000 on the Red Main River in northern Bavaria, south-central Germany. It is famous for its Beyreuth Festival, featuring the music of local boy Wagner. There are also many museums, parks, and historic buildings.

HI Bayreuth, Europa-Jugendherberge, Universitätsstr. 28, Bayreuth (Bavaria); *hihostels.com/, T:+49/921764380, jhbayreuth@djh-bayern.de*; $30Bed, Kitchen:Y, B'fast:Y, Pvt.room:N, Locker:Y, Recep:ltd; Note: billiards, laundry, bag hold, prkng

80 Hostels) BERLIN is Germany's capital and largest city and is documented from the 13th century. It was the capital of Prussia before becoming the capital of a united, then redivided, Germany. The city as well as the country was divided of course, and nothing was a better symbol of the Cold War than the isolated enclave of West Berlin struggling to survive while surrounded by Communist East Germany. With the fall of the Berlin Wall and the eventual reunification of the country (a fact which never ceases to amaze me), Berlin resumed its role as the country's undivided capital, and party central. That's *party* party, not Communist party.

Berlin is famous for its museums, including the Dahlem Museum complex in Dahlem district, the Egyptian Museum, the new National Gallery and Museum of Arts and Crafts, the Brucke-Museum, the Berlin Museum and the museum of Transport and Technology, for starters. Other landmarks include the Berlin Wall, of course, or at least what's left of it, and the controversially restored Reichstag building — Hitler's old stomping grounds.

Then there are the Philharmonic Hall, the New National Gallery of modern art, the Hall for Chamber Music, the Charlottenburg Palace, St. Nicholas Church, Palace of the Republic, the Church of Mary, Town Hall, St. Hedwig's Cathedral, Brandenburg Gate, and Museum Island, with its healthy handful of monuments to knowledge. Hostels here are pretty good. Kitchens are optional, though, and breakfasts will usually cost you bucks, though the many that have restaurants means that other meals are available also, not to mention beer.

Metropol Hostel, Mehringdamm 32, Berlin; T:03025940890, *info@ metropolhostel-berlin.com/*; $18bed, Kitchen:N, B'fast:$, Pvt.room:Y, Locker:Y, Recep:24/7; Note: wh/chair ok, bar/café, tour desk, parking, lift, bag hold

Inn-Berlin, Prinzenallee 49, Berlin; T:03049301901, *info@ inn-berlin.de/*; $18bed, Kitchen:Y, B'fast:$, Pvt.room:Y, Locker:Y, Recep:ltd; Note: parking, bike hire, forex, TV, private bath, bit distant, min. stay 2 nights

Grand Hostel Berlin, Tempelhofer Ufer 14, Berlin; *grandhostel-berlin. de/*, T:03020095450; $14bed, Kitchen:N, B'fast:$, Pvt.room:Y, Locker:Y, Recep:24/7; Note: no bunks, bar, café, bike hire, laundry, TV, stairs, min. stay 2 nights

EastSeven Berlin Hostel, Schwedter Strasse 7, Berlin; *eastseven.de/*, T:03093622240, *info@even.de*; $24bed, Kitchen:Y, B'fast:$, Pvt.room:Y, Locker:Y, Recep:7a>12m; Note: c.c. ok, tours, bag hold, dinners, pub crawl

U Inn Berlin, Finowstrasse 36, Berlin; T:03033024410, *info@ uinnberlinhostel. com/*; $14bed, Kitchen:Y, B'fast:$, Pvt.room:Y, Locker:Y, Recep:7a>1a; Note: left luggage, books, c.c. ok, parking, tour, safe, suburb

Comebackpackers, Adalbertstrasse 97, Berlin; *comebackpackers.com/*, T:03060057527; $21bed, Kitchen:Y, B'fast:$, Pvt.room:N, Locker:Y, Recep:24/7; Note: bar, café, bikes, laundry, tours, cheap beer!

Heart of Gold Hostel, Johannisstrasse 11, Berlin; *heartofgold-hostel.de/*, T:03029003300; $16bed, Kitchen:N, B'fast:$, Pvt.room:Y, Locker:Y, Recep:24/7; Note: bar, c.c. ok, free tour, travel desk

Pfefferbett Hostel, Christinenstrasse 18, Berlin; T:03093935858, *info@ pfefferbett.de/*; $13bed, Kitchen:N, B'fast:$, Pvt.room:Y, Locker:Y, Recep:24/7; Note: bar, restaurant, laundry, bikes, lift, c.c. ok, tour

Swimming Hostel Berlin, Zur Alten Flussbadeanstallt 5, Berlin; *swimming-hostel-berlin.de/*, T:01725463760; $12bed, Kitchen:Y, B'fast:$, Pvt. room:Y, Locker:N, Recep:ltd; Note: parking, TV, laundry, converted barge, not central, hard find

PART II: Central Europe

Main Station Hostel, Quitzowstrasse 110, Berlin; T:03039409750, *hostel@ mainstationhostel.de/*; $14bed, Kitchen:Y, B'fast:$, Pvt.room:Y, Locker:Y, Recep:24/7; Note: bar, parking, tours, laundry, c.c. ok, non-party hostel, modern, far

Wombats City Hostel, Alte Schönhauser St. 2, Berlin; T:0308471082/0, *office@ wombats-miunich.de/*; $17bed, Kitchen:Y, B'fast:$, Pvt.room:Y, Locker:Y, Recep:24/7; Note: bar, café, lift, cc ok, laundry, roof bar

Three Little Pigs Hostel, Stresemannstrasse 66, Berlin; T:03026395880, *info@ three-little-pigs.de/*; $16bed, Kitchen:Y, B'fast:$, Pvt.room:Y, Locker:Y, Recep:24/7; Note: café, bar, laundry, parking, c.c. ok, tours, bike hire, computers

Pangea People Hostel, Karl-Liebknecht-Strasse 34, Berlin; *pangeapeople. de/*; T:030886695815; $13bed, Kitchen:N, B'fast:N, Pvt.room:N, Locker:Y, Recep:24/7; Note: bar, café, lift, tour, bikes, travel desk, no computers, central

Schlafmeile Hostel, Weichselstrasse 25, Berlin; *schlafmeile.de/*, T:03096514676; $14bed, Kitchen:Y, B'fast:N, Pvt.room:Y, Locker:Y, Recep:ltd; Note: bar, café, c.c. ok, tour, bikes

Backpacker Berlin, Knorrpromenade 10, Berlin; *backpackerberlin.com/*, T:03029369164, *backpackerberlin@yahoo.de*; $14bed, Kitchen:Y, B'fast:Y, Pvt. room:Y, Locker:Y, Recep:8a>12m; Note: c.c. ok, city tour, bikes, tour desk, laundry

Helter Skelter Hostel, Kalkscheunenstrasse 4, Berlin; *helterskelterhostel. com/*, T:03028044997; $19bed, Kitchen:Y, B'fast:$, Pvt.room:Y, Locker:Y, Recep:24/7; Note: bar, tour, c.c. ok, safe dep., party hostel, smoking indoors

Amstel House, Waldenserstr. 31, Berlin; T:0303954072, *info@ amstelhouse. de/*; $14bed, Kitchen:N, B'fast:$, Pvt.room:Y, Locker:Y, Recep:24/7; Note: bar, tours, c.c. ok, laundry

CityHostel Berlin, Glinkastr. 5-7, Berlin; *cityhostel-berlin.com/*, T:+49(0)30238866850; $17bed, Kitchen:N, B'fast:Y, Pvt.room:Y, Locker:Y, Recep:24/7; Note: wheelchair ok, bar, lounge, parking, beer garden, terrace, central

Plus Berlin, Warschauer Platz 6, Berlin; *plushostels.com/*, T:03021238501; $13bed, Kitchen:N, B'fast:$, Pvt.room:Y, Locker:Y, Recep:24/7; Note: wheelchair ok, resto/bar, parking, free tour, lift, laundry, pool

Residenz 2000, Unter den Eichen 96, Berlin; *info@ residenz-2000. de/*, T:03081056253; $16bed, Kitchen:Y, B'fast:$, Pvt.room:N, Locker:Y, Recep:7a>10p; Note: c.c. req, lift, parking, dry cleaning, solarium, restaurant, not central

Singer109 Apartment-Hostel, Singerstrasse 109, Berlin; T:0308687870, *office@ singer109.com/*; $14bed, Kitchen:N, B'fast:$, Pvt.room:Y, Locker:Y, Recep:24/7; Note: resto/bar, lift, tour desk, smoking, TV, c.c. ok, near train not central

Citystay Mitte, Rosenstrasse protest 16, Berlin; T:03023624031, *info@ citystay.de/*; $22bed, Kitchen:N, B'fast:$, Pvt.room:Y, Locker:Y, Recep:24/7; Note: bar/café, tour desk, luggage room, laundry, central

Academy Hotel, Dennewitzstrasse 7, Berlin; *academy-hotel.de/*, T:03089049730; $32bed, Kitchen:Y, B'fast:$, Pvt.room:Y, Locker:Y, Recep:8a>7p; Note: café, parking, lift, luggage room, laundry, tour desk, c.c. ok

Globetrotter Hostel Odyssee, Grünberger Strasse 23, Berlin; T:03029000081, *odyssee@ globetrotterhostel.de/*; $13bed, Kitchen:Y, B'fast:$, Pvt. room:Y, Locker:Y, Recep:24/7; Note: resto/bar, bag hold, laundry, tour desk, c.c. ok, central, stairs

Sunflower Hostel, Helsingforser Strasse 17, Berlin; T:03044044250, *hostel@ sunflower-hostel.de/*; $16bed, Kitchen:N, B'fast:$, Pvt.room:Y, Locker:Y, Recep:24/7; Note: café, bar, bike rent, luggage room, TV, parking, c.c. ok

Hostel Die Etage East, Langhansstrasse 8, Berlin; *info@ die-etage-east.de/*, T:030548190; $17bed, Kitchen:Y, B'fast:N, Pvt.room:Y, Locker:Y, Recep:ltd; Note: east side, wheelchair ok, parking, free tour, travel desk, luggage room

Berlin Intl. YH, Kluckstrasse 3, Berlin; *hihostels.com/*, T:0302611097, *jh-berlin@jugendherberge.de*; $20bed, Kitchen:N, B'fast:Y, Pvt. room:N, Locker:Y, Recep:24/7; Note: resto/bar, parking, tour desk, luggage room, laundry, c.c. ok

Pegasus Hostel, Strasse der Pariser Kommune 35, Berlin; T:0302977360, *hostel@ pegasushostel.de/*; $16bed, Kitchen:Y, B'fast:$, Pvt. room:Y, Locker:Y, Recep:24/7; Note: resto/bar/café, 5th Fl no lift, laundry, lift, parking, tours, c.c. ok

Pension - Maximun, Lückstrasse 17, Berlin; *info@ pension-maximum.de,* T:03085617480; $29bed, Kitchen:N, B'fast:$, Pvt.room:Y, Locker:N, Recep:24/7; Note: luggage room, laundry, parking, far from center close to tube, market

Lette'm Sleep Hostel, Lettestrasse 7, Berlin; T:03044733623, *info@ backpackers.de/*; $16bed, Kitchen:Y, B'fast:N, Pvt.room:Y, Locker:Y, Recep:ltd; Note: wheelchair ok, bike rent, luggage ok, tour desk, c.c. ok, coffee/tea

Smart-hostel Berlin, Genter Strasse 53, Berlin; *smarthostel-berlin.de/*, T:03045486454; $13bed, Kitchen:N, B'fast:$, Pvt.room:Y, Locker:N, Recep:24/7; Note: wheelchair ok, lift, parking, luggage rm, tour desk, c.c. ok

Corner Hostel, Driesener Strasse 17, Berlin; *corner-hostel.de/*, T:03043734353; $17bed, Kitchen:Y, B'fast:$, Pvt.room:Y, Locker:Y, Recep:24/7; Note: wheelchair ok, bar/café, bike rent, luggage ok, laundry, free tour

All In Hostel/Hotel, Grünberger Str. 54, Berlin; *stay@ all-in-hostel. com/*, T:+49/302887683; $17bed, Kitchen:N, B'fast:$, Pvt.room:Y, Locker:Y, Recep:24/7; Note: wheelchair ok, resto/bar, pet ok, lift, bike rent, free tour, laundry

Design Hotel DDR, Wriezener Karree 5, Berlin; T:03025768660, *contact@ ostel.eu/*; $20bed, Kitchen:N, B'fast:$, Pvt.room:Y, Locker:Y, Recep:24/7; Note: bar/club, parking, luggage room

Check !N Hostel, Markgrafenstrasse 68, Berlin; *info@ check-in-hostel.de/*; T:03025923797; $10bed, Kitchen:N, B'fast:$, Pvt.room:N, Locker:Y, Recep: 24/7; Note: wheelchair ok, resto/café, luggage room, c.c. ok, new

St Christopher's Berlin, Rosa-Luxemburg-Str 39, Berlin; T:+49/3081453960, *berlin1@ st-christophers.co.uk/*; $17Bed, Kitchen:Y, B'fast:Y, Pvt.room:Y, Locker:Y, Recep:24/7; Note: bar, bikes, tour desk, luggage room, Sat TV

Alcatraz Backpacker Hostel, Schoenhauser Allee 133a, Berlin; T:03048496815, *alcatraz-backpacker.de/*; $18Bed, Kitchen:Y, B'fast:$, Pvt.room:Y, Locker:Y, Recep:24/7; Note: bikes, tour desk, bag hold, books, tour desk, parking

ONE80° Hostel Alexanderplatz, Otto-Braun-Strasse, Berlin; *Info@ one80hostels.com/*, T:+49(0)302804462-0; $14Bed, Kitchen:N, B'fast:$, Pvt. room:Y, Locker:Y, Recep:24/7; Note: resto/club, bikes, lift, wh/chair OK, laundry, bag hold

Eastener Hostel, Novalisstr. 14, Berlin; *contact@ eastener-hostel. de/*, T:01751123515; $17Bed, Kitchen:Y, B'fast:N, Pvt.room:Y, Locker:Y, Recep:10a>9p; Note: non-party, bikes, minimart, luggage room, tour desk, books, maps

Circus Hostel, Weinbergsweg 1a, Berlin; *Info@ circus-berlin.de/*, T:03020003939; $27Bed, Kitchen:N, B'fast:$, Pvt.room:Y, Locker:Y, Recep:24/7; Note: café/bar, bikes, lift, free meals/tours/beer Mondays, luggage rm, wh/chair ok

36 ROOMS Berlin Kreuzberg, Spreewaldplatz 8, Berlin Kreuzberg, Berlin; T:03053086398, *Info@ 36rooms.com/*; $17Bed, Kitchen:Y, B'fast:$, Pvt.room:Y, Locker:Y, Recep:24/7; Note: pool$, bikes, luggage rm, café/bar, nr metro, bohemian

Industriepalast Hostel Berlin, Warschauer Straße 43/44, Berlin; *rezeption@ ip-hostel.com/*; T:03074078290; $16Bed, Kitchen:Y, B'fast:$, Pvt.room:N, Locker:Y, Recep:24/7; Note: lift, wh/chair ok, bar, billiards, bag hold, laundry, tours

Riverside Lodge Berlin, Hobrechtstr. 43 cnr Maybachufer, Berlin; T:017631129791, *welcome@ riverside-lodge.de/*; $30Bed, Kitchen:Y, B'fast:$, Pvt.room:Y, Locker:Y, Recep:11a>9:30p; Note: resto/bar, bikes, bag hold, min 2N

Happy Go Lucky Hotel & Hostel, Stuttgarter Platz 17, Berlin; *Info@ happygoluckyhotel.com/*, T:03032709072; $14Bed, Kitchen:N, B'fast:$, Pvt.room:Y, Locker:Y, Recep:24/7; Note: birthdays free, luggage rm, tea/cof, nr train, bohemian

Eastern Comfort Hostelboat Berlin, Mühlen Str 73-77, Berlin; *captn@ eastern-comfort.com/*, T:03066763806; $23Bed, Kitchen:N, B'fast:$, Pvt.room:Y, Locker:N, Recep:8a>12m; Note: pool, café/bar, bikes, laundry, luggage rm, prkng

Comfy Little Corner, Zwinglistrasse 39, Berlin; *paulascomfycorner. com/*, T:01742865461, *paulascomfycorner@googlemail.com;* $18Bed, Kitchen:Y, B'fast:$, Pvt.room:Y, Locker:N, Recep:ltd; Note: arpt trans, lift, laundry, bag hold, no bunks!

Berlin City Lounge, Pariser Strasse 19, Berlin; *berlincityhostel.com/*, T:+49(30)8812145, *info@berlincitylounge.com;* $20Bed, Kitchen:N, B'fast:N, Pvt.room:Y, Locker:N, Recep: ltd; Note: lift, tour desk, parking, far, self-service

Aletto Kudamm Hotel & Hostel, Hardenbergstraße 21, Berlin, *kudamm@ aletto.de/*, T:030233214100; $18Bed, Kitchen:N, B'fast:Y, Pvt. room:Y, Locker:N, Recep:24/7 ; Note: bar, bikes, billiards, lift, wh/chair ok, bag hold, maps, games

Happy Bed Hostel - Hallesches Ufer, Hallesches Ufer 30, Berlin; *Info@ happybed.de/*, T:0307933647; $18Bed, Kitchen:Y, B'fast:N, Pvt.room:Y, Locker:Y, Recep:24/7; Note: café, lift, wh/chair ok, billiards, laundry, luggage rm

The Cat's Pajamas Hostel, Urbanstrasse 84, Berlin; T:03061620534, *thecatspajamashostel.com/*; $18Bed, Kitchen:Y, B'fast:Y, Pvt.room:Y, Locker:Y, Recep:24/7; Note: bikes, lift, wh/chair, laundry bag hold, tour desk, books, maps

Hostelxberger, Schlesische Straße 22, Berlin; T:+49/3069531863, *Info@ hostelxberger.com/*; $12Bed, Kitchen:Y, B'fast:N, Pvt.room:Y, Locker:Y, Recep:24/7; Note: wh/chair ok, billiards, luggage room, parking, party

Jugendgästehaus Lichterfelde, Osdorfer Straße 121, Berlin; *Info@ ju-li. de/*, T:+49/3071391734; $20Bed, Kitchen:Y, B'fast:Y, Pvt.room:Y, Locker:N, Recep:ltd; Note: no WiFi, laundry, tour desk, parking, not central, luggage room

Hotel 103, Schönhauser Allee 103, Berlin, *hotel103.de/*, T:+49/3043659103; $23Bed, Kitchen:N, B'fast:$, Pvt.room:Y, Locker:N, Recep:24/7; Note: bar, bikes, wh/chair ok, luggage room, maps, near subway

Bearinn Hostel, Bürgerstraße 29, Berlin Britz, *bearinn.de/*, T:+49/3068058093; $21Bed, Kitchen:$, B'fast:N, Pvt.room:Y, Locker:N, Recep:3>7p; Note: no WiFi

SleepCheapHostel, Spandauer Damm 101, Berlin; T:03070223991; *Info@ sleepcheaphostel.de/*; $14Bed, Kitchen:N, B'fast:N, Pvt.room:Y, Locker:Y, Recep:24/7; Note: pool, café, bikes, tour desk, luggage room

Green Hostel Berlin, Berliner Allee 39, Berlin; T:+49/3055878946, *service@ green-hostel-berlin.de*; $14Bed, Kitchen:N, B'fast:N, Pvt.room:Y, Locker:Y, Recep:24/7; Note: central, parking, luggage room, tour desk

2A Hostel, Saalestraße 76, Berlin, T:+49/3063226330, *Info@ 2a-hostel.de*; $18Bed, Kitchen:Y, B'fast:$, Pvt.room:Y, Locker:Y, Recep: 24/7; Note: café/

bar, bikes, laundry, lift, wh/chair ok, luggage room, parking, not central, near subway

Hostel Anlema, Zwinglistraße 3A, Berlin; T:+49/1747000331, *Info@ hostel-anlema.de/*; $17Bed, Kitchen:Y, B'fast:$, Pvt.room:Y, Locker:Y, Recep:2>10p; Note: luggage room, café, parking, tea/coffee, cash only

City 54 Hotel & Hostel, Chausseestrasse 54, Berlin; T:030200736430, *info@ city54hostel.de/*; $17Bed, Kitchen:N, B'fast:Y, Pvt.room:Y, Locker:N, Recep:24/7; Note: buffet brek, bikes, bag hold, tour desk, wh/chair ok, parking, near subway, WiFi $

Jugendgaestehaus Hauptbahnhof, Lehrter Straße 68; Berlin; T:0303983500, *jgh-hauptbahnhof.de/*, $21Bed, *gaestehaus@berliner-stadtmission.de*; Kitchen:Y, B'fast:$, Pvt.room:Y, Locker:N, Recep:24/7; Note: bikes, laundry, lift

Hotel Transit, Hagelberger Straße 53, Berlin; *welcome@ hotel-transit. de/*, T:+49/30789047x0; $30Bed, Kitchen:N, B'fast:Y, Pvt.room:Y, Locker:N, Recep:24/7; Note: lift, hotel-like, bar, near subway, eclectic 'hood

Rixpack Hostel, Karl-Marx-Straße 75, Berlin; T:03054715140, *mail@ rixpack.de/*; $17Bed, Kitchen:Y, B'fast:N, Pvt.room:Y, Locker:Y, Recep:24/7; Note: bikes, laundry, books, maps, tea/coffee, bag hold, not central, nr subway

Georghof Hostel, Gürtelstraße 39/41, Berlin, *tulip-inn-berlin.com/*, T:+49/30293830, *Info@georghof-berlin.de*; $17Bed, Kitchen:N, B'fast:N, Pvt. room:Y, Locker:N, Recep:24/7; Note: smoking, lift, wh/chair ok, parking, near metro

John's Cozy Castle, Waldenser Str 30; *johnshostel@yahoo.de*, T:03023273736

David's Cozy Little Moonshine Palace, Bredowstr. 35b, Berlin; *david-berlin.de/*, T:(030)21463156, *davidshostel@yahoo.de*; $7Bed, Kitchen:Y, B'fast:$, Pvt.room:Y, Locker:Y, Recep:9a>12m; Note: café, laundry, bikes, basic

Generator Berlin Mitte, Oranienburger Str 65; *berlinm@*, T:030921037680

Generator Hostel Berlin, Storkower Strasse 160, Berlin; T:0304172400, *berlin@ generatorhostels.com/*, $13bed, Kitchen:N, B'fast:$ Pvt.room:Y, Locker:Y, Recep:24/7; Note: wh/chair ok, resto/bar, tours, bikes, c.c. ok

Jetpak Flashpacker, Pariserstrasse 58; *city@jetpak.de*, T:0307844360

Jetpak Alternative, Görlitzer Str. 38, T:+49/3062908641, *alt@jetpak.de*, $28

Jetpak Eco-Lodge, Pücklerstr. 54, Berlin; *eco@ jetpak.de/*, T:0308325011; $20bed, Kitchen:N, B'fast:Y, Pvt.room:Y, Locker:Y, Recep:ltd; Note: in forest, close to bus, solar power, parking, luggage room

A&O Berlin Hauptbahnhof, Lehrter Straße 12, Berlin; T:0303229204200

A&O Berlin Friedrichshain, Boxhagener Str. 73, Berlin, T:0302977815400

A&O Berlin-Mitte, Köpenicker Strasse 127-129, Berlin, Germany; *aohostels. com/*, T:030809475200; $16bed, Kitchen:N, B'fast:$, Pvt.room:Y, Locker:Y, Recep:24/7; Note: bar, parking, tour desk, luggage room, pets ok, TV, lift

Baxpax Downtown Hostel, Ziegelstrasse 28, Berlin; T:03027874880, *info@ baxpax-downtown.de*; $10bed, Kitchen:N, B'fast:$, Pvt.room:Y, Locker:Y, Recep:24/7; Note: bar, café, parking city tour, bike hire, c.c. ok, laundry, linen fee

Baxpax Kreuzberg, Skalitzer Str. 104; *kreuzberg@baxpax.de*, T:03069518322

Baxpax Mitte Hostel, Chausseestr. 102, Berlin; T:+49(0)3028390965, *info@ backpacker.de/*; $9bed, Kitchen:Y, B'fast:N, Pvt.room:Y, Locker:Y, Recep:24/7; Note: bar, tour, laundry, c.c. ok, bike rent, luggage room

Meininger Berlin Airport, Alexander-Meissner-Strasse 1, T:03031878911

Meininger Mitte Humboldthaus, Oranienburgerstr 67/68, T:03031879816

Meininger Berlin Prenzlauer Berg, Schönhauser Allee 19; T:03098321074

Meininger Berlin Central Station, Ella-Trebe-Straße 9, Berlin; *welcome@ meininger-hotels.com/*, T:+49(0)3098321073; $14Bed, Kitchen:Y, B'fast:$, Pvt.room:Y, Locker:Y, Recep:24/7; Note: bar, gaming area, luggage rm, laundry, prkng

BIELEFELD is a city of some 325,000 in the northwest, and once known as the 'city of linen' back in the days of the Hanseatic League. More recently in the 1920's it made '*stoffgeld*,' money of fabric, prized by collectors. There is a castle and historic church.

Bielefeld JBB, Hermann-Kleinewächter-Straße 1, Bielefeld, T:0521522050, *jgh-bielefeld@ djh-wl.de/*; $44Bed, Kitchen:N, B'fast:Y, Pvt.room:Y, Locker:Y, Recep:ltd; Note: resto/bar, gym, lift, wh/chair, luggage room, parking, WiFi $

2 Hostels) BOCHUM is a city of 365,000 in the west-central Ruhr region of the country. Originally established by Charlemagne in the 9th century, Bochum suffered the Kristallnacht slaughter of its Jews and other indignities in WWII . Today it is a cultural center for Westphalia state, with many museums, and much art and architecture.

YH Bochum, Humboldtstr 59-63, Bochum; *hihostels.com/*, T:023441757990, *jgh-bochum@djh-wl.de*; $45Bed, Kitchen:N, B'fast:Y, Pvt. room:Y, Locker:N, Recep:24/7; Note: resto/bar, lift, wh/chair, parking, hotel-like, central, killer brek

BOLA Culture Hostel Ruhr, Herbergsweg 1, Bochum; T:0234494163, *gruppenunterkuenfte.de/*, $28Bed, *hostel@prokulturgut.net*; Kitchen:N, B'fast:$, Pvt.room:Y, Locker:N, Recep: call; Note: art/music/culture/healing/ veg-oriented

3 Hostels) BONN is a city of 328,000 in the center-west of Germany with the distinction of having been the *de facto* capital of the country while East Germany was Communist for 50 years, a function it still continues in part today. There are parks, museums, Beethoven's birthplace, and historic churches and buildings, like Old Town Hall.

Max Hostel, Maxstraße 7, Bonn; T:+49/22882345780, *Info@ max-hostel.de/*; $31Bed, Kitchen:N, B'fast:N, Pvt.room:Y, Locker:N, Recep:4>8p; Note: WiFi $, café, parking, maps, central, nr train, c.c. ok

Bonn YH, Haager Weg 42, Bonn; *hihostels.com/*, T:+49/228289970, *bonn@djh-rheinland.de*; $30Bed, Kitchen:N, B'fast:Y, Pvt.room:Y, Locker:Y, Recep:24/7; Note: resto/bar, lift, wh/chair ok, luggage rm, not central, WiFi $

Basecamp Bonn, In der Raste 1, Bonn, T:+49(0)22893494955; *stay@ basecamp-bonn.de/*; $31Bed, Kitchen:Y, B'fast:Y, Pvt.room:N, Locker:Y, Recep:ltd; Note: cash only, meals $, laundry, tour desk, parking, minimart, RV camp

PART II: Central Europe

BOTTROP is another city in the central-west Ruhr industrial region, population 116,000 and 40% Polish. There are festivals, museums, historic buildings and countless churches.

Chillten Bottrop, Gungstraße 3, Bottrop: *chillten.de/*, T:+49/204137858x0; $23Bed, Kitchen:M, B'fast:$, Pvt.room:Y, Locker:N, Recep:6:30a>10:30p; Note: resto, billiards, lift, wh/chair ok, luggage room

BRAUNLAGE is a town of 6000 and health resort in the Harz Mountains of north central Germany. There is skiing nearby and a 1.7mi/2.8km gondola lift.

Hostel Braunlage, Harzburger Straße 22A, Braunlage, T:+49/55205060101, *customers@ hostel-braunlage.de/*; $21Bed, Kitchen:N, B'fast:N, Pvt.room:Y, Locker:N, Recep:ltd; Note: books, parking, central

5 Hostels) BREMEN is another north German Hanseatic city with much medieval history and the architecture to prove it. For tourist sights Roland, the city's mythic protector immortalized in a statue on the main plaza, sounds like the hot ticket, unless you prefer statues of the donkey, dog, cat, and rooster from the Grimm Brothers' fairy tale. The old town also includes the Gothic Town Hall, the marketplace and the 11th C. cathedral. Then there's Becks Brewery, for when the clock strikes beer:30.

Townside Hostel, Am Dobben 62, Bremen; T:042178015, *info@ townside. de/*; $22bed, Kitchen:Y, B'fast:$, Pvt.room:Y, Locker:Y, Recep:>11p; Note: bike rent, parking, laundry, luggage ok, special meal deals, central

Gasthaus Bremer B'packer Hostel, Emil-Waldmann-Strasse 5, Bremen; *bremer-backpacker-hostel.de/*, T:04212238057; $27bed, Kitchen:Y, B'fast:$, Pvt. room:N, Locker:Y, Recep:ltd; Note: linen fee, bag hold, laundry, cash, train/ctr

Hostel-Posty, An der Weide 50, Bremen; *hostel-posty.de/*, T:042133456000, *hostel-posty@live.de*; $27bed, Kitchen:Y, B'fast:Y, Pvt.room:Y, Locker:N, Recep:24/7; Note: coffee & tea, close to train, stairs, no lift

The Grand Hostel Bremen, Feuerkuhle 30, Bremen; T:04216437209, *info@ thegrandhostel.com/*; $21bed, Kitchen:Y, B'fast:$, Pvt.room:Y, Locker:Y,

Recep:ltd; Note: parking, luggage room, TV, c.c. ok, linen free for 3N stay, central

Southend Hostel, Jakobistraße 23, Bremen; T:+49/42169620561; *Info@ southendhostel-bremen.de/*; $21Bed, Kitchen:Y, B'fast:$, Pvt.room:Y, Locker:Y, Recep:9a/9p; Note: bikes, lift, laundry, luggage room, tour desk, basic

8 Hostels) COLOGNE (Koeln) is a western German trading city of the same vintage as Hamburg, Germany's fourth largest, and part of the massive Rhine-Ruhr metropolitan area which totals more than ten million. This all started as a tiny Germanic village pre-BC, and expanded in 50 AD into a Roman "Colonia" (Colonia=Cologne, get it?). It was an important trade center. The Franks took over in 459 until it became part of the Holy Roman Empire later. Napoleon occupied it briefly, and then Prussia in 1815 until the creation of the German state. Meanwhile Cologne was absorbing smaller towns and becoming heavily industrialized. Cologne was occupied by the British and French under the terms of the Versailles Treaty ending WWI, and devastated during WWII. It has since rebuilt, based less on heavy industries and more on services, insurance, and media.

Tourism is also important, with green spaces, prominent museums, fairs and festivals, and dozens of restaurants and pubs. But the entertainment is still a little tamer than Hamburg and elsewhere. The big deal here is the Carnival, which starts on 11-11 at 11:11 and continues until Ash Wednesday (?). Prominent sights include the Gothic cathedral, which is a UNESCO World Heritage site, and is the city's symbol. Other prominent churches in Romanesque style include those of Sankt Gereon, S. Severin, Ursula, Maria im Kapitol, Kunibert, Pantaleon, Aposteln, and Gross Sankt Martin. Roman remains include portions of the original wall, a banquet hall floor, remains of the North Gate and a large part of the Praetorium. Three of the original twelve gates in the medieval wall survive. Hostel quality here is good.

Pathpoint Cologne, Allerheiligenstrasse 15, Cologne; T:022113056860, *info@ pathpoint-cologne.de/*; $30bed, Kitchen:Y, B'fast:$, Pvt.room:Y, Locker:Y, Recep:24/7; Note: c.c. ok, laundry, games, convenient, no lift

Weltempfanger Backpacker Hostel, Venloer Str. 196, Cologne; *info@ koeln-hostel.de/*,T:022199579957; $27bed, Kitchen:Y, B'fast:$, Pvt.room:Y, Locker:Y, Recep:7a>12m; Note: bar, bag hold, bikes, c.c. ok, not central, E20 key deposit

Station Hostel Backpackers, Marzellenstrasse 44, Cologne; T:02219125301, *station@ hostel-cologne.de/*; $24bed, Kitchen:Y, B'fast:$, Pvt.room:Y, Locker:Y, Recep:24/7; Note: bar, c.c. ok, lift, laundry, near train, smoke-friendly

YH Cologne-Riehl, An der Schanz 14, Cologne; T:0221976513-0, *koeln-riehl@ jugendherberge.de/*; $40bed, Kitchen:N, B'fast:Y, Pvt.room:Y, Locker:N, Recep:24/7; Note: bar, resto, lift, laundry, c.c. ok, lots of students, clinically clean

A&O Koln Neumarkt, Mauritiuswall 64-66, Cologne; *aohostels.com/ en/* T:0221467064700; $17bed, Kitchen:N, B'fast:$, Pvt.room:Y, Locker:Y, Recep:24/7; Note: bar, parking c.c. ok, travel desk, linen fee, bag hold, WiFi:$,

Black Sheep Hostel, Barbarossaplatz 1, Cologne, *blacksheephostel.com/*, T:022130290960, *kontakt@blacksheephostel.de*; $26Bed, Kitchen:Y, B'fast:Y, Pvt. room:Y, Locker:Y, Recep:8a>11:30p; Note: bikes, lift, laundry, bag hold

Meininger Hotel Köln City Center, Engelbertstraße 33-35, Köln; *welcome@ meininger-hotels.com/*, T:022199760965; $15Bed, Kitchen:Y, B'fast:$, Pvt.room:Y, Locker:Y, Recep:24/7; Note: bar, bikes, lift, laundry, bag hold, tour desk

404 Hostel, Neusser Straße 404, Cologne, *booking@ 404-hostel.de/*, T:+49/2218205830; $23Bed, Kitchen:Y, B'fast:Y, Pvt.room:Y, Locker:Y, Recep:10a//10p; Note: cash only, luggage room, tea/coffee, books, nr subway

DACHAU is a small city of 45,000 in the southern region of Upper Bavaria and only 12mi/20km north of Munich. It is famous for its WWII concentration camp. There is a historic center.

München (North Munich)–Dachau, Rosswachtstr. 15, Dachau; *hihostels. com/*, T:08131322950, *dachau@jugendherberge.de/*; $28Bed, Kitchen:N, B'fast:Y, Pvt.room:Y, Locker:Y, Recep:7:30a>12m; Note: resto/bar, lift, wh/chair ok

DORTMUND is largest of the Ruhr Valley industrial cities, with a population of 580,000. There is medieval architecture, including castles and churches. After a history of coal mining, it is now known as the "green metropolis."

A & O Dortmund Hauptbahnhof, Koenigswall 2, Dortmund; *aohostels. com/*; T:030809475109, $16Bed, Kitchen:N, B'fast:$, Pvt.room:Y, Locker:N, Recep:24/7; Note: bar, billiards, lift, wh/chair ok, laundry, bag hold, tour desk, central

6 Hostels) DRESDEN is an East German cultural city, in a Saxon area with Slavic roots. Its central core received 3900 tons of incendiary bombs from 1300 UK and US heavy bombers which destroyed thirty-nine square kilometers of the city in four raids between 13-15 February, 1945. Ouch! Those bombs killed 25,000 people, an event immortalized in *Slaughterhouse Five* by Kurt Vonnegut, and still controversial to this day. Dresden became a major industrial center in Communist East Germany and Vladimir Putin was stationed there from 1985-90 as a KGB agent while the Wall fell farther north.

The nearby Elbe valley is a UNESCO world heritage site for its parks and monuments, and Dresden is now regaining its status as a major cultural center. Its heart is still the Rococo-style Zwinger in the old city and a cluster of Baroque churches: the Frauenkirche, the Hofkirche, and the Kreuzkirche. Besides the Zwinger museums there are the Semper Gallery and the Japanese palace. There is also the Opera House, the Dresden State Theatre, and the Dresden Philharmonic Orchestra.

Hostel Kangaroo-Stop, Erna-Berger-Str. 8-10, Dresden; T:0351314345-5; *info@ kangaroo-stop.de/*; $18bed, Kitchen:Y, B'fast:$, Pvt.room:Y, Locker:Y, Recep:24/7; Note: bar, parking, linen fee, near train

Hofgarten 1824, Theresienstrasse 5, Dresden; T:03512502828; *reservierung@ hofgarten1824.de/*; $22bed, Kitchen:N, B'fast:$, Pvt.room:N, Locker:Y, Recep:ltd; Note: bar, parking, travel desk, bag hold, near train & old town

Hostel Lollis Homestay, Görlitzer Str. 34, Dresden; T:03518108458; *lolli@ lollishome.de/*; $18bed, Kitchen:Y, B'fast:$, Pvt.room:Y, Locker:Y, Recep:24/7; Note: free bikes, tea & coffee, dinners, laundry, linen fee, hippie-ish

Hostel Mondplast, Louisenstrasse 77, Dresden; T:03515634050; *info@ mondpalast.de/*; $14bed, Kitchen:Y, B'fast:$, Pvt.room:Y, Locker:Y, Recep:24/7; Note: bar, restaurant, c.c. ok, travel desk, near nightlife

PART II: Central Europe

A&O Dresden Hauptbahnhof, Strehlener Strasse 10, Dresden; *aohostels. com/*; T:03514692715900; $16bed, Kitchen:N, B'fast:$, Pvt.room:Y, Locker:Y, Recep:24/7; Note: rooftop bar, parking, games, travel desk, c.c, ok, near train

Louise 20, Louisenstraße 20, Dresden, T:+49/3518894894, *Info@ louise20. de/*; $17Bed, Kitchen:Y, B'fast:$, Pvt.room:Y, Locker:Y, Recep:7a>11p; Note: resto/bar, luggage room, parking, games, central, coffee/tea

DUISBERG is a city of almost 500,000 in the western Ruhr region, and the largest inland seaport in the world. It is a blast furnace center; its specialty is steel. They also brew beer.

Dorms & Dorms City Hostel, Friedenstraße 85, Duisburg, T:+49/2039356362; $33Bed, Kitchen:Y, B'fast:N, Pvt.room:Y, Locker:Y, Recep:11a>1p (!); Note: tour desk, tea/coffee, central

3 Hostels) DUSSELDORF is a center of German fashion, advertising, telecommunications, and… beer, *altbier*, that is, old-school, the top-fermenting pre-lager, hoppier, crisper kind: black gold, Westphalia tea. They have a lively regional competition going with Cologne, including the annual Carnival that starts on 11-11 at 11:11, etc. Landmarks in the city include the 13th–14th C. Lambertuskirche (Lambertus Church), and the old town hall, Jägerhof Castle, Benrath Castle, and remains of the palace of Frederick I (Barbarossa).

A&O Dusseldorf Hbh, Corneliusstrasse 9, Dusseldorf; *aohostels.com/*; T:+49(0)21133994–4800; $17bed, Kitchen:Y, B'fast:$, Pvt.room:Y, Locker:Y, Recep:24/7; Note: bar, parking, tour desk, luggage room, laundry, c.c. OK, near train

City YH Düsseldorf, Düsseldorfer St. 1, Düsseldorf; T:+49(0)211557310, *duesseldorf.jugendherberge.de/*; $48bed, Kitchen:N, B'fast:Y, Pvt.room:Y, Locker:Y, Recep:24/7; Note: HI fee, resto/bar, luggage room, laundry, c.c. ok, tour desk

Backpackers Dusseldorf, Fürstenwall 180, Dusseldorf; T:02113020848; *info@ backpackers-germany.de/*; $23bed, Kitchen:Y, B'fast:Y, Pvt.room:N, Locker:Y, Recep:>10p; Note: luggage room, parking, TV/DVD's

2 Hostels) ERFURT is city of more than 200,000 near the geographic center of the country. With roots in prehistory, it enters the annals in 742 and was an important trade center of the Middle Ages, dealing in woad, a blue dye. The oldest synagogue of Europe is here, and some of the earliest *pogroms*. There are numerous museums and historic architecture.

Opera Hostel, Walkmühlstraße 13, Erfurt; *opera-hostel.de/*, T:036160131360 $20Bed, Kitchen:Y, B'fast:$, Pvt.room:N, Locker:Y, Recep:24/7; Note: arpt trans, resto/bar, bikes, books, tour desk, luggage room, parking, minimart, central

Re4hostel, Puschkinstraße 21, Erfurt, *mail@ re4hostel.com/*, T:+49/3616000110 $24Bed, Kitchen:N, B'fast:$, Pvt.room:Y, Locker:Y, Recep:7a>9p; Note: café, billiards, laundry, bag hold, parking, tour desk, maps, books, central

7 Hostels) FRANKFURT is not Germany's largest city, but it may be its most international. Prior to the establishment of the Holy Roman Empire, Frankfurt was little more than a shallow spot in the River Main suitable as a ford for the Franks, yep. It is notable that the Frankfurt *Messe* (Trade Fair), for which it is famous today, was mentioned as long ago as 1150. It was heavily damaged during WWII and little remains of the medieval city. Today it is Germany's fifth-largest city and the financial center of it and Europe both, home to major banks, major trade fairs and a stock exchange. It is also home to people of some 180 nationalities. Follow the money.

Notable landmarks include the city's Zoological Garden, the Stadel Art Institute and Municipal Gallery, the Senckenberg Natural History Museum, and the Liebeighaus museum of Sculpture. There is also a major red-light district near the train station, a veritable shopping center of sex, if that's your thing. You wouldn't believe how hotel prices soar during trade fairs. Since much of its tourism is of the business sort, there are only a few hostels in Frankfurt; too bad. There is a porn theater in the airport.

Five Elements Hostel, Moselstrasse 40, Frankfurt; T:06924005885, *welcome@ 5elementshostel.de/*; $25bed, Kitchen:Y, B'fast:$, Pvt.room:Y, Locker:Y, Recep:24/7; Note: close to train, theme nights, café/bar, free tour, bike rent, lift

Frankfurt Hostel, Kaiserstrasse 74, Frankfurt; T:0692475130; *info@ frankfurt-hostel.com/*; $21bed, Kitchen:Y, B'fast:Y, Pvt.room:N, Locker:Y, Recep:24/7; Note: close to train, café/bar, luggage room, laundry, lift, c.c. ok, pasta

United Hostel, Kaiserstraße 52, Frankfurt am Main, T:069256678000, *Info@ united-hostel-frankfurt.com/*; $24Bed, Kitchen:Y, B'fast:$, Pvt.room:N, Locker:Y, Recep:24/7; Note: resto/bar/club, lift, forex, luggage rm, tours, minimart, nr train stn

Meininger Frankfurt Airport, Bessie-Coleman-Straße 11, T:06995797965

Meininger Hotel Frankfurt/Main Messe, Europaallee 64, Frankfurt; T:06940159052, *welcome@ meininger-hotels.com/*; $22Bed, Kitchen:Y, B'fast:N, Pvt.room:Y, Locker:Y, Recep:24/7; Note: bar, bikes, lift, laundry, luggage rm

Frankfurt Central Hostel, Mainzer Landstrasse 341, Frankfurt; *Info@ frankfurt-central-hostel.com/*, T:06987203908&9; $24Bed, Kitchen:N, B'fast:$, Pvt. room:Y, Locker:Y, Recep:24/7; Note: arpt trans, bar, bikes, gym, lift, 2km>ctr

A & O Frankfurt, Mainzer Landstraße 226-230, Frankfurt; *aohostels. com/*, T:030809475109; $12Bed, Kitchen:N, B'fast:$, Pvt.room:Y, Locker:Y, Recep:24/7; Note: bar, billiards, lift, tour desk, tea/coffee, parking, central

FREIBURG is a city of 230,000 in the far southwest of Germany, in a major wine-producing region and at the entrance to the Black Forest. The climate is sunny, the standard of living is high, and the Greens are politically strong. There is a medieval university and cathedral, and a Merchants Hall and Old Town Hall from the 1500's.

Gaestehaus Jacoby, Rieselfeldallee 23, Freiburg, *gaestehausjacoby.de/*, T:07614764389; $35Bed, Kitchen:$, B'fast:N, Pvt.room:Y, Locker:Y, Recep:3>7p (late check-in $); Note: svc fees, wh/chair ok, tea/coffee, laundry, parking, hard find

4 Hostels) FUSSEN is a town of 14,000 only 3mi/5km from the Austria border and at an elevation of 2600ft/800mt. There is a castle nearby, a river, mountains, and a history that dates back to the Romans.

House L.A.-City Hostel, Wachsbleiche 2, Füssen; T:+49/8362607366, *housela.de/*; $25Bed, Kitchen:N, B'fast:N, Pvt.room:Y, Locker:Y, Recep:ltd; Note: central, bikes, wh/chair ok, laundry, bag hold, parking, maps

Mainstation Hostel, Bahnhofstr. 10, Fussen; *Info@ mainstation-hostel. de/*, T:08362-9300975; $28Bed, Kitchen:N, B'fast:N, Pvt.room:Y, Locker:N, Recep:8a//7p; Note: bikes, parking, tour desk, maps, central, nr train stn

HI Fuessen, Mariahilfer Straße 5, Füssen; *hihostels.com/*, T:083627754, *fuessen@jugendherberge.de*; $31Bed, Kitchen:N, B'fast:Y, Pvt.room:N, Locker:Y, Recep:ltd; Note: laundry, luggage room, parking, 1km>center

Old Kings Hostel, Franziskanergasse 2, Fussen; T:083628837385, *Info@ oldkingshostel.com/*, $31Bed, Kitchen:Y, B'fast:$, Pvt.room:Y, Locker:Y, Recep:7a//9p; Note: cash only, family-run, bikes, maps, laundry, bag hold, central

2 Hostels) GARMISCH-PARTENKIRCHEN is a town of 25,000 in Germany's far south-central Bavarian region, near its highest peak, Zugspitze — 9714ft/2961mt a.s.l. Partenkirchen was originally the Roman town, Garmisch the German district; the two are still distinct.

Hostel 2962-Garmisch, Partnachauenstraße 3, Garmisch-Partenkirchen; T:0882195750, *contact@ hostel2962-garmisch.com/*; $28Bed, Kitchen:N, B'fast:$, Pvt.room:Y, Locker:N, Recep:ltd; Note: bar, tours, luggage rm, prkng, maps, central

Haus der Athleten, Wildenauer Straße 15, Garmisch-Partenkirchen, *hausderathleten.de/*, T:088219692940, *info@hostel-gapa.de*; $31Bed, Kitchen:Y, B'fast:N, Pvt.room:Y, Locker:Y, Recep:ltd; Note: tours, luggage rm, parking, sauna

GERSFELD is a town of almost 6000 in the center of Germany, on the Fulda River.

Jugendbildungsstätte Wasserkuppe, Wasserkuppe 10, Gersfeld; T:06654918330, *jugendbildungsstaette-wasserkuppe.de/*; $29Bed, Kitchen:N, B'fast:Y, Pvt.room:Y, Locker:N, Recep:ltd; Note: resto, parking, luggage, tour desk, remote

PART II: Central Europe

GOERLITZ is a city of 54,000 on Germany's far east-central Polish border. Originally a Sorbian village in upper Lusatia, it has made the rounds of ownership between Saxony, Prussia, Bohemia, etc. Welcome to central Europe. Tarantino shot some of *Basterds* here.

Hostel eol777, Bahnhofstraße 1A, Görlitz, *hosteleol777.com/*, T:01748485918; $18Bed, Kitchen:Y, B'fast:N, Pvt.room:N, Locker:N, Recep:24/7; Note: arpt trans, parking, laundry, luggage room, cash only, central

GOTTINGEN is a city of 130,000 in the center of the country on the River Leine. It was a wealthy member of the Hanseatic League in the Middle Ages, trading in textiles, mostly. Today it is famous for its Georg-August-Universitat. There is a Handel Festival.

Hostel 37, Groner Landstr. 7, Gottingen; T:+49/55163445177, *Info@ hostel37.de/*; $28Bed, Kitchen:N, B'fast:N, Pvt.room:Y, Locker:Y, Recep:advise arrival; Note: parking, wh/chair ok

HALLE is a city of 234,000 in the central German region and only 21mi/35km away from Leipzig. There is the Medieval Giebichenstein Castle and the Renaissance-era Moritzburg castle, a Market Square, churches and parks, theaters and museums. Its early history was based on the presence of salt, evidence of Celts pre-dating the Germans.

Citystation Hostel, Raffineriestraße 16a, Halle, *hostel-halle.de/*, T:+49/1743154413, *citystationhostel@yahoo.de*; $23Bed, Kitchen:N, B'fast:$, Pvt. room:N, Locker:N, Recep:ltd; Note: lift, hard find, central

13 Hostels) HAMBURG sits at the base of the Jutland Peninsula where it joins Europe, strategically located with the North Sea close by to the west—and connected to Hamburg by river—and the Baltic Sea close by to the east, where its historic trading partner Lubeck is located. It is Germany's second city and a major trading port since the days of the Hanseatic League and the old Holy Roman Empire, long before the idea of a unifed Germany had even been imagined. It was a free city-state, in fact, for much of its history, and was the

point from which ethnic Germans, including my ancestors, typically left for America. These days it is still a major port, Europe's second largest in fact, but tourism is a major economic factor now, also.

Hamburg has more than 2000 bridges over its numerous canals and rivers, giving it a romantic look to match its romantic setting of architecture and arts. There is an old town, too, though with little traditional architecture aside from the five churches of Sankt Jacobi, S. Petri, S. Katharinen, S. Nikolai, and S. Michaelis. Museums include the Kunsthalle, Museum of Arts and Crafts, and Museum of Ethnology and Prehistory.

Seamen need their outlets and entertainment, too, of course, and Hamburg's got that, home to Europe's largest red-light district, claiming among its residents and victims many a St. Pauli girl and the Beatles, who prepared for stardom here. Take a stroll along the *Reeperbahn* in the evening to soak up the atmosphere. Looking's free. Hamburg is home to many musicians and artists, and many good festivals. Many hostels are converted brothels; give them an "A" for atmosphere.

Generator Hostel Hamburg, Steintorplatz 3, Hamburg; *generatorhostels. com/*; T:040226358460; $17bed, Kitchen:N, B'fast:$, Pvt.room:Y, Locker:Y, Recep:24/7; Note: bar, laundry, tour, c.c. ok, lift, near train & center

A&O Hamburg Reeperbahn, Reeperbahn 154; T:04031769990-4600

A&O Hamburg Hauptbahnhof, Amsinckstr. 2-10; T:0406442104-5600

A&O Hamburg City, Spaldingstraße 160; T:040181298-4000; $14bed

A&O Hamburg Hammer Kirche, Hammer Landstr.170, Hamburg; *aohostels.com/*; T:04064421045500; $18bed, Kitchen:N, B'fast:$, Pvt.room:Y, Locker:Y, Recep:24/7; Note: bar, parking, wh/chair ok, c.c. ok, nr metro/ctr, WiFi:$

Wira Hostel, Königstrasse 16a, Hamburg; *wirahostel.hostel.com/*, T:04076997202; $22bed, Kitchen:Y, B'fast:$, Pvt.room:Y, Locker:Y, Recep:8a>10p; Note: c.c. +3%, laundry, free tour, $ for extras, Thai food

Kastanien Hostel, Kastanienallee 27, Hamburg; T:04053253364; *kontakt@ kastanien-hotel.de/*; $28bed, Kitchen:N, B'fast:N, Pvtroom:Y, Locker:N, Recep:10a>10p; Note: bar, parking, ex-brothel, linen fee, colorful area

Kiezbude, Lincolnstrasse 2, Hamburg, North Sea Coast; T:04074214269; *kontakt@ kiezbude.com/*; $35bed, Kitchen:N, B'fast:N, Pvt. room:Y, Locker:N, Recep:>10p; Note: min. stay 3N, ex-brothel, bar, café, free tour, tours, hard find

Meininger Hotel Hamburg City Center, Goetheallee 11, Hamburg; T:+49(0)4028464388, *welcome@ meininger-hotels.com/*; $18Bed, Kitchen:Y, B'fast:$, Pvt.room:Y, Locker:Y, Recep:24/7; Note: bar, lift, laundry, bag hold, central

Backpackers St. Pauli, Bernstorffstraße 98 Hamburg, T:+49/4023517043, *Info@ backpackers-stpauli.de/*;$18Bed, Kitchen:Y, B'fast:N, Pvt.room:N, Locker:Y, Recep:9a>9p; Note: cash only, café/bar, bikes, bag hold

Jugendherberge Hamburg "Auf dem Stintfang", Alfred-Wegener-Weg 5; T:0405701590, *stintfang@ jugendherberge.de/*; $31Bed, Kitchen:Y, B'fast:Y, Pvt.room:Y, Locker:N, Recep:24/7; Note: bar, bikes, billiards, wh/chair ok, lift, center

Arena Hostel Hamburg, Fangdieckstraße 20, Hamburg, T:04054801585, *contact@ arena-hostel-hamburg.de*, $Bed, Kitchen:Y, B'fast:N, Pvt.room:Y, Locker:Y, Recep:2-7p; Note: lift, luggage room, books, maps, not central

Hamburg-Horner Rennbahn, Rennbahnstr. 100, Hamburg; *hihostels. com/*, T:405701590, *hamburg-horn@jugendherberge.de*; $33Bed, Kitchen:Y, B'fast:Y, Pvt.room:Y, Locker:Y, Recep:24/7; Note: café, parking, no WiFi, wh/chair ok, far

3 Hostels) HANOVER is a city of over a half million in north-central Germany. It is a major commercial city, hosting many trade fairs and one of the largest oktoberfests in the world. It has an old town and spectacular zoo, too, and a 'Red Thread,' a 3mi/4.2km line on the sidewalk that starts at the Tourist Info office, and connects the city's 36 most important tourist sites.

Hostel Hannover, Lenaustr. 12 a, Hannover, T.0511 1319919, *info@ hostelhannover.de/*, $21Bed, Kitchen:N, B'fast:N, Pvt.room:N, Locker:Y, Recep:ltd; Note: no party, laundry, central, cash only

Bed n Budget City Hostel, Osterstraße 37; T:05113606107, *cityhostel@*

Bed n Budget Hostel, Hildesheimer Straße 380, Hanover; T:051112611504, *reservation@ bednbudget.de/*; $25Bed, Kitchen:Y, B'fast:N, Pvt.,room:Y, Locker:Y, Recep: 24/7; Note: resto/bar, bikes, minimart, luggage rm, parking, WiFi $

3 Hostels) HEIDELBERG is not one of Germany's largest cities, but it has certainly seen some history. The half-million-year-old (give or take a couple 100K) "Heidelberg Man" was discovered here and since his time the area has been claimed by various tribes — Celts, Romans, Germans, and Holy Romans — until the foundation of the modern German state. Heidelberg was a stronghold of the Nazi party. Now Heidelberg is best known for its university and tourism. The Castle above town is the main attraction, but the old town and bridge are nice, too. Other landmarks include the Heiliggeistkirche and the Marstall, the Knight's House, the town hall, and the Jesuitenkirche.

Lotte–Backpackers Hostel Heidelberg, Burgweg 3 Heidelberg; T:062217350725, *info@ lotte-heidelberg.de/*; $33bed, Kitchen:Y, B'fast:N, Pvt. room:Y, Locker:Y, Recep:8a>10p; Note: parking, bag hold, laundry, c.c. ok, central

Steffis Hostel Heidelberg, Alte Eppelheimer Str. 50, Heidelberg; *stefffi@ hostelheidelberg.de/*, T:062217782772; $24bed, Kitchen:Y, B'fast:N, Pvt.room:N, Locker:Y, Recep:8a>10p; Note: bar/club, parking, tour desk, bag hold, c.c. ok, nr mkt

Sudpfanne Hostel, Hauptstraße 223, Heidelberg; T:06221163636, *info@ heidelberger-sudpfanne.de/*; $26bed, Kitchen:N, B'fast:$, Pvt.room:Y, Locker:Y, Recep:>12m; Note: resto/bar, cash only, one-off linen fee, central

2 Hostels) KARLSRUHE is a city of almost 300,000 on the western border with France, and known for its radial street plan, similar to D.C. in the US. Not an ancient city, its architecture is more 'neo' than classical. Once a center of Judaism in Germany, many have since come back. *Das Fest* and the African Summer Festival are in July.

Gaestehaus Kaiserpassage, Kaiserpassage 10, Karlsruhe, *gaestehaus-kaiserpassage.de/*, T:072140243459; $23Bed, Kitchen:Y, B'fast:N, Pvt.room:Y, Locker:Y, Recep:11a>12m; Note: lift, wh/chair ok, tours, parking, maps, tea/cof

A&O Karlsruhe Hauptbahnhof, Bahnhofplatz 14, Karlsruhe; *aohostels. com/*, T:072137154100; $13Bed, Kitchen:N, B'fast:NPvt.room:Y, Locker:N Recep:24/7; Note: nr train stn, bar, billiards, lift, laundry, bag hold, tours, maps, parking

3 Hostels) KIEL is a city of some 242,000 in Germany's far north, 56mi/90km from Hamburg. Near the sea, its beaches are popular, as is shopping. There are lakes and parks.

HI Kiel, Johannesstr. 1, Kiel, *hihostels.com/*, T:+49/431731488; *kiel@ jugendherberge.de/*; $28Bed, Kitchen:N, B'fast:Y, Pvt.room:N, Locker:Y, Recep:ltd; Note: bikes, wh/chair ok, luggage room, meals $, WiFi $

Bekpek Kiel, Kronshagener Weg 130a, Kiel; *info@   bekpek-kiel. de/*, T:04318888009; $33Bed, Kitchen:Y, B'fast:N, Pvt.room:Y, Locker:N, Recep:8a//8p; Note: cash only, bikes, bag hold, tour desk, life, parking, not central

Peanuts Hostel, Harriesstraße 2, Kiel, *Info@   peanuts-hostel.de/*, T:+49/4313642208; $28Bed, Kitchen:Y, B'fast:N Pvt.room:Y, Locker:Y Recep:5-7p (!); Note: coffee/tea, no TV, books, central, parking, games

9 Hostels) LEIPZIG is a city of over 500,000 in East Germany, 90mi/150km south of Berlin. Significant in instigating the fall of Communism, it has changed significantly since then, with much new construction and reconstruction. A center of trade since the Middle Ages, it is now one of the world's most livable cities. The historic downtown is mostly Renaissance in era and style. It's lively.

A&O Leipzig Hauptbahnhof, Brandenburger Str. 2, Leipzig; *aohostels. com/*, T:0341250794900; $12Bed, Kitchen:N, B'fast:$, Pvt.room:Y, Locker:Y, Recep:24/7; Note: Wifi $, bar, billiards, wh/chair ok, lift, laundry, bag hold, parking

Hostel Absteige, Harkortstraße 21, Leipzig, T.149/3116106717, room@ *absteigeninleipzig.de*; $25Bed, Kitchen:N, B'fast:N, Pvt.room:Y, Locker:Y, Recep:ltd; Note: central, pool, bar, parking, central

Sleepy Lion Hostel, Jacobstraße 1, Leipzig; T:03419939480, *Info@ hostel-leipzig.de/*; $16Bed, Kitchen:Y, B'fast:$, Pvt.room:Y, Locker:Y, Recep:24/7;

Note: central, wh/chair OK, lift, bag hold, laundry, books, maps, games, tea/cof

HomePlanet-Hostel, Bornaische Str. 56, Leipzig; *homeplanethostel.de/*, T:015787677523, *homeplanethostel@googlemail.com*; $16Bed, Kitchen:Y, B'fast:N, Pvt.room:Y, Locker:Y, Recep:2>10p; Note: bikes, laundry, tours, parking, not central

Say Cheese Leipzig, Kleine Fleischergasse 8, Leipzig; T:034135583196, *leipzig@ say-cheese.net/*; $17Bed, Kitchen:Y, B'fast:$, Pvt.room:Y, Locker:Y, Recep:3>6p (confirm); Note: café/bar, wh/chair OK, lift, bag hold, tours, tea/cof

Hostel Unschlagbar, Karl-Liebknecht-Straße 1A, Leipzig, T:034125668070, *Info@ unschlagbar-leipzig.de/*; $27Bed, Kitchen:Y, B'fast:N, Pvt.room:Y, Locker:Y, Recep:5>8p; Note: resto, laundry, bag hold, parking, lift, maps, coffee/tea, central

Central Globetrotter Hostel, Kurt-Schumacher-Straße 41, Leipzig; T:03411498960, *Info@ globetrotter-leipzig.de/*; $14Bed, Kitchen:Y, B'fast:$, Pvt. room:Y, Locker:Y, Recep:24/7; Note: bar, laundry, bag hold, parking

Space Hotel, Wurzner Straße 4, Leipzig, T:+49/1805772232, *booking@ space-hotel.de/*; $14Bed, Kitchen:N, B'fast:$, Pvt.room:Y, Locker:$, Recep:4>8p; Note: WiFi $, central, luggage room, tour desk, parking

B&B-Hostel-Elisa, Elisabethstraße 21, Leipzig; T:+49/34169945984, *Info@ bb-elisa.de/*; $25Bed, Kitchen:Y, B'fast:$, Pvt.room:Y, Locker:Y, Recep:9a//7p; Note: bikes, tour desk, parking, tea/coffee, maps

2 Hostels) LINDAU is a town and island of almost 25,000 in the far south of the country where it shares borders with Austria and Switzerland. Along with lake-based activities, there is a medieval center, with lighthouse, churches, town hall, promenade, and shopping street.

HI Lindau, Herbergsweg 11, Lindau; *landau@ jugendherberge.de/*, T:+49/83829671-0; $30Bed, Kitchen:N, B'fast:Y, Pvt.room:N, Locker:Y, Recep:3>9p; Note: resto/bar, bikes, wh/chair ok, tour desk, bag hold, parking

Dasmietwerk, Holdereggenstraße 11, Lindau, *willkommen@dasmietwerk.de/* T:+49/83825041130; $38Bed, Kitchen:N, B'fast:$, Pvt.room:Y, Locker:Y,

PART II: Central Europe

Recep:3>9p; Note: café, wh/chair ok, lift, laundry, bag hold, minimart, books, maps

2 Hostels) LUEBECK is a city of 200,000 that has been declared a UNESCO world heritage site. Its size belies its previous importance as capital of the Hanseatic League, a very important phase in European history. City's a monument to brick. Got marzipan?

Sleepin' YMCA Luebeck, Große Petersgrube 11, Lubeck; T:+49/4513999410, *Info@ cvjm-luebeck.de/*; $35Bed, Kitchen:N, B'fast:$, Pvt. room:Y, Locker:N, Recep:>8p; Note: pool, tour desk

HI Lübeck-Vor dem Burgtor, Am Gertrudenkirchhof 4, Lübeck, *hihostels. com/*, T:045133433; *luebeck@jugendherberge.de*; $29Bed, Kitchen:N, B'fast:Y, Pvt. room:N, Locker:Y, Recep:6a>12m; Note: bar, pool, wh/chair ok, lift, laundry

MAINZ is a city of 200,000 in Germany's center, famous for the invention of the movable-type printing press. It lies on the Rhine. There are sand dunes and Roman ruins. The city was 80% destroyed during WWII. The cathedral, Iron Tower, and Wood Tower are still there, though, plus many newer structures and many museums.

Wanderlust Hostel in Flörsheim, Jahnstraße 15, Flörsheim am Main, T:061457737, *Info@ monteur-unterkunft.com/*; $28Bed, Kitchen:N, B'fast:Y, Pvt. room:Y, Locker:Y, Recep:6a>11p; Note: arpt trans, bikes, café/bar, tours

MUENSTER is a city of 270,000 in the northwest part of the country, the name referring to the monastery. In the Middle Ages, it was a member of the Hanseatic League. Today it is 'bicycle capital of Germany.' There are many museums and much historic architecture.

Sleep Station, Wolbecker Straße 1, Munster, *sleep-station.de/*, T:2514828155; $23Bed, Kitchen:Y, B'fast:Y, Pvt.room:Y, Locker:Y, Recep: 8a//9:30p; Note: café, lift, coffee/tea, luggage room, maps

11 Hostels) MUNICH is now Germany's third-largest city and the largest in Bavaria. It rates highly on liveability indices and has much less crime than

Germany's largest metropli, but is also more expensive, almost in proportion to its proximity to the Alps. It dates from at least the twelfth century when it was a settlement of Benedictine monks. It derived income from a monopoly on the salt trade and grew enough to become the capital of Bavaria in the early 1500's. It soon became a center of the Counter-Reformation and brown beer. Hitler's Beer Hall Putsch in 1923 occurred here, resulting in his arrest and imprisonment. I guess they should have drunk lager.

Munich was a stronghold when Hitler came to power ten years later. The Nazi's first concentration camp at Dachau was only 10mi/16km away. It suffered seventy-one air raids during the subsequent war. Since then Munich has focused on rebuilding and it is more than a little ironic that Israeli athletes were murdered at the Summer Olympics here in 1972. Oktoberfest is the big deal for entertainment here, and is held annually every — September. With culinary specialties that include baked sausage loaf, pork knuckle, and *beuscherl* (look it up), the strudel-ly desserts come as something of a relief.

Then there are the beer gardens and the famous *Hofbrauhaus*. *Kultfabrik* should be worth checking out. Three of the seven original 14th century town gates still stand, and other medieval buildings include the cathedral, the Frauenkirche, and the old Town Hall. Munich's oldest church, Peterskirche, has been rebuilt. Museums include the Bavarian State Picture Galleries, the Neue Pinakothek, and the Deutches Museum. Hostel quality is not bad, with kitchens optional, but breakfast usually pricey, and services costing extra.

Wombats City Hostel, Senefelderstrasse 1, Munich; T:01799484144; *office@ wombats-munich.de/*; $15bed, Kitchen:N, B'fast:$, Pvt. room:Y, Locker:Y, Recep:24/7; Note: bar, parking, laundry, lift, tours, near train, free drink

Euro Youth Hostel, Senefelderstrasse 5, Munich; *info@ euro-youth-hotel.de/*, T:08959908811; $22bed, Kitchen:N, B'fast:$, Pvt.room:Y, Locker:Y, Recep:24/7; Note: bar, laundry, bikes, lift, c.c.+%, close to train, dorm age >35

Easy Palace City Hostel, Mozartstrasse 4, Munich; T:0895587970; *info@ easypalace.de*; $27bed, Kitchen:Y, B'fast:$, Pvt.room:N, Locker:N, Recep:24/7; Note: bar, parking, laundry, c.c. ok, tours, far, near Oktoberfest, WiFi $

Easy Palace Station Hotel, Schützenstrasse 7, Munich; T:0895525210, *station@ easypalace.de*; $26bed, Kitchen:N, B'fast:$, Pvt.room:Y, Locker:N, Recep:24/7; Note: bar, parking, tour, c.c. ok, WiFi $

The 4You Hostel Munich, Hirtenstraße 18, Munich; *the4you.de/*, T:0895521660; $31bed, Kitchen:N, B'fast:Y, Pvt.room:Y, Locker:Y, Recep:24/7; Note: bar, parking, tours, laundry, travel desk, near train & center

Jaeger's Munich, Senefelderstraße 3, Munich; *office@ jaegershotel.de/*, T:089555281; $27Bed, Kitchen:N, B'fast:$, Pvt.room:Y, Locker:Y, Recep:24/7;

Note: @Hbf, 18-35 dorm age, bar, lift, laundry, bag hold, tours, parking, books

Meininger Hotel München City Center, Landsberger Straße 20, München; T:08954998023, *welcome@ meininger-hotels.com/*; $63Bed, Kitchen:Y, B'fast:$, Pvt.room:Y, Locker:Y, Recep:24/7; Note: bar, bikes, billiards, tours, lift, bag hold

Smart-Stay Hotel Station, Schutzenstrasse 7; *station@*, T:0895525210

Smart-Stay Munich City, Mozartstraße 4, Munich, *munichcity@ smart-stay.de/*, T:0895587970; $21Bed, Kitchen:Y, B'fast:$, Pvt.room:N, Locker:Y, Recep:24/7; Note: café/bar, billiards, central, bikes, bag hold, lift, parking

CVJM/YMCA Muenchen, Landwehrstraße 13, Munich, *hotel@ cvjm-muenchen.org/*, T:+49/89552141x0; $42Bed, Kitchen:N, B'fast:Y, Pvt.room:N, Locker:N, Recep: 8a>0:30a; Note: central, bag hold, lift, tours

Hostel Nanina, Breslauer Straße 34, Gröbenzell; T:081425805368, *Info@ hostel-nanina.de*; $26Bed, Kitchen:Y, B'fast:Y, Pvt.room:Y, Locker:N, Recep:5>9p; Note: no WiFi, 7-day cancel, lift, wh/chair OK, parking, tea/coffee

A&O München Hauptbahnhof, Bayerstr. 75, T:089452357-5700, $49

A&O München Hackerbrücke, Arnulfstr. 102, München; *aohostels. com/*, T:089452359-5800; $34Bed, Kitchen:N, B'fast:$, Pvt.room:Y, Locker:Y, Recep:24/7; Note: bar, billiards, lift, laundry, bag hold, parking, tea/coffee

3 Hostels) NUREMBERG is a city of 500,000 in the country's center, once the unofficial capital of the Holy Roman Empire, and more recently the site of Hitler's annual Nazi propaganda rallies and subsequent war crimes' trials. Albrecht Durer mapped the stars from here and illustrated the Nuremberg Chronicles around 1500. There are three castles, a medieval market, a lepers' colony, and many churches and museums. Got bratwurst?

A&O Nürnberg Hauptbahnhof, Bahnhofstraße 13, Nürnberg; *aohostels. com/*, T:0911309168-4400; $15Bed, Kitchen:Y, B'fast:$, Pvt.room:Y, Locker:N, Recep:24/7; Note: bar, wh/chair ok, lift, laundry, bag hold, parking, tours, central

City Hostel Nuernberg, Klaragasse 12, Nuremberg, *city-hostel-nuernberg. de/*, T:091180192146; $23Bed, Kitchen:Y, B'fast:$, Pvt.room:Y, Locker:Y, Recep:2-11p; Note: 12n checkout, café, bikes, books, bag hold, parking, tea/cof, WiFi $

Five Reasons Hostel, Frauentormauer 42, Nuremberg, T:091199286625 *booking@ five-reasons.de/*; $25Bed, Kitchen:Y, B'fast:$, Pvt.room:Y, Locker:Y, Recep:24/7; Note: central, café/bar, lift, bag hold, parking, maps, central, modern

OSNABRUCK is a city of 150,000 in the northwest, founded by Charlemagne himself in 780. It was a Hanseatic League member in the Middle Ages. Much of that Old Town still remains. Hyde Park and Alando provide tunes to dance to. It is also a railway hub, bub.

Penthouse Backpackers, Möserstraße 19, Osnabrück; T:05416009606, *Info@ penthousebp.com/*; $20Bed, Kitchen:Y, B'fast:Y, Pvt.room:Y, Locker:Y, Recep:8a//8p; Note: pool, sauna, laundry, bag hold, books, roof terrace

3 Hostels) REGENSBURG is a city of 140,000 at the confluence of the Danube and Regen rivers in the south. The medieval center is a UNESCO world heritage site. There are Roman ruins also. The Bavarian Forest lies to the East.

Brook Lane Hostel Regensburg, Obere Bachgasse 21, Regensburg, *kontakt@ hostel-regensburg.de/*; T:09416900966; $22Bed, Kitchen:Y, B'fast:$, Pvt. room:Y, Locker:N, Recep:8a>9p; Note: minimart, tours, bag hold, central

HI Regensburg, Wöhrdstr. 60, Regensburg; *hihostels.com/*, T:09414662830, *regensburg@jugendherberge.de;* $33Bed, Kitchen:N, B'fast:Y, Pvt.room:N, Locker:N, Recep: 7a>12m; Note: parking, group-oriented, laundry

Abotel Regensburg, Donaustaufer Straße 70, Regensburg, *abotel-regensburg.de/*, T:094164090585, *abotel@arcor.de;* $24Bed, Kitchen:N, B'fast:$, Pvt.room:Y, Locker:N, Recep:4-6p; Note: parking, no staff, not central

2 Hostels) ROSTOCK is a city of over 200,000 on the northeast Baltic Coast, and a Hanseatic city back in the day. The university dates to 1419. Once East Germany's major port, it has lost population since reunification. With the Hanse Sail and jazz festivals, it is now reinventing itself for tourism.

Hanse Hostel Rostock, Doberaner Straße 96, Rostock, *haus2@ hanse-hostel.de/*; T:038125299980; $21Bed, Kitchen:Y, B'fast:$, Pvt.room:N, Locker:Y, Recep:7:30a-10p; Note: bikes, wh/chair ok, tours, laundry, bag hold, parking, not central

Jellyfish Hostel, Beginenberg 25, Rostock; T:03814443858, *Info@ jellyfish-hostel.com/*; $21Bed, Kitchen:Y, B'fast:$, Pvt.room:Y, Locker:Y, Recep:8a>11p; Note: laundry, luggage room, tour desk, central

ROTHENBURG is a town of 11,000 in south central Germany famous for its pristine medieval old town. The old town walls are still intact. There are many museums.

YH Rothenburg ob der Tauber, Mühlacker 1, Rothenburg; *hihostels. com/*, T:0986194160, *rothenburg@jugendherberge.de*; $32Bed, Kitchen:N, B'fast:Y, Pvt.room:Y, Locker:Y, Recep:ltd; Note: resto, billiards, parking, laundry, bag hold

2 Hostels) STUTTGART is located in southwestern Germany in the state of Baden-Wurttemberg and historically has been home to various Germanic groups and the Frankish Merovingians. Nowadays it's best known as the home of the Mercedes-Benz. Despite the heavy industry, Stuttgart is green and ranks high in liveability, and the nearby Alps and Black Forest are tourist delights. Historic landmarks include the old castle, the Rosenstein Palace, the Gothic Leonhardskirche, and the Stiftskirche (collegiate church), a 12th C. Romanesque basilica. The Cannstatter Folk Festival is held nearby every autumn, and there are mineral springs, too.

Inter-Hostel, Paulinenstraße 16, Stuttgart, T:071166482797, *Info@ inter-hostel.com*; $32Bed, Kitchen:Y, B'fast:$, Pvt.room:N, Locker:Y, Recep:2>11p; Note: a/c, bag hold, parking, laundry, five floors no lift, central

Hostel Alex30, Alexanderstraße 30, Stuttgart, *alex30-hostel.de/*, T:0711838895x0; $26Bed, Kitchen:Y, B'fast:$, Pvt.room:N, Locker:Y, Recep:24/7; Note: bar, bag hold, tours, parking, books, beer garden, 12n checkout, 3 fl no lift

WEIMAR is a city of 65,000 in the center of Germany, where Germany's post-WWI constitution was signed and where the Bauhaus art movement was started, both in 1919 (numerology, anyone?). There are many UNESCO sites here, and it dates back to 899.

Weimar Hostel, Goetheplatz 6, Weimar; T:+49/3643811822, *Info@ weimar-hostel.com/*; $21Bed, Kitchen:Y, B'fast:$, Pvt.room:Y, Locker:Y, Recep:ltd; Note: tour desk, luggage room, books, maps, tea/coffee, central

WERNIGERODE is a city of 35,000 in central Germany, on the north slopes of the Harz Mountains. There is a new town and an old town, containing Gothic architecture. A railway goes to Brocken, Harz's highest peak at 3743ft/1141mt.

Harz Hostel, Schmatzfelder Straße 50, Wernigerode, T:+49/3943501826, *Info@ harz-hostel.de/*; $23Bed, Kitchen:Y, B'fast:$, Pvt.room:N, Locker:Y, Recep:8a>6p; Note: luggage room, parking, tour desk, quiet

2 Hostels) WURZBERG is a city of 130,000 in Germany's center, halfway between Frankfurt and Nuremberg. Most of the old city was destroyed on 16 March, 1945 by a British air raid. Many historic buildings now standing are replications. Summer festivals include the Afrika Festival, Mozartfest, and the Kiliani Volksfest. There are museums.

Babelfish Hostel, Haugerring 2, Würzburg, T:09313040430, *Info@ babelfish-hostel.de/*; $24Bed, Kitchen:Y, B'fast:$, Pvt.room:Y, Locker:Y, Recep:7:30a-12m; Note: bar, wh/chair ok, lift, laundry, bag hold, tour desk, maps, central

HI Würzburg, Fred-Joseph-Platz 2, Würzburg; *hihostels.com/*, T:+49/93142590, *wuerzburg@jugendherberge.de*; $33Bed, Kitchen:N, B'fast:Y, Pvt.room:Y, Locker:N, Recep:7a>1a; Note: wh/chair ok, lift, luggage room

9) Luxembourg

Luxembourg is a city and state that grew up around a castle. Strategically, it was home for a succession of Bourbons, Habsburgs and Hohenzollerns, before France and Netherlands and Germany. It finally became a modern state at the same time as Belgium, to which it lost half its territory, all French-speaking, and with which it now forms a trade partnership, along with the Netherlands.

Like Belgium and Switzerland, Luxembourg is a north-south border nation that is effectively divided between Romance and Germanic sectors. The standard of living is high. The Old Town is a UNESCO World Heritage site. The major cultural institution of Luxembourg is the Grand Ducal Institute. Then there's The National Museum of History, National Library, the National Archives, and the Music Conservatory of the City of Luxembourg. The currency is Euro, the phone code is +352, and languages are French, German, and Luxembourgish.

Luxembourg City Hostel, 2 Rue du Fort Olisy, L-2261; T:(+352)22688920, *luxembourg@ youthhostels.lu/*; $32bed, Kitchen:N, B'fast:Y, Pvt.room:N, Locker:Y, Recep:24/7; Note: resto/bar, parking, terrace, lift, walkable to town

10) Netherlands

In every language the translation is the same, "low lands," and that is the distinguishing feature of the Netherlands, aka "Holland," the fact that much of the country is at or below sea level. The Netherlands were settled early in the Common Era by more or less the same tribes as the ones who settled France, the Franks, southern tribes becoming Romanized while the northern ones maintained their Germanic roots and language, a single linguistic group that forms a continuum across the contiguous German plains.

That process of choosing the southern or northern culture still goes on to some extent to this day down south in Belgium. Many of the Jews expelled from Spain in 1492 went to the Netherlands, and the rest is history. Though tiny, once the Kingdom of the Netherlands freed itself from imperial Spain it went on to establish the next great empire after that of Portugal and Spain, including colonies in South Africa (before the Bantu-speaking Africans themselves got there by the way), Indonesia, South America, and... oh yeah, New Amsterdam, now better known as Nueva York.

The English put the kibosh on that little fantasy, of course, but by then Holland was a thoroughly capitalist state, perhaps the first, a step beyond mere free trade, and featuring a stock exchange, insurance, retirement funds, boom-bust cycles, asset-inflation, corporate raiders, short sellers, whew!—and well positioned for the future (?!). Today the Netherlands are a bastion of liberal democracy and a founding member of NATO and EU. Stayokay is a hostel chain here with market penetration like I've never seen before, maybe a new paradigm. Dutch is the language; Euro is currency; phone code is +31.

35 Hostels) AMSTERDAM has much the same history as the Netherlands, of course, as its longtime capital and major city, but these days Netherlands' much-touted liberalism has become stock-in-trade for Amsterdam, in particular its liberal drug laws, which have spawned a cottage industry of cannabis "coffee shops" and related industries. I can't recommend any of this, of course, any more than I can recommend drinking any one of a large number of alcoholic drinks to be found in literally thousands of public houses around the world.

This industry threatens to supplant the more traditional sex industry which Amsterdam has long been famous for, in which a red-blooded male can get his rocks off from girls of any one of several dozen different nationalities from all over the world, all here for the same reason—to study (I'm half-joking). They line the windows that line the canals that line the walls of your imagination. It's a boy's dream.

For the less degenerate tourists, there are lovely canals, excellent bike paths, superb museums, and a multitude of entertainment venues. Museums include the Rijksmuseum, the Stedelijk museum, the Van Gogh Museum, and the Anne Frank House. Ancient buildings in the old part of Amsterdam include the Old Church and the New Church, the Royal Palace, the Mint Tower, the South Church, the West Church, the Trippenhuis, and the Old Man's House Gate.

Amsterdam has come a long way since its origins as a dam on the River Amstel. It is also well-connected to the rest of Europe, but be forewarned that your Eurolines bus may be searched on arrival in Paris, complete with skunk-sniffing dogs. Amsterdam's motto is *"Leef en laat leven;"* sounds good to me. With Islamic politics and problems from drug tourists, though, there are signs that the famed tolerance is undergoing challenges. Better hurry. C U at the *Melkveg.*

Hostel Van Gogh, Van de Veldestraat 5, Amsterdam Oud-Zuid; T:0202629200, *info@ hotelvangogh.nl/*; $15bed, Kitchen:Y, B'fast:$, Pvt. room:Y, Locker:N, Recep:24/7; Note: dorm age 18-40, a/c, bikes, laundry, lift, tea/coffee

Stayokay Amsterdam Zeeburg, Timorplein 21, *Zeeburg@*, T:0205513190

Stayokay Stadsdoelen, Kloveniersburgwal 97; T:0206246832, *stadsdoelen@*

Stayokay Vondelpark, Zandpad 5, Amsterdam Oud-Zuid; T:0205898996, *vondelpark@ stayokay.com/*; $30bed, Kitchen:N, B'fast:Y, Pvt.room:Y, Locker:Y, Recep.24/7; Note: bar, café, wh/chair ok, laundry, bag hold, lift, billiards, bikes

Cocomama, Westeinde 18, Amsterdam, T:0206272454, *info@ cocomama. nl*; $36bed, Kitchen:Y, B'fast:N, Pvt.room:N, Locker:Y, Recep:9a>9p; Note: bikes, laundry, bag hold, tea/cof, tours, c.c.+2%, ex-brothel, "boutique-y", not central

St. Christopher's Inn-Winston, Warmoesstraat 131, Binnenstad; *winston.nl/*, T:0206231380; $27bed, Kitchen:N, B'fast:Y, Pvt.room:Y, Locker:Y, Recep:24/7; Note: resto/bar, c.c. ok, tours, lift, billiards, tea/coffee, bag hold, red light dist

Flying Pig Beach, Parallel Bl 208, Noordwijk; *BeachHostel@*, T:0713622533

Flying Pig Downtown, Nieuwendijk 100, *downtown@*, T:0204206822

Flying Pig Uptown Hostel, Vossiusstraat 46, Amsterdam Oud-Zuid; T:0204004187, *uptown@ flyingpig.nl/*; $22bed, Kitchen:Y, B'fast:Y, Pvt.room:N, Locker:Y, Recep:24/7; Note: ages 18-40, bar, café, bikes, bag hold, min. 2N

The Bulldog, Oudezijds Voorburgwal 220, Amsterdam; T:06270295, *info@ bulldoghotel.com/*; $38bed, Kitchen:N, B'fast:Y, Pvt.room:Y, Locker:Y, Recep:24/7; Note: resto/bar, billiards, wh/chair ok, lift, tours, bag hold, laundry, min. 2N

Hotel Hostel Mevlana, NZ. Voorburgwal 160, Amsterdam; *mevlanahotel. com/*, T:0203306641, *hotelmevlana@hotmail.com*; $16bed, Kitchen:N, B'fast:N, Pvt.room:Y, Locker:Y, Recep:24/7; Note: resto/bar, bag hold, minimart, tours, central

Inner Amsterdam, Wanningstraat 1, Amsterdam; T:0206625792, *info@ innerhotel.nl/*; $28bed, Kitchen:N, B'fast:Y, Pvt.room:Y, Locker:N, Recep:24/7; Note: lift, luggage room, tours, c.c. ok, central, BYOB

Hans Brinker Hotel, Kerkstraat 136, Amsterdam; T:0206220687, *sybil@ hans-brinker.com/*; $28bed, Kitchen:N, B'fast:Y, Pvt.room:Y, Locker:Y, Recep:24/7; Note: re-confirm, bar, restaurant, club, bag hold, c.c. ok, central, lift

Hostel Cosmos Amsterdam, Nieuwe Nieuwstraat 17, Amsterdam; *Info@ hostelcosmos.com/*; T:+31/206252438, $38Bed, Kitchen:N, B'fast:$, Pvt.room:Y, Locker:Y, Recep:24/7; Note: bikes, tour desk, luggage room, parking

YH Meetingpoint, Warmoesstraat 14, Amsterdam; T:0206277499, *Info@ hostel-meetingpoint.nl/*; $19Bed, Kitchen:N, B'fast:$, Pvt.room:N, Locker:Y, Recep:24/7; Note: café/bar, billiards, bag hold, central/red-light, smoking room

Durty Nelly's Inn, Warmoesstraat 117, Amsterdam, *durtynellys.nl/*, T:0206380125, *nellys@xs4all.nl*; $35Bed, Kitchen:N, B'fast:Y, Pvt.room:Y, Locker:Y, Recep:24/7; Note: resto/bar, bikes, billiards, tours, bag hold, party hard

PART II: Central Europe

Shelter City, Barndesteeg 21, T:+31(0)206253230, $24bed

Shelter Jordan (Christian Hostel), Bloemstraat 179, Amsterdam, T:0206244717; *shelter.nl/*; $26Bed, Kitchen:N, B'fast:Y, Pvt.room:N, Locker:Y, Recep: 24/7; Note: no drugs/alc, café, bikes, luggage room, maps, games, meals $

International Budget Hostel, Leidsegracht 76, Amsterdam; T:0206242784, *internationalbudgethostel.com/*; $25Bed, Kitchen:N, B'fast:Y, Pvt.room:Y, Locker:Y, Recep:24/7; Note: bikes, maps, games, central, smoke room

Amsterdam Hostel Leidseplein, Korte Leidsedwarsstraat, Amsterdam; *bookings@ amsterdamhostelleidseplein.com/*, T:+31/204208014; $21Bed, Kitchen:N, B'fast:Y, Pvt.room:N, Locker:N, Recep:24/7; Note: tours, forex, party, tea/cof

Hostel the Globe Center, Oudezijds Voorburgwal 3, Amsterdam, T:0204217424; *Info@ hotel-theglobe.nl/*; $28Bed, Kitchen:N, B'fast:$, Pvt.room:Y, Locker:Y, Recep:24/7; Note: resto/bar, billiards, bag hold, maps

Euphemia Hotel, De Weteringschans, Amsterdam; T:0206229045, *Info@ euphemiahotel.com/*; $34Bed, Kitchen:N, B'fast:$, Pvt.room:Y, Locker:Y, Recep:8a>11p; Note: bikes, tour desk, bag hold, maps, books

Amsterdam Hostel Annemarie, Jan Willem Brouwerstraat 14, Amsterdam, *bookings@ amsterdamhostelannemarie.com/*, T:0204703007, $37Bed, Kitchen:Y, B'fast:Y, Pvt.room:Y, Locker:N, Recep:24/7; Note: bikes, tours, maps, games, cash

The White Tulip Hostel, Warmoesstraat 87A, Amsterdam, T:0206255974, *Info@ wittetulp.nl*; $28Bed, Kitchen:N, B'fast:$, Pvt.room:Y, Locker:Y, Recep:24/7 Note: resto/bar, bikes, tours, maps, drug-free, c.c.+5%, pub crawl, red-light

Amsterdam Hostel Orfeo, Leidsekruisstraat 12, Amsterdam, T:0206231347, *booking@ amsterdamhostelorfeo.com/*; $35Bed, Kitchen:Y, B'fast:Y, Pvt.room:Y, Locker:N, Recep:24/7; Note: bag hold, tours, maps, tea/coffee, fax, stairs

Amsterdam Hostel Janson, Frans van Mierisstraat 69A-1HG, Amsterdam; T:0206797203, *bookings@ amsterdamhosteljanson.com/*; $41Bed, Kitchen:N, B'fast:Y, Pvt.room:N, Locker:N, Recep:24/7; Note: bikes, bag hold, tours, prkng

Bostel Amsterdamse Bos, Kleine Noorddijk 1, Amstelveen; T:0206416868, *campingamsterdamsebos.nl/*, $13Bed, *Info@campingamsterdam.com*; Kitchen:Y, B'fast:$, Pvt.room:Y, Locker:N, Recep:3p>; Note: far, mkt, prkng

Hostel Slotania, Slotermeerlaan 133, Amsterdam, T:+31/206134568; *Info@ nieuwslotania.nl/*; $21Bed, Kitchen:N, B'fast:$, Pvt.room:Y, Locker:N, Recep:24/7; Note: lift, wh/chair ok, tour desk, parking, bag hold, maps

Hotel My Home, Haarlemmerstraat 82, Amsterdam, T:0206242320, *reservations@ amsterdambudgethotel.com/*; $41Bed, Kitchen:N, B'fast:Y, Pvt. room:Y, Locker:N, Recep:ltd; Note: min 2N, egg brek, maps, bag hold, red-light dist.

Amsterdam Hostel Centre, Leidsekruisstraat 13, Amsterdam, T:0203204600, *Info@ amsterdamhostelcentre.com/*; $28Bed, Kitchen:N, B'fast:$, Pvt.room:Y, Locker:Y, Recep:24/7; Note: cash only, bag hold, parking, party central

Travel Hotel Amsterdam, Beursstraat 23, Amsterdam, *travelhotel-amsterdam.com/*, T:0206266532, *info@travelhotel.nl*; $41Bed, Kitchen:N, B'fast:$, Pvt.room:N, Locker:Y, Recep:12m; Note: bar, tours, WiFi $, basic, stairs

Amsterdam Hostel Uptown, Korte Leidsedwarsstraat 147 Amsterdam, T:0204283125, *bookings@ amsterdamhosteluptown.com/*; $41Bed, Kitchen:N, B'fast:N, Pvt.room:Y, Locker:N, Recep:24/7; Note: bag hold, tours, cash only

Budget Hotel Tourist Inn, Spuistraat 52, Amsterdam; T:0204215841; *info@ tourist-inn.nl/*; $31Bed, Kitchen:N, B'fast:Y, Pvt.room:Y, Locker:N, Recep:24/7; Note: bar, lift, bag hold, maps, safe dep, a/c, TV, nr train

Amsterdam Hostel Sarphati, Sarphatipark 58, Amsterdam, T:0204702035 *Bookings@ amsterdamhostelsarphati.com/*; $32Bed, Kitchen:N, B'fast:Y, Pvt. room:Y, Locker:N, Recep:24/7; Note: bikes, tours, bag hold, a/c, cash, stairs

Aivengo Hostel, Spuistraat 6, Amsterdam, T:+31/204213670, *aivengoyouthhostel.com/*; $30Bed, Kitchen:Y, B'fast:N, Pvt.room:Y, Locker:Y, Recep:6a>4a; Note: 16-35 y.o., cash only, books, maps, bag hold, parking, stairs

APELDOORN is a city of 150K at 60mi/100km SE of Amsterdam. There is a good zoo.

Stayokay Apeldoorn, Asselsestraat 330, Apeldoorn, T:0553553118, *Apeldoorn@ stayokay.com/*, $30Bed, Kitchen:N, B'fast:Y, Pvt.room:Y, Locker:N, Recep:ltd; Note: resto/bar, bikes, wh/chair ok, luggage rm, tours, prkng, not central

ARNHEM is a city of 150,000 in the eastern part of the country. The city is famous for its parks and greenery. There is an open air museum that features traditional ways of life.

Stayokay Arnhem, Diepenbrocklaan 27, Arnhem; T:0264420114, *Arnhem@ stayokay.com/*, $28Bed, Kitchen:N, B'fast:Y, Pvt.room:Y, Locker:N, Recep:ltd; Note: nr natl park, resto/bar, bikes, wh/chair ok, billiards, parking, tours

BERGEN OP ZOOM is a city of 65,000 located in the south of the country. There is a museum, cultural center, and picturesque architecture.

Stayokay Bergen op Zoom, Boslustweg 1, Bergen op Zoom; *bergenopzoom@ stayokay.com/*, T:0164233261; $30Bed, Kitchen:N, B'fast:Y, Pvt.room:Y, Locker:N, Recep:ltd; Note: resto/bar, bikes, wh/chair ok, bag hold, in forest

DELFT is a city of 100,000 in the country's south, between Rotterdam and The Hague, famous for its blue pottery, its association with the royal family, and its historic town center with canals. When thiry tons of stored gunpowder exploded in 1654, the reverberations are still being felt.

Jorplace Delft, Voldersgracht 16, Delft, T:+31/158875088, *delft@ jorplace. nl*; $26Bed, Kitchen:Y, B'fast:$, Pvt.room:N, Locker:N, Recep:ltd; Note: resto/ bar, maps, luggage room, tea/coffee, central

DEN BURG is a burg of 7000 on the island of Texel in the north. It is the island's least touristy town, yet features a historic center, town hall, and open market.

Stayokay Texel, Haffelderweg 29, Den Burg, T:0222315441; *Texel@ stayokay.com/*, $25Bed, Kitchen:N, B'fast:Y, Pvt.room:Y, Locker:N, Recep:ltd;

Note: resto/bar, wh/chair ok, bikes, billiards, lift, tours, parking, island w/ ferry

DOMBURG is a beach town of 1500 on the North Sea, inhabited since antiquity.

Stayokay Domburg, Duinvlietweg 8, Domburg; T:0118581254, *Domburg@ stayokay.com/*; $24Bed, Kitchen:N, B'fast:Y, Pvt.room:Y, Locker:N, Recep: ltd; Note: bikes, resto/bar, tours, luggage rm, "Medieval castle rises out of…forest near…sea"

DORDRECHT is a city of almost 120,000 and Holland's oldest city, documented from the Viking raids of 844. It was an important market city of the Middle Ages, dealing in wood and wine. Almost 1000 of the monuments of that era still stand, plus seven churches and six museums. Events include the *Wantijfestival* out-doors music festival and World Jazz days, a Fun Fair and International Puppet Festival.

Stayokay Dordrecht, Baanhoekweg 25, Dordrecht; T:0786212167, *Dordrecht@ stayokay.com/*, $28Bed, Kitchen:N, B'fast:Y, Pvt.room:Y, Locker:N, Recep:3>10p; Note: resto/bar, bikes, billiards, bag hold, tours, wh/chair ok

EGMOND is a former town in North Holland, now merged with Bergen, a municipality of 31,000. There was a 10th century abbey and castle, destroyed in 1573. There is a music festival in August and an arts festival in October.

Stayokay Egmond, Herenweg 118, Egmond, T:0725062269, *Egmond@ stayokay.com/*, $34Bed, Kitchen:N, B'fast:Y, Pvt.room:Y, Locker:N, Recep: ltd; Note: bulb fields, Dune Reserve, resto/bar, bikes, wh/chair ok, bag hold

EINDHOVEN is a city of over 400,000 located in the south. They are largely foreign-born, with many students. It is known as the 'City of Lights,' home to the Phillips Company. The Eindhoven Museum is open-air archeological, and the Van Abbemuseum has contemporary art, including Picasso. The Public Space has large numbers of artworks and the Effenaar is tops for musical and cultural venues, Plaza Futura for cinema.

3BE Backpackers Bed, Stratumsedijk 31, Eindhoven, T:0402120416 *Info@ 3be.nl*; $35Bed, Kitchen:Y, B'fast:$, Pvt.room:N, Locker:Y, Recep:2/11p; Note: café, bar, billiards, wh/chair ok, laundry, bag hold, games, central

Stayokay Valkenswaard, P. Heerkensdreef 20, Valkenswaard, Eindhoven, *Valkenswaard@ stayokay.com/*, T:0402015334; $24Bed, Kitchen:N, B'fast:Y, Pvt. room:Y, Locker:N, Recep:ltd; Note: resto/bar, bikes, bag hold, not ctr

GORSSEL is a town in eastern Netherlands, now merged with Lochem.

Stayokay Gorssel, Dortherweg 34, Gorssel; T:+31(0)573431615, *Gorssel@ stayokay.com/*; $24Bed, Kitchen:N, B'fast:Y, Pvt.room:Y, Locker:N, Recep:ltd; Note: resto/bar, bikes, luggage room, parking

GRONINGEN is a city of 190,000 in the north, and former member of the medieval Hanseatic League, with an original settlement traceable to the 3rd Century AD. It has the second-oldest university in the Netherlands. There are theaters and museums and the bars don't close until seven in the morning. What else? Okay, so there are two red-light zones.

Budget Hostels, Rademarkt 3, Groningen, T:+31/505886558, *Recepte@ budgetthostels.nl/*; $31Bed, Kitchen:N, B'fast:$, Pvt.room:Y, Locker:Y, Recep:24/7; Note: bikes, lift, luggage room, a/c, minimart

2 Hostels) HAARLEM is a city of over 150,000 in its own right and at the northern end of the Randstaat that with Amsterdam is one of the largest megalopoli of Europe. It is the historic center of the tulip-bulb business, and was once a wealthy medieval city because of it…and textiles…and printing and beer production. Gradually the gravitas of commerce has shifted to Amsterdam, leaving Haarlem as a living museum of medieval architecture. There are museums, theaters, festivals, and nightlife.

Hello I'm Local Boutique Hostel, Spiegelstraat 4, Haarlem, T:0238446916, *mail@ helloimlocal.nl/*; $32Bed, Kitchen:N, B'fast:$, Pvt.room:Y, Locker:N, Recep:ltd; Note: café, bar, laundry, bag hold, tours, bikes, tea/coffee, parking

Stayokay Haarlem, Jan Gijzenpad 3, Haarlem, T:0235373793, *Haarlem@ stayokay.com/*, $24Bed, Kitchen:N, B'fast:Y, Pvt.room:Y, Locker:Y, Recep:ltd; Note: resto/bar, bikes, billiards, wh/chair ok, laundry, bag hold, parking

HEEG is a town of 2250 in the Frisian part of the Netherlands. There are marinas and shipyards. Did you know that Frisian is the modern language closest to Old English?

Stayokay Heeg, 't Eilân 65, Heeg; *Heeg@ stayokay.com/*, T:+31(0)515442258, $24Bed, Kitchen:N, B'fast:Y, Pvt.room:Y, Locker:N, Recep:3>10P; Note: resto/ bar, lift, bikes, parking, lake, sailing school

HEEMSKERK is a city of almost 40,000 in North Holland. There is a castle.

Stayokay Heemskerk, Tolweg 9, Heemskerk; T:+31(0)251232288, *Heemskerk@ stayokay.com/*, $33Bed, Kitchen:N, B'fast:Y, Pvt.room:Y, Locker:Y, Recep:3>11p; Note: resto/bar, bikes, luggage room, tour desk

HOLLUM-AMELAND is a village on one of the Frisian Islands off the north coast of the Netherlands, village population 1400, island 3500. The dune landscape creates a unique flora and fauna. There are ferries to the mainland, or you can wait for the tide to fall.

Stayokay Ameland, Oranjeweg 59, Hollum-Ameland; *Ameland@ stayokay. com/*, T:+31/519555353; $19Bed, Kitchen:N, B'fast:Y, Pvt.room:Y, Locker:N, Recep:3>10p; Note: resto/bar, bikes, wh/chair ok, bag hold, tours

MAASTRICHT is a city of 122,000 in the far southeast, capital of the province of Limburg. It dates back to Roman times and was prominent in the empire of Charlemagne. It has 1677 national heritage sites, second only to

Amsterdam. It is best known to modern students of history for the treaty of the same name that created the European Union.

Stayokay Maastricht, Maasboulevard 101, Maastricht; T:0437501790, *Maastricht@ stayokay.com/*, $30Bed, Kitchen:N, B'fast:Y, Pvt.room:Y, Locker:Y, Recep:24/7; Note: resto/bar, billiards, books, bikes, wh/chair ok, maps

NOORDWIJK is a city of 25,000 on the South Holland seacoast. Originally a fishing village, now there are more fishers of men…and women: tourists. It is also a pilgrimage destination, in honor of Priest Jeroen, who lost his head to ransacking Normans in 857.

Stayokay Noordwijk, Langevelderlaan 45, Noordwijk; T:0252372920, *Noordwijk@ stayokay.com/*, $30Bed, Kitchen:N, B'fast:Y, Pvt.room:Y, Locker:Y, Recep:3>10p; Note: resto/bar, bikes, parking, tours, bag hold, remote

3 Hostels) ROTTERDAM began in 1270 as a dam on the river Rotte, and was until recently the busiest port in the world as well as the sixth most populous conurbation in Europe. A lively competition exists with Amsterdam and The Hague, and, despite Rotterdam's reputation as the workhorse of the group, a lively cultural life exists. Things to see and do include the Boymans-van Beuningen Museum, the Museum of Ethnology, the Prince Henry Maritime Museum, the Historical Museum… and the zoo, of course.

Hostel ROOM Rotterdam, Van Vollenhovenstraat 62, Rotterdam; T:0102827277, *Info@ roomrotterdam.nl*; $23Bed, Kitchen:Y, B'fast:Y, Pvt.room:Y, Locker:Y, Recep:24/7; Note: café, bar, laundry, tours, bikes, bag hold, central

Stay Inn Rotterdam, Mijnsherenlaan 9, Rotterdam; T:0102794112, *Info@ stayinn.nl/*; $38Bed, Kitchen:N, B'fast:Y, Pvt.room:Y, Locker:N, Recep:24/7; Note: resto, lift, tea/coffee, maps, aka "Art Hotel", hotel-like

Stayokay Rotterdam Cube Hostel, Overblaak 85-87, Rotterdam, *Rotterdam@ stayokay.com/*, T:0104365569; $29Bed, Kitchen:N, B'fast:Y, Pvt.room:Y, Locker:Y, Recep:24/7; Note: resto/bar, bikes, lift, bag hold, wh/chair ok, architecture

SNEEK is a city of 33,000 in Southwest-Friesland, in northern Netherlands. It is known for its canals and water gate. There is also an ancient wall around the city, still stsnding.

Stayokay Sneek, Oude Opperhuizerweg 17, Sneek; T:0515412132; *Sneek@ stayokay.com/*, $24Bed, Kitchen:N, B'fast:Y, Pvt.room:Y, Locker:Y, Recep:24/7; Note: resto/bar, bikes, lift, bag hold, wh/chair ok, laundry, parking

SOEST is a city of 45,000 in the center of the country, not far from Utrecht. Originally an agricultural area, it has residents now that are mostly commuters.

Stayokay Soest (bei Utrecht), Bosstraat 16, Soest; T:0356012296, *Soest@ stayokay.com/*, $33Bed, Kitchen:N, B'fast:Y, Pvt.room:Y, Locker:N, Recep:3>10p; Note: resto/bar, wh/chair ok, bag hold, parking, bikes, tours

3 Hostels) THE HAGUE (Den Haag) is the Netherlands' third city, with a half million inhabitants in the city proper. The Hague is the seat of government, though Amsterdam is the constitutional capital. The entertainment is tamer here, meeting at French-style sidewalk cafes on the city's three squares by day, congregating in the sea-front bars and clubs at night. The Maritshuis Museum carries the Dutch masters and the Escher musem has you-know-who, to mention but two of the dozen or so. Summer festivals feature more jazz then rock, more wine than pot. I guess there is life after Amsterdam.

Jorplace, Keizerstraat 296, The Hague–Scheveningen; T:0703383270, *Info@ jorplace.nl/*; $26Bed, Kitchen:Y, B'fast:$, Pvt.room:Y, Locker:Y, Recep:>10p; Note: resto/bar, parties, billiards, gym, tours, laundry, bag hold, parking, beach

Stayokay Den Haag (Hague), Scheepmakersstraat 27, The Hague, *DenHaag@ stayokay.com/*, T:0703157888; $37Bed, Kitchen:N, B'fast:Y, Pvt. room:Y, Locker:Y, Recep:3>10p; Note: resto/bar, billiards, bikes, lift, parking, @train, no party

F.A.S.T., Strandweg 1A, 2586 JK Scheveningen, The Hague; *Info@ fastthehague.com*, T:0703586749; $28Bed, Kitchen:Y, B'fast:$, Pvt.room:N, Locker:Y, Recep:ltd; Note: surf/lessons, resto/bar/club, parking, cash, container cribs

4 Hostels) UTRECHT is the Netherlands fourth city, with more than 320,000 inhabitants, but second culturally, after Amsterdam. Its origins go back to Roman fortifications in the area, until they left in 270. In the Middle Ages it became an important trade and ecclesiastical center, until Amsterdam eclipsed it in importance in the Golden Age. The old medieval inner city is largely intact, with canals and walls. Utrecht University is the largest in the country, and there are many museums, galleries, and the Letters of Utrecht, an endless poem in the cobblestones of the street.

Stone Hotel & Hostel, Biltstraat 31, Utrecht; T:0302682315; *contact@ stonehotel.nl/*; $24Bed, Kitchen:Y, B'fast:$, Pvt.room:Y, Locker:Y, Recep:3>11p; Note: bikes, bag hold, coffee/tea, maps, TV, fax, central

Hostel Strowis, Boothstraat 8, Utrecht; T:0302380280; *Info@ strowis.nl/*; $25Bed, Kitchen:Y, B'fast:$, Pvt.room:Y, Locker:Y, Recep:8a>12m; Note: curfew 2a, café, bar, tour desk, bikes, books, laundry, bag hold, tea/coffee, central

Hostel B&B Utrecht City Center, Lucasbolwerk 4, Utrecht, T:0303100155 *Info@ hostelutrecht.nl/*; $27Bed, Kitchen:Y, B'fast:Y, Pvt.room:N, Locker:N, Recep:>9p; Note: c.c. ok, meals, maps, laundry, safe dep, tea/cof, ctr

Stayokay Utrecht - Bunnik, Rhijnauwenselaan 14, Bunnik, Utrecht, T:0306561277, *Bunnik@ stayokay.com/*, $30Bed, Kitchen:N, B'fast:Y, Pvt. room:Y, Locker:Y, Recep:3>11p; Note: rural, resto/bar, bikes, tours, luggage rm

VLISSINGEN (English: "Flushing") is a city of 45,000 on the far southeast seacoast. Originally a fishing village, it became an important seaport in the Dutch Golden Age.

City Hostel Vlissingen, Kerkstraat 10, Vlissingen; *cityhostel-vlissingen.nl/*, T:0118415200; $31Bed, Kitchen:N, B'fast:Y, Pvt.room:Y, Locker:N, Recep:8a>6p; Note: cash only, resto/bar, bikes, books, laundry, bag hold, parking

TERSCHELLING is a Frisian island of 4700 in the North Sea to the Netherlands' far northwest. Once a province of sailors, tourism is now king. Local specialties are cranberries and the scavenging of driftwood (esp. shipwrecks) for construction purposes.

Stayokay Terschelling, Burg. van Heusdenweg 39, West-Terschelling; T:0562442338; *Terschelling@ stayokay.com/*, $24Bed, Kitchen:N, B'fast:Y, Pvt. room:Y, Locker:N, Recep:3>11p; Note: resto/bar, bikes, billiards, wh/chair ok

11) Poland

Poland has always had the unique position of being intermingled with the West and the East, with many Germans and Jews, among others, lying within its borders, borders that are flexible and changing with the tides of politics. Details are sketchy, but its origin as a state is closely identified with the adoption of Christianity in 966. It once tasted greatness starting in the 1500's in partnership with Lithuania before being decimated and deposed in 1795. It regrouped and there was a brief independence between WW's I & II, before final independence with the fall of Communism in 1989.

The drive to undermine Communism began right here, with Lech Walesa and the Solidarity movement in the shipyards of Gdansk. Prime tourist destinations today include Nazi concentration camps and many national parks, featuring lakes, rivers, forests, and even a desert. A desert in Poland? You heard it here first. Poland also has thirteen — count 'em — UNESCO World Heritage sites. It is truly one of the unpolished travel gems of Europe. Polish is the language; *zloty* is the currency; phone code is +48.

9 Hostels) GDANSK ('Danzig' in German), on the northern Baltic coast, is Poland's largest seaport and fourth-largest city. Like Wroclaw, Gdansk also has swung back-and-forth between German and Polish overlordship. It was founded in the earliest years of the Common Era by Goths in migration, and then Slavic Pomeranians. With the arrival of Teutonic knights and the foundation of the Hanseatic League, Germans returned to a position of dominance, a situation in effect until the end of WWII, when the city was returned to Poland and German residents left.

Since then Gdansk has always been a scene of unrest. This is the birthplace of Solidarity, which put the first chinks in Soviet armor that eventually led to the downfall of Communism in Europe. Historical architecture is the main attraction today. Long Street and Long Market are the main tourist areas. The National Museum and the Maritime Museum are important, as is the Dominican Fair, which originated in 1260.

La Guitarra Hotel Gdansk, Grodzka 12, Gdansk; T:510795535, *gdansk@ lagitarra.com/*; $9bed, Kitchen:Y, B'fast:Y, Pvt.room:Y, Locker:Y, Recep:24/7; Note: coffee/tea, bag hold, laundry, parking c.c. ok, central, new

Happy Seven Hostel, Grodzka 16, Gdańsk; T:583208601, *booking@ happyseven.com/*; $16bed, Kitchen:Y, B'fast:Y, Pvt.room:Y, Locker:Y, Recep:24/7; Note: coffee/tea, bar, parking, bag hold, tours, c.c. ok, shoes off

Hostel Wolna Chata, Krzywoustego 8, Gdańsk; **T:**587463351, *info@ hostelwolnachata.com/*; $12bed, Kitchen:Y, B'fast:Y, Pvt.room:Y, Locker:Y, Recep:ltd; Note: parking, bag hold, bikes, non-tourist area

Grand Hostel Gdansk, Kołodziejska 2, Gdańsk; *grandhostel.pl/*, T:666061350, *grand.hostel.gda@gmail.com*; $14bed, Kitchen:Y, B'fast:Y, Pvt. room:Y, Locker:Y, Recep:24/7; Note: bikes, bag hold, laundry, a/c, central, shoes off, no lift

Old Town Hostel, Długa Grobla 7, Gdańsk; *hostel@ hostel. gda.pl*; $10bed, Kitchen:Y, B'fast:Y, Pvt.room:Y, Locker:Y, Recep:24/7; Note: bike rent, parking, bag hold, laundry, c.c. ok, walk>center

Hostel Zappio, Świętojańska 49, Gdańsk; T:583220174, *zappio@ zappio. pl/*; $15bed, Kitchen:Y, B'fast:$, Pvt.room:Y, Locker:Y, Recep:24/7; Note: bikes, bar/cafe, bag hold, forex, c.c. ok, Sat TV, central

Riverside Hostel, Powroźnicza 18, Gdansk; *info@ riverside-hostel. pl/*, T:+48/587183854; $12bed, Kitchen:Y, B'fast:Y, Pvt.room:Y, Locker:Y, Recep:24/7; Note: bag hold, bikes, café, wh/chair ok, tea/coffee, tours, old town

Hostel Przy Targu Rybnym, Grodzka 21, Gdańsk; *gdanskhostel.com. pl/*, T:583015627, *gdanskhostel@hotmail.com*; $9bed, Kitchen:Y, B'fast:Y, Pvt. room:Y, Locker:Y, Recep:24/7; Note: coffee/tea, bag hold, laundry, prkng, c.c. ok

Baltic Downtown Hostel , ulica Zaroślak 12, Gdańsk; *baltichostel.com.pl/*, T:587219657; $10bed, Kitchen:Y, B'fast:$, Pvt.room:Y, Locker:N, Recep:24/7; Note: central, luggage room, laundry, arpt trans

26 Hostels) KRAKOW (pronounce 'w' as 'v') is the second largest and oldest city in Poland. It dates back to the seventh century and served as capital for most of the time since Poland's origin as a state. It was almost completely destroyed by the Mongols before being able to repel them. It was a trade city of the Hanseatic League and capital of the Polish-Lithuania Commonwealth before that entity was partitioned. After that Krakow became known as a center of art and culture and education. In the 20th century it was a center of Jewish culture and Zionism, and the city closest to Auschwitz.

Today the entire historic center is a world heritage site and the architecture here is a Renaissance monument. Besides Auschwitz, prime tourist sights include Wawel Castle and the old Jewish quarter, one of the largest in the world. Krakow had more than a hundred synagogues prior to WWII. Its architecture fared better than its Jewish population, and includes St. Mary's Church, Wawel Cathedral, The Barbican, the 13th C. Florian Gate, and Cloth Hall. Hostels are of high quality, and demand is equally high, advance payments sometimes being required in high season.

Greg & Tom (Jr.) Party Hostel, Zyblikiewicza 9, Kraków, T:124225525, *junior@ gregtomhostel.com/*; $18bed, Kitchen:Y, B'fast:Y, Pvt.room:Y, Locker:Y, Recep:24/7; Note: age 18-40, bar, lounge, laundry, dinner, parties

Flamingo Hostel, Szewska 4, Kraków; *Krakow@ flamingo-hostel.com/*, T:124220000; $12bed, Kitchen:Y, B'fast:Y, Pvt.room:Y, Locker:Y, Recep:24/7; Note: restaurant, laundry, luggage room, free tour/travel info

Football Corner Hostel, Ul. Wróblewskiego 3, Kraków; *footballcorner. com.pl/*, T:503764365, *footballcorner@home.pl* $11bed, Kitchen:Y, B'fast:Y, Pvt. room:Y, Locker:Y, Recep:24/7; Note: printer, tea/cof, laundry, luggage ok, nr train

Pink Panther's Hostel, Ul. Św Tomasza 8, 2 piętro, Kraków; T:124220935, *hostel@ pinkpanthershostel.com/*; $13bed, Kitchen:Y, B'fast:Y, Pvt.room:Y, Locker:Y, Recep:24/7; Note: tours, bag hold, tea/coffee, TV, party, central

PART II: Central Europe

AAE Mosquito Hostel, Rynek Kleparski 4, Kraków; T:660926190, *info@ mosquitohostel.com/*; $19bed, Kitchen:Y, B'fast:Y, Pvt.room:Y, Locker:Y, Recep:24/7; Note: free tour/info, laundry, luggage ok, c.c. ok, near old town, vodka

Cracow Hostel, Rynek Główny 18, Kraków; *cracowhostel.com/*, T:124291106, *hostel@ cracowhostel.nazwa.pl/*; $12bed, Kitchen:Y, B'fast:Y, Pvt.room:Y, Locker:Y, Recep:24/7; Note: café, lounge, tours, stairs no lift, near market sq

One World Hostel, Westerplatte 8, Kraków; T:0124446546, *Cracow@ oneworldhostel.eu/*; $9bed, Kitchen:Y, B'fast:Y, Pvt.room:Y, Locker:Y, Recep:24/7; Note: arpt trans, laundry, bag hold, tours, tea/cof, central, party

Flower Hostel, świętego Tomasza 5, Kraków; T:123505918, *office@ flowerhostel.pl/*; $17bed, Kitchen:N, B'fast:Y, Pvt.room:Y, Locker:Y, Recep:24/7; Note: bike rent, laundry, bag hold, tours, travel info, central

Traveller's Inn, Plac Na Groblach 8, Kraków; *info@ travellersinn.pl/*, T:602555753; $16bed, Kitchen:Y, B'fast:Y, Pvt.room:Y, Locker:Y, Recep:advise ETA; Note: bike rent, luggage room, laundry, parking, tour desk

Mundo Hostel, Józefa Sarego 10, Kraków; T:124226113, *info@ mundohostel. eu/*; $15bed, Kitchen:Y, B'fast:Y, Pvt.room:Y, Locker:N, Recep:24/7; Note: bar, luggage room, laundry, c.c. ok, in courtyard, pancakes!

Elephant on the Moon, Ul. Białe Wzgórze 8, Kraków; *elephantonthemoon. com/*, T:695949604, *hostel24@hotmail.com*; $17bed, Kitchen:Y, B'fast:Y, Pvt. room:Y, Locker:Y, Recep:24/7; Note: bag hold, laundry, TV, walk>ctr

Deco Hostel, Mazowiecka 3A, Kraków; T:126310745, *hostel@ hosteldeco. pl/*; $10bed, Kitchen:Y, B'fast:Y, Pvt.room:Y, Locker:N, Recep:24/7; Note: free tour/info, luggage, laundry, theme rooms, 20 min walk>town

Mama's Hostel-Main Market Sq, Bracka 4, Kraków, T:124295940, *hostel@ mamashostel.com.pl/*; $12bed, Kitchen:Y, B'fast:Y, Pvt.room:Y, Locker:Y, Recep:24/7; Note: free tour, travel desk, party, luggage ok, TV, c.c. ok, off main sqare

Ars Hostel, Koletek 7 St, Krakow, Poland; *arshostel.pl/*, T/F:124223659, *info@ krakowtravels.pl/*; $15bed, Kitchen:Y, B'fast:Y, Pvt.room:Y, Locker:Y, Recep:24/7; Note: cash, bar, bikes, luggage rm, laundry, forex, off main sq

Atlantis Hostel, ul. Dietla 58, Kraków, Poland; *atlantishostel.pl/*, T:124210861, *atlantis@hostel.pl*; $11bed, Kitchen:Y, B'fast:N, Pvt.room:Y, Locker:N, Recep:24/7; Note: free tour/info, bag hold, c.c. ok, coffee/tea, central

Hostel Benedykta, Juliana Dunajewskiego 5, Kraków; T:124210285, *hostel@benedykta.pl/*; $8bed, Kitchen:Y, B'fast:Y, Pvt.room:N, Locker:Y, Recep:24/7; Note: bag hold, laundry, pets ok, 3-deck bunks, non-party, bikes, tours, tea/cof

Highlife Hostel, Starowiślna 16, Kraków; T:0530144469, *booking@highlifehostel.com/*; $10bed, Kitchen:N, B'fast:Y, Pvt.room:Y, Locker:Y, Recep:ltd; Note: bar, parking, TV, luggage room, laundry

City Hostel, Świśtego Krzyża 21, Kraków; T:124261815, *cityhostel@cityhostel.pl/*; $12bed, Kitchen:Y, B'fast:Y, Pvt.room:Y, Locker:Y, Recep:24/7; Note: luggage room, laundry, c.c. OK, travel info, central, modern

Dizzy Daisy Hostel Krakow, ul.Pędzichów 9, Kraków; *krakowhostel.pl*, T:122920171, *krakow@hostel.pl*; $10bed, Kitchen:Y, B'fast:$, Pvt. room:Y, Locker:Y, Recep:ltd; Note: café, bag hold, laundry, bikes, c.c. ok, no lift, central

Momotown Hostel, Miodowa 28, Kraków; T:124296929, *info@momotownhostel.com/*; $12bed, Kitchen:Y, B'fast:Y, Pvt.room:Y, Locker:Y, Recep:24/7; Note: bar, parking, bag hold, laundry, bikes, forex, 4 fl. no lift

Tutti Frutti Hostel, Kraków, 29 Floriańska St; *tuttifruttihostel.com/*, T:0124280028, *office@tfhostel.com*; $13bed, Kitchen:Y, B'fast:Y, Pvt.room:Y, Locker:N, Recep:24/7; Note: bar/club, parking, tours, party, c.c. ok, nr transport

Premium Hostel, Pomorska 2, Kraków; *premiumhostel.pl/*, T:122922211, *premium@hostel.pl*; $11bed, Kitchen:N, B'fast:Y, Pvt.room:Y, Locker:Y, Recep:24/7; Note: parking, tours, bag hold, c.c. ok, 20 min. walk to town

Hostel Rynek 7, Rynek Główny 7, Kraków; T:607073252, *hostel@hostelrynek7.pl/*; $14bed, Kitchen:Y, B'fast:Y, Pvt.room:Y, Locker:N, Recep:24/7; Note: bar, tour desk, luggage room, c.c. ok, front of Old Square

GlobArt Hostel, Basztowa 15, Kraków; *globarthostel.pl/*, T:124300099, *globart@hostel.pl*; $13bed, Kitchen:Y, B'fast:$, Pvt.room:Y, Locker:Y, Recep:24/7; Note: lift, laundry, luggage room, tour info, c.c. ok, central

Giraffe Hostel, 31 Krowoderska St, Krakow; T:+48/124300150, *info@ hostelgiraffe.com/*; $13bed, Kitchen:Y, B'fast:Y, Pvt.room:Y, Locker:Y, Recep:24/7; Note: bar/café, gym, laundry, luggage room, tour info, c.c. ok, parties

Orange Hostel, Józefa Dietla 64, Kraków; T:124212712, *info@ orangehostel. pl/*; $10bed, Kitchen:Y, B'fast:Y, Pvt.room:Y, Locker:Y, Recep:24/7; Note: parking, tour info, luggage room, laundry, coffee/tea

2 Hostels) LODZ is located in almost the exact geographic center of Poland. Once an economic boomtown based on the production of cotton textiles, it went from a village of a few hundred to a half million over the course of the 19th century. WWII was hard on Lodz, and the textile industry has gone elsewhere, but today Lodz survives and thrives as Poland's third city because of its central location and foreign investment in its manufacturing base. Though an ancient village, it is a relatively modern city, with few historical buildings. Still it is a cultural center, with The Museum of Modern Art, the Museum of Textiles, a flourishing art community and a film industry that has produced filmmakers like Andrzej Wajda and Roman Polanski.

Music Hostel, Piotrkowska 60, Łódź; *rezerwacje@ music-hostel.pl/*, T:533533263; $13bed, Kitchen:N, B'fast:Y, Pvt.room:Y, Locker:Y, Recep:24/7; Note: café, parking, luggage room, laundry, central, hard to find 1st time

Flamingo Hotel Lodz, Henryka Sienkiewicza 67, Łódź; T:426611888, *lodz@ flamingo-hostel.com/*; $13bed, Kitchen:N, B'fast:Y, Pvt.room:Y, Locker:Y, Recep:24/7; Note: bag hold, c.c. ok, bikes, bar, café, parking, no lift to top floors, tours

LUBLIN is located far to the east and has a castle. It was a great center of Jewish scholarship for the Talmud and Kabbalah in the 1500's. Four hundred years later, the Lublin Ghetto's residents would be sent to Belzec for extermination. Labor strikes in Lublin in 1980 were an impetus for the Solidarity movement a month later. These days Lublin is a center of the IT industry. It also has several universities and many students. The poverty of the surrounding region and subsequent low wages and costs make it an attractive place of investment. There are music, art, and festivals. Landmarks include the medieval castle and the Chapel of the Holy Trinity which houses the Lublin Museum. At the concentration camp is a museum and memorial park.

Hostel Lublin, ul Lubartowska 60, Lublin; T:792888632, *poczta@ hostellublin.pl/*; $13bed, Kitchen:Y, B'fast:Y, Pvt. room:Y, Locker:N, Recep:24/7; Note: parking, bag hold, safety deposit, central, near bus station, cafe

7 Hostels) POZNAN is Poland's fifth-largest city and one of its oldest. Located in the west of the country, Poznan, as elsewhere, has long had a significant number of ethnic German residents. That's only changed within the last century, though the Nazi occupation attempted a reversal. Poznan was devastated during WWII. They stubbornly resisted Communist rule here, too. Today Poznan is a trade city, as it was in the past. Old Town is the main tourist attraction. Notable landmarks include the cathedral (erected 968) and Poznan''s 16th C. town hall with clock tower. Besides the National Museum there are museums of archaeology and of musical instruments.

Hill Hostel, Zamkowa 1/2, Poznań; T:618530910, *info@ hillhostel.pl*; $9bed, Kitchen:Y, B'fast:Y, Pvt.room:Y, Locker:Y, Recep:24/7; Note: luggage room, tour desk, a/c, c.c ok, central

Frolic Goats Hostel, Wrocławska 16, Poznań; T:618524411, *bookings@ frolicgoatshostel.com*;$9bed, Kitchen:Y, B'fast:Y, Pvt.room:Y, Locker:Y, Recep:24/7; Note: advance dep, tours, bag hold, laundry, parking, c.c. ok

La Guitarra Hostel Poznan, Aleje Karola Marcinkowskiego 20, Poznań; T:618522074, *poznan@ lagitarra.com/*; $9bed, Kitchen:Y, B'fast:Y, Pvt.room:Y, Locker:Y, Recep:24/7; Note: prkng, wh/chairs ok, bag hold, tours, central

Melange Hostel, Rybaki 4/6, Poznań; *hostel@ melangehostel.com/*, T:507070107; $10bed, Kitchen:N, B'fast:Y, Pvt.room:Y, Locker:N, Recep:24/7; Note: some rooms w/o windows, central, parking, tours, bag hold

Fusion Hostel & Hotel, Święty Marcin 66/72, Poznań; T:618521230, *office@ fusionhostel.pl/*; $18bed, Kitchen:N, B'fast:Y, Pvt.room:N, Locker:Y, Recep:24/7; Note: c.c. ok, futuristic design, convenient

Cinnamon Hostel, Gwarna 10/2, Poznan; T:618515757, *poznan@ cinnamonhostel.com/*; $10bed, Kitchen:Y, B'fast:Y, Pvt.room:Y, Locker:Y, Recep:24/7; Note: tour desk, bag hold, laundry, TV, c.c. ok, near old town

Retro Hostel, Kramarska 1, Poznan, T:+48/612236061, *info@ retrohostel. pl/*; $9bed, Kitchen:Y, B'fast:$, Pvt.room:Y, Locker:Y, Recep:24/7; Note: tour desk, luggage room, tea/coffee, old town

3 Hostels) TORUN is the birthplace of Nicolaus Copernicus. It is one of the oldest Polish cities, with roots going back to the Lusatian culture in 1100 BC, with a subsequent Slavonic and then Teutonic occupation that had to be terminated by force, and their castle destroyed in the Thirteen Years War. Due to the mixed Polish/German populace, the Protestant Reformation carried serious repercussions here. "Germanization" was even forced upon the populace, and Hitler annexed it outright. Poles couldn't reclaim it as their own until after WWII. Its medieval old town is a UNESCO world heritage site, and well preserved. It is built entirely of brick. Highlights of the historic city include the 13th C. Church of St. John, the ruins of a Teutonic castle and the Gothic Church of Mary.

Angel Hostel, Rynek Staromiejski 8, Toruń, Poland; *angelhostel.com/*, T:696528664, *torun.hostel@gmail.com*; $12bed, Kitchen:N, B'fast:$, Pvt.room:Y, Locker:Y, Recep:ltd; Note: resto/bar/club, luggage rm, call check-in, centre

Hostel Orange, Prosta 19, Toruń; T:566520033, *rezerwacje.torun@ hostelorange.pl/*, $12bed, Kitchen:Y, B'fast:N, Pvt.room:Y, Locker:Y, Recep:24/7; Note: travel info, laundry, luggage room, two locations

Freedom Backpackers, Szeroka 31, Toruń; *freedomtorun.pl/*, T:790704785, *freedom.backpackers@gmail.com*; $12bed, Kitchen:Y, B'fast:Y, Pvt.room:Y, Locker:Y, Recep:24/7; Note: cash, laundry, bag hold, Sat TV, central, hard find

10 Hostels) WARSAW, near the center of the country, is Poland's capital and largest city. Like many of Europe's major cities, its roots go back to the beginning of the last millennium. It became capital of the Polish-Lithuanian Commonwealth and, after turns with Germany and Russia, was capital of independent Poland after WWI. Unfortunately it was 80% destroyed during WWII and hundreds of thousands of Jews were annihilated during the Warsaw Ghetto Uprising there.

Another Warsaw Uprising near the end of the war resulted in most of the city's original architecture being systematically destroyed by the Nazis while Russian troops camped on the city's outskirts. Since WWII the old town has been reconstructed to the original plan, and has the somewhat unique distinction that that reconstruction has been declared a World Heritage site in its own right. The only original medieval buildings are the Gothic St. John's Cathedral and the red-brick Barbican fortifications.

Other significant structures include the Church of the Holy Cross, the Royal Castle, Belvedere Palace, the Alexander Citadel and the palace of Culture and Science, built by the Soviets. There are the National Museum and the Zachęta National Gallery of Art in addition to many specialized museums. The Saxon Gardens and Royal Baths are two of the best parks. Wianki is a traditional summer festival. There are music and film festivals also.

Hostel Krokodyl, Czapelska St. 24, Warszawa; T:228101118, *info@ hostelkrokodyl.com/*; $14bed, Kitchen:Y, B'fast:Y, Pvt.room:Y, Locker:Y, Recep:24/7; Note: luggage room, laundry, parking, TV, c.c. ok, tram to center 20 min.

Hostel Helvetia, Sewerynów 7, Warsaw, Poland; *info@ hostel-helvetia.pl/*, T:228267108; $10bed, Kitchen:Y, B'fast:Y, Pvt.room:Y, Locker:Y, Recep:24/7; Note: bikes, laundry, bag hold, minimart, tea/coffee, tours, books, central

New World Street Hostel, Nowy Świat St 27, Warsaw; *newworldst-hostel. pl/*, T:228281282, *hostel@nws-hostel.pl*; $11bed, Kitchen:N, B'fast:$, Pvt.room:Y, Locker:Y, Recep:24/7; Note: bikes, laundry, bag hold, central, tea/cof

Oki Doki Hostel, Plac Jana Henryka Dąbrowskiego 3, Warsaw; T:224231212, *okidoki@ okidoki.pl/*; $12bed, Kitchen:N, B'fast:$, Pvt.room:Y, Locker:Y, Recep:24/7; Note: bar, bikes, café, tours, bag hold, laundry, c.c. ok, parking

Tamka Hostel, Tamka 30, Warsaw; *tamkahostel.com/*, T:228263095, *tamka@ hostel.pl*; $12bed, Kitchen:Y, B'fast:Y, Pvt.room:Y, Locker:Y, Recep:24/7; Note: bikes, tours, bag hold, laundry, c.c. ok, tea/coffee, parking

Old Town Hostel Kanonia, Jezuicka 2, Warsaw; T:226350676, *hostel@ kanonia.pl/*; $14bed, Kitchen:Y, B'fast:$, Pvt.room:Y, Locker:Y, Recep:24/7; Note: luggage room, laundry, c.c. ok, old town location

Nathan's Villa Hostel, Piękna 24/26, Warsaw; T:226222946, *warsaw@ nathansvilla.com/*; $14bed, Kitchen:Y, B'fast:N, Pvt.room:Y, Locker:Y, Recep:24/7; Note: laundry, bag hold, tours, c.c. ok, tea/coffee, books, maps

Camera Hostel, Jasna 22, Warsaw; T:228288600, *info@ camerahostel.pl/*; $15bed, Kitchen:Y, B'fast:Y, Pvt.room:Y, Locker:Y, Recep:24/7; Note: luggage room, laundry, parking, lift, café

Hostel Witt, Emilii Plater 9/11, Warsaw; T:603632588; *rezerwacja@ hostelwitt.pl/*; $15bed, Kitchen:Y, B'fast:N, Pvt.room:Y, Locker:Y, Recep:ltd; Note: scooter & bike rental, parking, TV, c.c. ok, nice old house

Hostel Fabryka, 11 Listopada 22, Warsaw; *hostelfabryka.pl/*, T:515464209, *hostelfabryka@gmail.com;* $10bed, Kitchen:Y, B'fast:Y, Pvt.room:Y, Locker:Y, Recep:24/7; Note: café, club, parking, bag hold, Praga club dist, tea/cof

10 Hostels) WROCLAW (pronounced something like "vrot swaf") is located in the southwest of Poland. Located at a central crossroads of Europe, Wroclaw, originally Silesian, has at various times been a member of Austria, Prussia, and Germany, besides Poland, and has different names in half a dozen different languages, creating today a modern city of mixed origins and cultures. Mostly it's been a swing city between the Germans and the Poles. It's always been Bohemian. The historic architecture here is a tourist attraction, a collective monument to the use of brick. Town Hall can't be missed; it's the wedding cake at the feast. Centennial Hall is a world heritage site. Other buildings of particular historical interest include the churches at Ostrów Tumski, and the Aula Leopoldina, a Baroque assembly hall at the university. There are music festivals.

Mleczarnia Hostel, Pawła Włodkowica 5, Wrocław; T:717877570, *rezerwacja@ mleczarniahostel.pl/*; $12bed, Kitchen:Y, B'fast:N, Pvt.room:Y, Locker:N, Recep:24/7; Note: resto/bar/café, pets ok, bag hold, laundry, c.c. ok, in old town

Boogie Hostel Deluxe, ul. Bialoskornicza 6, Wroclaw, *wroclaw@*, T:713421160

Boogie Hostel Wroclaw, Ruska 35, Wrocław; T:713424472, *hostel@ boogiehostel.com/*; $10bed, Kitchen:Y,B'fast:Y, Pvt.room:Y, Locker:Y, Recep:24/7; Note: tour desk, luggage room, laundry, c.c. ok, near center

Babel Hostel, Księdza Hugona Kołłątaja 16/3, Wrocław; T:694896921; *rezerwacje@ babelhostel.pl/*; $13bed, Kitchen:Y, B'fast:N, Pvt.room:N, Locker:Y, Recep:24/7; Note: free tour, luggage room, laundry, TV

Absynt Hostel, świętego Antoniego 15, Wrocław; T:713444469, *biuro@ absynthostel.pl/*; $10bed, Kitchen:Y, B'fast:N, Pvt.room:Y, Locker:N, Recep:24/7; Note: lift, tour desk, a/c, c.c. ok

Hostel Cinema, Kazimierza Wielkiego 17, Wrocław, Poland; *hostelcinema. pl/*, T:717957755, *hostelcinema@o2.pl*; $13bed, Kitchen:Y, B'fast:N, Pvt.room:Y, Locker:N, Recep:24/7; Note: coffee/tea, bag hold, laundry, c.c ok, central

Cinnamon Hostel, Kazimierza Wielkiego 67, Wrocław; T:713445858, *wroclaw@ cinnamonhostel.com/*; $11bed, Kitchen:Y, B'fast:Y, Pvt.room:Y, Locker:N, Recep:24/7; Note: tours, bag hold, laundry, central, checkout 12n, bikes

Centrum Hostel, Świętego Mikołaja 16/17, Wrocław; *centrumhostel.pl/*, T:717930870, *hostelcentrum@o2.pl*; $13bed, Kitchen:Y, B'fast:N, Pvt.room:Y, Locker:N, Recep:24/7; Note: confirm res. 1 day B4, central, laundry, safe dep

Hostel Europa, Ul. Grabiszynska 61-65, Wroclaw, Poland; *hosteleuropa. pl/*, T:+48/713437024; $11bed, Kitchen:Y, B'fast:$, Pvt.room:Y, Locker:N, Recep:24/7; Note: club, parking, luggage room, 15 min. walk to center

Corner Hostel, Świdnicka 13, Wrocław; *hostel-centrum.wroclaw.pl/*, T:713441095, *wroclaw@cornerhostel.com*; $10bed, Kitchen:Y, B'fast:Y, Pvt.room:Y, Locker:Y, Recep:24/7; Note: café, wh/chair ok, pets ok, parking, bag hold

4 Hostels) ZAKOPANE lies at the southernmost tip of Poland, where it pokes into the hilly border of Slovakia, at an elevation of some 1000m/4000ft. A former mining town, today it is a center of winter sports in the winter and a hikers' mecca in the summer. Zakopane also serves as the cultural centre for the area, with the Chałubin´ski Memorial Tatra Museum, containing ethnographic and geologic displays, and the Exhibition Hall of the Union of Polish Arts.

Target Hostel, Henryka Sienkiewicza 3b, Zakopane; T:182074596, *kontakt@ targethostel.pl/*; $11bed, Kitchen:Y, B'fast:N, Pvt.room:N, Locker:Y, Recep:24/7; Note: parking, laundry, luggage room, near bus & Tesco, quiet

Goodbye Lenin Hostel, Chłabówka 44, Zakopane; *zakopane.goodbyelenin. pl/* T:182001330; $13bed, Kitchen:Y, B'fast:Y, Pvt.room:Y, Locker:Y, Recep:24/7; Note: prkng, luggage ok, laundry, c.c. ok, natl. park, 40 min>town

Top Hostel, Krupówki 24, Zakopane, T:+48/184487771, *zakopane@ tophostel.pl/*; $14bed, Kitchen:Y, B'fast:$, Pvt.room:Y, Locker:Y, Recep:2p>12m; Note: cash only, bikes, cafe, laundry, luggage room, tea/coffee, party

Hostel Stara Polana, ul. Nowotarska 59, Zakopane; T:182068902, *rezerwacje@ starapolana.pl/*; $13bed, Kitchen:Y, B'fast:Y, Pvt.room:Y, Locker:Y, Recep:24/7; Note: parking, tour desk, luggage room, laundry

12) Slovakia

The nation that is now Slovakia (long form = "Slovak Republic"), enters the history books during the fifth and sixth centuries around the same time that the Roman Empire was falling and the entire continent of Europe was entering a period of intense migration. It was part of several of the earliest Slavic states to coalesce as "Samo's kingdom" and Greater Moravia. After that it was an important part of the Kingdom of Hungary and the Austrian-Habsburg Empire, then Czechoslovakia, before finally achieving independence last century. The Czech and Slovak republics separated in 1993, but are still close politically. Today Slovakia is a market-oriented multi-party capitalist democracy with a bright future. Tourism is based on medieval towns and castles, natural landscapes, and ski resorts. Slovak is the (main) language, Euro is currency and the phone code is +421.

8 Hostels) BRATISLAVA is Slovakia's capital and largest city and is known variously throughout history as Pressburg, Presporik and Pozsony. Bratislava's moment in the spotlight came when the Hungarian capital was relocated here following the Ottoman Empire's occupation of Budapest in 1526. This period lasted more than three hundred years from the sixteenth to nineteenth centuries. Prior to WWI and Czechoslovakia's creation, the Slovak population in Pressburg was less than one in five, the remainder German and Hungarian.

After WWII the population was 90% Slovak and the name was Bratislava. Communist Warsaw Pact troops occupied the city during Prague Spring of 1968, and it wasn't until the Velvet Revolution of 1989 that Communism was defeated. The Velvet Divorce separated the two countries in 1993. Today Old Town and Bratislava Castle are major tourist attractions. It is only 40mi/60km from Vienna, Austria.

Hostel Blues, Špitálska 2205/2, Staré Mesto-Bratislava I; T:0905204020, *bookings@ hostelblues.sk/*; $15bed, Kitchen:Y, B'fast:N, Pvt.room:Y, Locker:Y, Recep:24/7; Note: bar/café, lift, free tour/info, laundry, bag hold, TV

Downtown Backpacker Hostel, Panenská 680/31, Bratislava; T:0254641191, *info@ backpackers.sk/*; $16bed, Kitchen:Y, B'fast:$, Pvt.room:Y, Locker:Y, Recep:24/7; Note: resto/bar/café, tours, luggage rm, laundry, c.c. ok, old town

Art Hostel Taurus, Zámocká 24, Staré Mesto-Bratislava 1; *hostel-taurus. com/*, T:0220722401, *art.hostel.taurus@gmail.com*; $18bed, Kitchen:N, B'fast:Y, Pvt.room:Y, Locker:Y, Recep:24/7; Note: parking, bag hold, laundry, bikes, no alcohol

Hostel Possonium, Šancová 3996/20, Bratislava-Old Town; T:0220720007, *info@ possonium.sk/*; $21bed, Kitchen:Y, B'fast:$, Pvt. room:Y, Locker:Y, Recep:24/7; Note: bar, parking, bag hold, laundry, c.c. ok, not central, nr train

Hostel Spirit, Vančurova 1694/1, Bratislava-Nové Mesto; *hotelgallery. eu/*, T:0254777561, *info@hotelpirit.sk*; $20bed, Kitchen:N, B'fast:Y, Pvt.room:Y, Locker:N, Recep:24/7; Note: parking, laundry, luggage ok, safe deposit

Patio Hostel, Špitálska 2196/35, Staré Mesto-Bratislava; *patiohostel.com/*, T:0252925797; $19bed, Kitchen:Y, B'fast:$, Pvt.room:Y, Locker:Y, Recep:24/7; Note: bar, parking, laundry, luggage ok, c.c. ok, , TV, central

A1 Hostel Bratislava, Heydukova 2138/1, Bratislava-Staré Mesto; *a1hostelbratislava.com/*, T:0944280288, *A1Bratislava@gmail.com*; $15bed, Kitchen:Y, B'fast:N, Pvt.room:Y, Locker:Y, Recep:ltd; Note: bikes, laundry, bag hold, ctr

Hotel Plus, Bulharská 1743/72, Bratislava, Ružinov-Ružinov; T:0243426350, *travel@ hotelyplus.sk/*, $14bed, Kitchen:N, B'fast:N, Pvt.room:Y, Locker:N, Recep:24/7; Note: resto/bar, parking, forex, tour desk, laundry, bag hold

PART III: Scandinavia

If central Europe in general, and the hostels there in particular, are a bit slicker, more modern and more urban than the British Isles, then Scandinavia is positively otherworldly. Even high-tech robot-friendly Asians get confused here. For one thing, you really need a cell-phone, not just so that you can call to advise your arrival and arrange check-in when necessary, but so that they can text you a code to open the door! That constitutes check-in, as often as not. They love codes, and credit cards, too. If you need to actually talk to someone – or pay cash – then they usually try to show up and man the desk for two or three hours, typically 3-6 p.m. Anything after that is 'late' check-in.

Sometimes they'll even expect you to clean up your bunk, too, or pay someone else to do it. They don't press their luck, though, so you can forget the kitchens, and the resto/bars, too. They're squeaky clean. And those linens usually carry a fee, also, unless you bring your own. Sleeping bags don't usually count. There's no midday lock-out, though, since you'll have the code. Social equality doesn't come cheap, I guess, nor does anything else here. That high linen fee should logically be a one-off, though. If they attempt to charge you that every day, then I'd protest vigorously (unless you actually plan to change your linen every day; yeah right).

It's all worth it, though, for this is one special part of the world. It's almost incredible to imagine that this was once the home of the Vikings, some of the most violent actors ever on history's stage. Finland is the only non-Viking country, they related to the area's earliest inhabitants. The others are all of an Indo-European linguistic group, related to Germans, Latins, Slavs and Indo/Iranians, and whose Scandinavian languages are all mutually intelligible to this day (except for Icelandic, an archaic form of the language). Today, these countries are not only the most socially equal, the most highly advanced, but also the most environmentally conscious, of any in the world. They're beautiful, too, and bathed by Gulf Stream waters that keep climates mild even north of the Arctic Circle. There, except in summer, you're likely to see the *aurora borealis*, and that's special.

13) Denmark

The narrow conglomeration of continent and islands that connects Europe to Scandinavia is today the country of Denmark, a small area of land whose people changed the world around the beginning of the Common Era. For it was here that highly successful and populous Germanic tribes soon to become Franks, Lombards, Alemanni, Saxons, and Goths, etc. first pushed southward in an epic era of expansion and migration that first displaced the ubiquitous Celts, then many smaller groups, and finally even the powerful Romans themselves. Others of course went to England and displaced the Celts there.

Denmark itself, though, remained most closely related to the northern countries and was part of the Viking era that rocked the world. Denmark was once in a union which included both Norway and Sweden, and still maintains oversight of Greenland and the Faroe Islands, which are otherwise self-governing today. Like Norway, Denmark has some North Sea oil that it exports. Politics tend to be environmental and progressive. The Danish *krone* is currency, Danish is the language, and the phone code is +45.

AARHUS is a city of 300,000 in the center of Denmark, with up to three times again that many in the environs. A university town, it has many young people and much entertainment, including festivals such as North Side Festival, Aarhus International Jazz Festival and Aarhus Festuge. It also has theme parks such as Old Town and Tivoli Friheden. Architecture includes the 13th century cathedral and Aarhus City Hall. For diversity, check out Arab-themed Bazar West. Aarhus is LGBT-friendly.

PART III: Scandinavia

City Sleep-in, Havnegade 20, Aarhus; T:+45/86192055, *sleep-in@ citysleep-in.dk/*; $34Bed, Kitchen:Y, B'fast:N, Pvt.room:Y, Locker:Y, Recep:8a//9p; Note: lift, tours, bag hold, laundry, billiards, games, nr beach, nr bus/train, basic, central

8 Hostels) COPENHAGEN is Denmark's capital and largest city. It has been a trading center since the Middle Ages, and was frequently attacked by the Hanseatic League. The straits that Denmark occupied between the Baltic and North Seas were prime passages to fuss over. They were later famously attacked by the British in 1807 and occupied by the Nazis in WWII. Things are calmer these days and Copenhagen has a rep as a modern and futuristic city, clean and green. In the center of the city is Tivoli Gardens, the second-oldest amusement park in the world, and featuring the oldest still-operating roller coaster and Ferris wheel in the world. The oldest amusement park is outside the city limits, Dyrehavsbakken in Klampenborg. Care for an apple, Mr. Disney?

Rådhuspladsen ("Town Hall Square") is the heart of the city, and other important buildings include Thott Palace, the Charlottenborg Palace, Christiansborg Palace, Bertel Thorvaldsen Museum, the Royal Arsenal Museum, the Royal Library, National Museum, the Church of Our Lady, the University of Copenhagen, the Petri Church, the 17th C. citadel, and the palace of Amalienborg. There is a major music festival at Roskilde. Via the recently-opened Oresund Bridge, Malmo in Sweden is now part of the metropolitan area of Copenhagen.

Danhostel Copenhagen Downtown, Vandkunsten 5, Kbh; *danhostel.dk/*, T:28960699, *info@copenhagendowntown.com;*$26bed, Kitchen:Y, B'fast:$, Pvt. room:Y, Locker:N, Recep:24/7; Note: resto/bar, bikes, wh/chair ok, lift, bag hold

Generator Hostel Copenhagen, Adelgade 7, Kbh; T:78775400, *copenhagen@ generatorhostels.com/*; $28bed, Kitchen:Y, B'fast:N, Pvt.room:Y, Locker:Y, Recep:24/7; Note: bar/café/club, lift, laundry, bag hold, billiards, wh/chair ok, central

Sleep in Heaven, Struensegade 7, København N; T:35354648, *morefun@ sleepinheaven.com/*; $24bed, Kitchen:N, B'fast:$, Pvt.room:Y, Locker:Y, Recep:24/7; Note: bar/café, luggage ok, tours, bikes, billiards, c.c.+4%, central

145

HI Danhostel Copenhagen City, H. C. Andersens Blvd. 50, København V; *danhostelcopenhagencity.dk/*, T:33118585; $26bed, Kitchen:Y, B'fast:$, Pvt.room:Y, Locker:Y, Recep:advise ETA; Note: resto/bar, bikes, wh/chair ok, lift, bag hold

Hotel Jorgensen, Rømersgade 11, Kbh; *hoteljoergensen.dk/*, T:33138186, *HotelJoergensen@mail.dk*; $24bed, Kitchen:N, B'fast:$, Pvt.room:Y, Locker:N, Recep:24/7; Note: c.c.+2.2%, bar, billiards, bag hold, central, near train

Woodah Hostel, Abel Cathrines Gade 1, Kbh V, *hello@ woodah-hostel.com/*; T:+45/23905563; $45Bed, Kitchen:N, B'fast:Y, Pvt.roomY, Locker:Y, Recep:ltd; Note: resto/bar, bikes, books, bag hold, maps, tours, near train

Danhostel C'hagen Bellahoej, Herbergvejen 8, Brønshøj, Kbh; *copenhagenhostel.dk/*, T:38289715, *bellahoej@danhostel.dk*; $30Bed, Kitchen:Y, B'fast:N, Pvt.room:Y, Locker:Y, Recep:3-5p (call); Note: bikes, fees, bag hold, far

Danhostel Copenhagen Amager, Vejlands Allé 200, Kbh; T:32522908, *danhostelcopenhagen.dk/*, $30Bed, *Copenhagen@danhostel.dk*; Kitchen:Y, B'fast:N, Pvt.room:Y, Locker:Y, Recep:24/7; Note: wh/chair ok, laundry, far, luggage rm

ODENSE is a city of 170,000 and occupies the island of Funen. Fixtures include St. Canute's Cathedral, Our Lady's Church, Odense Palace, City Hall, Odense Zoo, Funen Village, Danish Railway Museum, and H.C. Andersen's house.

Odense Danhostel City, Østre Stationsvej 31, Odense; *odensedanhostel.dk/* T:63110425, *info@cityhostel.dk*; $52Bed, Kitchen:Y, B'fast:Y, Pvt.room:Y, Locker:Y, Recep:4-5p(Call); Note: lift, luggage storage, near transport

14) Finland

Finns are related to the original inhabitants of Scandinavia and other tribal groups that inhabited the vast northern lands between the Urals and the Atlantic, and if linguistics imply races, maybe all the way to the Altai four-corners region where China meets Russia meets Kazakhstan meets Mongolia. After being colonized for centuries by Sweden until Russia took a turn in the 1800's, Finland finally achieved total independence last century, with a distinct policy of not bugging the Russians.

Now Finland is a full-fledged member of modern Europe and modern Scandinavia, and the only Scandinavian country using the Euro as currency. The first work written in Finnish was the New Testament in the 16th century. *Kalevala* is the national folk epic. There is a lively music and arts scene. The phone code is +358 and Finnish, Swedish, and Sami are the languages.

5 Hostels) HELSINKI is the capital and largest city in Finland, and home to approximately twenty percent of all Finns. Though founded in 1550, it didn't grow much until the 19th century. Today it is less expensive than the other Scandinavian capitals, so not a bad place to hang for a while. There are ferry services to Stockholm, St. Petersburg and Tallinn only some 50mi/80km across the water in Estonia. The city is small enough to walk around easily and the architecture is lovely. Much of it is clustered around Senate Square, such as the state council building and the Lutheran cathedral. Uspenski Orthodox Cathedral is a vestige of previous Russian rule. In the Hollywood tradition of "day for night," Helsinki was used frequently in cold-war movies as the cinematic equivalent of Russia, art imitating life. This is the place to try a reindeer burger. Enjoy.

Eurohostel, Linnankatu 9, Helsinki; T:096220470, *eurohostel@ eurohostel.fi/*; $38bed, Kitchen:Y, B'fast:$, Pvt.room:Y, Locker:Y, Recep:24/7; Note: restaurant, bar, lift, luggage room, laundry, c.c. ok, free sauna, central

Stadion, Pohjoinen Stadiontie, Helsinki; T:094778480, *info@ stadionhostel. fi/*; $32bed, Kitchen:Y, B'fast:$, Pvt.room:Y, Locker:Y, Recep:24/7; Note: HI member, laundry, bag hold, parking, tea/coffee, tours, non-party, far

Hostel Erottajanpuisto, Uudenmaankatu 9, Helsinki; *Info@ erottajanpuisto. com/*, T:+358(0)9642169; $38Bed, Kitchen:Y, B'fast:N, Pvt.room:Y, Locker:Y, Recep:24/7; Note: central, 3rd floor no lift, quiet

CheapSleep Helsinki, Sturenkatu 27, Helsinki; *reservations@ cheapsleep.fi/*, T:0458456188; $24Bed, Kitchen:Y, B'fast:N, Pvt.room:Y, Locker:Y, Recep:ltd; Note: lift, wh/chair ok, mart, parking, maps, books, not central, easy>airport

Hostel Suomenlinna, Suomenlinna C9, Helsinki, *hostelhelsinki.fi/*, T:+358/96847471, *hostel@snk.fi*; $35Bed, Kitchen:Y, B'fast:N, Pvt.room:Y, Locker:Y, Recep:9a>4:45p; Note: luggage room, parking, tea/coffee, island w/ ferry

ROVANIEMI is a city of 61,000 located north of Finland's Arctic Circle, and the northern terminus of its electric railway. Unspoiled nature and the Northern Lights are top tourist attractions.

Hostel Rudolf, Koskikatu 41, Korkalonkatu 29, Rovaniemi, *rudolf.fi/*, T:016321321, *Rudolf@santashotels.fi/*; $56Bed, Kitchen:Y, B'fast:$, Pvt.room:Y, Locker:Y, Recep:24/7; Note: lift, wh/chair ok, luggage room, parking, central

TAMPERE is an inland city of over 200,000 and Finland's third-largest. There are museums, an amusement park, a film festival, and a rock music festival.

Tampere Dream Hostel, Åkerlundinkatu 2, Tampere; T:0452360517, *Info@dreamhostel.fi/*; $31Bed, Kitchen:Y, B'fast:N, Pvt.room:Y, Locker:Y, Recep:ltd; Note: bikes, wh/chair ok, laundry, bag hold, parking, mart, coffee/tea

TURKU is a city of 180,000 in the region of 'Finland Proper,' so-called because it was likely the first and now oldest city there. It is also bilingual, with a significant Swedish-speaking contingent. The Russian occupation of Finland in 1809 moved the capital eastward to Helsimki. Besides historic architecture, there are many festivals.

Hostel Turku, Slottsgatan 39, Turku; *hostelturku.fi/*, T:022627680, *hostel@turku.fi*; $32Bed, Kitchen:Y, B'fast:$, Pvt.room:Y, Locker:Y, Recep:3>9p; Note: bikes, wh/chair ok, laundry, luggage room, parking, central

15) Iceland

Iceland was settled by Norsemen in the ninth century AD, but there is good reason to think that Irish monks had already been there. The fact that the Norse apparently took Gaelic slaves (and maybe wives) there would make genomic evidence inconclusive. It belonged first to Norway, then to Denmark, before gaining independence in 1944. Today it is home to over 300,000 people, most of whom have traditionally made their living from the sea. That all changed in the early years of the current millennium when Iceland got the brilliant idea to become a financial center, with all the shenanigans that advanced capitalism is famous for. That was a disaster, of course, and Iceland is still recovering, a terrible shame for a country with a reputation as having one of the lowest income disparities in the world.

On a lighter note, the pop music is some of the best in the world—Bjork, Sigur Ros, and all the rest. The language is closer to Old Norse than any modern Scandinavian language. The main source of energy is geothermal and the island is full of volcanoes and geysers. The northern tip of the island kisses the Arctic Circle. There is a road that rings the island, which I figure would make an excellent two-three day tour under the summer's midnight sun. Icelandic Air has some of the cheapest flights between Europe and the East Coast of the US. They'll let you stopover at no extra charge for three days. Icelandic is the language; *krona* (ISK) is currency; phone code is +354.

2 Hostels) AKUREYRI is a town of almost 18,000 and Iceland's second-largest metropolis after Greater Reykjavik. Nearby mountains serve as windbreaks, so it's not as cold as you'd think. There is folk culture and summer festivals. I hope you like fish.

HI Akureyri YH, Störholt 1, 603 Akureyri; *hihostels.com/*, T:8944299, *akureyri@hostel.is*; $30Bed, Kitchen:Y, B'fast:$, Pvt.room:Y, Locker:N, Recep:8a>9:30p; Note: wh/chair ok, bag hold, laundry, parking, tea/coffee

Akureyri Backpackers, Hafnarstræti 98, Akureyri, T:5783700, *akureyri@backpackers.is/*; $22Bed, Kitchen:Y, B'fast:$, Pvt.room:Y, Locker:Y, Recep:ltd; Note: resto/bar, laundry, luggage room, tour desk, maps

DALVIK is a town of 1400 in Iceland's north, and a port for commerce and fishing. There is skiing nearby and the *Fiskidagurinn mikli* festival in August; free fish!

HI Gimli Hostel, Vegamót, Hafnarbraut 4, Dalvik, *hihostels.com/*, T:8658391; *dalvik@hostel.is*; $33Bed, Kitchen:Y, B'fast:$, Pvt.room:Y, Locker:Y, Recep:9a//6:30p; Note: trans<Akureyri $, arpt trans, minimart, laundry, prkng

HAFNARFJORDUR is a city of 26,000 in Iceland's southwest, and site of an annual Viking festival and Bright Days festival. Many rock bands started here.

Lava Guest House, Hjallabraut 51, Hafnarfjörður; T:5650900, *info@ hafnarfjordurguesthouse.is/*; $43Bed, Kitchen:Y, B'fast:$, Pvt.room:N, Locker:N, Recep:9a>10p; Note: arpt trans, laundry, bag hold, tours, maps, books, parking

HVOLSVOLLUR is a town of 860 in Iceland's south. There is a Saga Centre here, dedicated to 'Njal's Saga', which is based here.

Volcano Huts Thorsmork, Húsadalur Þórsmörk, Hvolsvollur; *volcanohuts@ volcanohuts.com*, T:5528300; $56Bed, Kitchen:Y, B'fast:$, Pvt. room:Y, Locker:N, Recep:7a>11p; Note: yoga, shuttle 4km, hot tub, bar, café, wh/chair ok

KEFLAVIK is a town of 14,000 not far from Reykjavik. Originally developed to process fish, now they process more tourists… through nearby KEF, the country's main airport.

Fit Hostel, Fitjabraut 6b, 260 Keflavik; *fithostel@ fithostel.is*, T:4218889; $28Bed, Kitchen:Y, B'fast:$, Pvt.room:Y, Locker:N, Recep:12n>6p; Note: HI member, bikes, parking, 5 min>arpt, 45 min>Reykjavik, absentee staff

14 Hostels) REYKJAVIK is the capital and largest (read: "only") city in Iceland. It was founded in 870, but didn't develop much as a city until the 18th century. Like its sister Nordic cities on the mainland, it is quite attractive, though much

smaller. It's expensive, though, the cheapest fast food around $10 USD and any sit-down meal easily $25. There are at least a hundred bars; they close at 4:30 a.m. on weekends, so the sun's already rising in summer. The Reykjavík Art Museum and the Sigurjón Ólafsson Museum are among the town's many museums and galleries. Hostels are good quality, albeit typically with linen fees (sleeping bags usually OK).

Reykjavík City, Sundlaugavegur 34, Reykjavík; *hihostels.com/*, T:5538110, *reykjavikcity@hostel.is*; $21Bed, Kitchen:Y, B'fast:$, Pvt.room:Y, Locker:Y, Recep:24/7; Note: not central, arpt trans, pool, bikes, wh/chair ok, café, laundry

Igdlo Guesthouse, Gunnarsbraut 46, Reykjavík, T:5645555, *booking@ igdlo.com/*; $29Bed, Kitchen:Y, B'fast:$, Pvt.room:Y, Locker:N, Recep:ltd; Note: bikes, maps, bag hold, safe dep, parking, games, tea/coffee, nr arpt bus/ctr

Reykjavik Downtown Hostel, Vesturgata 17, Reykjavik, Iceland; *hostel. is/*, T:5538120, *reykjavikdowntown@hostel.is*; $29bed, Kitchen:Y, B'fast:$, Pvt. room:Y, Locker:N, Recep:24/7; Note: linen $, bag hold, prkng, tours, c.c. ok, member disc.

Kex Hostel, Skúlagata, Reykjavik; T:5616060, *info@ kexhostel.is/*; $32bed, Kitchen:Y, B'fast:$, Pvt.room:Y, Locker:N, Recep:24/7; Note: resto/bar, laundry, luggage room, c.c. ok, linen fee

Aurora Guesthouse, Freyjugata 24, Reykjavik; T:354/8991773, *book@ aurorahouse.is/*; $32bed, Kitchen:Y, B'fast:N, Pvt.room:Y, Locker:N, Recep:24/7; Note: laundry, travel desk, c.c. ok, near center & bus

Reykjavik Backpackers, Laugavegur 28, Reykjavik; T:5783700, *bookings@ reykjavikbackpackers.is/*; $26bed, Kitchen:Y, B'fast:$, Recep:Y, Locker:$, Recep:24/7; Note: bar, laundry, bag hold, travel desk, c.c. ok

Domus Guesthouse, Hverfisgotu 45, Reykjavik; *domusguesthouse. is/*, T:+354/561 1200, *domus@simnet.is*; $26bed, Kitchen:N, B'fast:$, Pvt. room:N, Locker:N, Recep:ltd; Note: parking, free laundry, bag hold, high linen fee

Capital Inn, Sudurhlíd 35d, Reykjavik; T:+354/5882100; *Info@ capitalinn.is/* $17Bed, Kitchen:Y, B'fast:$, Pvt.room:Y, Locker:N, Recep:ltd; Note: basic, not central, basement rooms, laundry

Hotel Gardur, Hringbraut 29, Reykjavík, T:+354/5716200, *info@ hotelgardur.is/*; $25Bed, Kitchen:N, B'fast:$, Pvt.room:Y, Locker:N, Recep:24/7; Note: luggage room, laundry, tour desk, parking, central

Hostel B47, Barónsstígur, Reykjavik, *hostelb47@ hostelb47.is/*, T:+354/4589000; $35Bed, Kitchen:Y, B'fast:$, Pvt.room:Y, Locker:Y, Recep: remote/code; Note: wh/chair ok, parking, maps, tea/coffee

Hlemmur Square, Laugavegur 105, Reykjavik, T:4151600, *booking@ hlemmursquare.com;* $22Bed, Kitchen:Y, B'fast:$, Pvt.room:Y, Locker:Y, Recep:24/7; Note: bikes, café, forex, parking, lift, laundry, bag hold, tour desk, central

Bus Hostel Reykjavik, Skógarhlíð, Reykjavik; T:5350350, *Info@ bushostelreykjavik.com/*; $24Bed, Kitchen:Y, B'fast:$, Pvt.room:Y, Locker:Y, Recep:24/7; Note: bar, bikes, lift, wh/chair ok, parking, bag hold, tours, books

Loft Hostel, Bankastræti 7, Reykjavík; *hihostels.com/*, T:+354/5538140, *loft@hostel.is;* $31Bed, Kitchen:Y, B'fast:$, Pvt.room:Y, Locker:Y, Recep:24/7; Note: lift, laundry, bag hold, tour desk, tea/coffee, games, books

AR Guesthouse, Braedraborgarstigur 3, Reykjavik; *arguesthouse.is/*, T:+354/8593979, *info@accommodation-reykjavik.is;* $42Bed, Kitchen:Y, B'fast:N, Pvt.room:Y, Locker:N, Recep:ltd; Note: laundry, central

STYKKISHOLMUR is a town of 1100 on the west coast. There is a 'Danish Days' festival every August. There are ferries to Flatey and Vestfirðir. I hope you like fish.

Harbour Hostel Stykkishólmur, Hafnargata 4, Stykkisholmur, *Info@ harbourhostel.is/*, T:+354/6600063; $Bed, Kitchen:Y, B'fast:$, Pvt.room:Y, Locker:Y, Recep:24/7; Note: bar, wh/chair ok, tour desk, parking, books, c.c. ok

16) Norway

When you think of countries that border Russia, you don't usually think of Norway, but there it is, sharing the Arctic Ocean with them and Alaska and Canada and Greenland, staking claims to a hypothetical pole and making claims to its hypothetical oil. The historical Norse are probably best remembered for their Vikings, of course, and if the Swedish variety were inward-looking toward the lands now called Russia, and the Danes mostly interested in setting up shop, and "Danelaw," in the lands now called Britain, the Norwegian branch of the brotherhood were anything but shy in their effort, expanding to the Faroe Islands, Iceland, Greenland, and even America.

After various permutations (Norway was absorbed into Denmark for four centuries) and occupation by German Nazis, today Norway, with the help of North Sea oil, is one of the richest countries in the world, and a nice place to hang, too, if you can afford it. Norwegian (Nynorsk and/or Bokmal) is the language, *krone* is the currency, and the calling code is +47.

ALESUND is a center of 43,000 on Norway's west coast, an important fishing port, now refitted to service North Sea oil exploration also. There is tourism, too, drawn to the fjords and picturesque town center.

HI Ålesund Hostel, Parkgata 14, Møre og romsdal, Alesund; T:+47/70115830, *alesund@ hihostels.no/*; $46Bed, Kitchen:Y, B'fast:Y, Pvt.room:Y, Locker:Y, Recep:8a//8p; Note: laundry, tour desk, c.c. ok, central

4 Hostels) BERGEN is Norway's second city, and its position on the West Coast makes it the capital of the North Sea oil industry in Norway. The Hanseatic-era wharf is a UNESCO world heritage site. Other sites are the 12th C. Saint Mary's Church, the city's oldest structure; Bergenhus fortress; and the Rosenkrantz Tower. Then there's the West Norway Museum of Decorative Art. The Bergen International Music Festival is an annual event. The Gulf Stream keeps temps mild in winter, but it rains like a mother.

HI Montana Y. H., Johan Blytts vei 30, Bergen; T:55208070, *bergen.montana@ hihostels.no/*; $35bed, Kitchen:Y, B'fast:Y, Pvt.room:Y, Locker:N, Recep:>10p; Note: linen fee $12, wh/chair ok, parking, laundry, c.c. ok, distant

Dorm.no Bergen, Marken 26, Bergen; *support@ dorm.no/*, T:+47/98238601, *dorm.no/*; $48Bed, Kitchen:Y, B'fast:$, Pvt.room:N, Locker:N, Recep: Call (must have cell phone); Note: c.c. ok, staff scarce, basic, absentee operation

Bergen YMCA Hostel, Nedre Korskirkeallmenningen 4, Bergen; *booking@ bergenhostel.com/*, T:55606055; $33Bed, Kitchen:Y, B'fast:$, Pvt.room:N, Locker:Y, Recep:8a>9p (call in winter); Note: lift, bag hold, tea/coffee, central

Marken Gjestehus, Tverrgaten, Bergen; *post@ marken-gjestehus.com/*, T:55314404; $37Bed, Kitchen:Y, B'fast:$, Pvt.room:Y, Locker:Y, Recep:9a>9p; Note: use c.c. as key-card, lift, laundry, bag hold, not central/near train, hotel-like

BODO is a city of 48,000 and Norway's largest above the Arctic Circle. It is a historic trade center, and is the northern terminus of the state railways. There is a national park and seventeen nature reserves nearby. Festivals include Nordland Musikfestuke and Parkenfestivalen in summer, and Bodø Hardcore Festival in winter.

Bodø Hostel, Sjøgata 57, Bodø; T:+47/75508048, *bodo@ hihostels.no/*; $57Bed, Kitchen:Y, B'fast:$, Pvt.room:N, Locker:Y, Recep:4>8p; Note: café, lift, wh/chair ok, laundry, luggage room, parking, TV, at train station

DRAMMEN is an industrialized river port city of 63,000 in south central Norway, and also has a historic brewery. There is a theater and museum.

Drammen Hostel, Stromso Torg 7, Drammen; *ambassadeur@firsthotels.no*, T:31012100, *drammenhostel.no/*; $52Bed, Kitchen:N, B'fast:$, Pvt.room:Y, Locker:N, Recep:24/7; Note:@4star hotel, resto/bar, gym, lift, arpt trans, bag hold

HELLESYLT is a village of a few hundred in the western fjord couintry. There is a ferry.

Hellesylt Hostel HI, Vandrarheimen, Møre og romsdal, Helleslyt; T:70265128, *hellesylt@ hihostels.no/*; $50Bed, Kitchen:N, B'fast:Y, Pvt.room:Y, Locker:N, Recep:8a//8p; Note:bikes, tour desk, mart, luggage rm, long-timers, views

NORDKAPP is the northernmost city in the world, they say. The town has a population of 3200 and receives scads of tourists in the summer.

HI Nordkapp Vandreerhjem, Kobbhullveien 10, Honningsvåg Nordkapp; T:91824156, *nordkapp@ hihostels.no/*; $58Bed, Kitchen:N, B'fast:Y, Pvt.room:Y, Locker:N, Recep:8a>8p; Note: wh/chair ok, bag hold, parking, northern lights?

LILLEHAMMER was the site of the 1994 Winter Olympics. The highway from Oslo to Trondheim on the west coast passes through. The city center is of 19th C. wood construction. The open-air Maihaugen folk museum has Norwegian art and architecture.

Lillehammer Hostel, Jernbanetorget 2, Lillehammer; T:80019572, *www.815mjosa.no/artikkel/les/160/87/*; $59bed, Kitchen:Y, B'fast:Y, Pvt.room:Y, Locker:N, Recep:ltd; Note:prkng, lift, a/c, c.c. ok, tours, @bus/train stn

6 Hostels) OSLO is Norway's largest city and capital. Though founded as long ago as 1049, its status as vassal to Denmark reduced its importance and development. Today much of its business is focused around its port and related maritime industries. It is regularly rated as one of the most expensive cities in the world. This is when hostels come in very handy. I'm only surprised that they don't have more of them, possibly because of the low Norwegian population in general.

Like its sister cities in the region, Oslo is clean and green, and sixty-degree north latitude means about eighteen hours of daylight in summer and only six in winter. The Gulf Stream keeps the temps moderate, though. There is a Historical Museum and the National Museum of Art, Architecture, and Design. At Tøyen, in the east of the city, are botanical gardens and several museums, including the Munch Museum. At Bygdøy are the Norwegian Folk Museum, Viking Ship Museum, Fram Museum, Kon-Tiki Museum, and Norwegian shipping museum. Enjoy.

Perminalen Hotel, Øvre Slottsgate 2, Oslo, Norway; *perminalen.no/*, T:24005500, *post.perminalen@iss.no*; $66bed, Kitchen:N, B'fast:Y, Pvt.room:N, Locker:N, Recep:24/7; Note: luggage room, lift, c.c. ok, clean, central

HI Oslo Y.H. Haraldsheim, Haraldsheimveien 4, Oslo; T:22222965, *oslo. haraldsheim@ hihostels.no/*; $48bed, Kitchen:Y, B'fast:Y, Pvt.room:Y, Locker:Y, Recep:24/7; Note: linen fee, bag hold, parking, wh/chairs ok, member discount

Sentrum Pensjonat, Tollbugata 8, Oslo; *post@ sentrumpensjonat.no/*, T:22335580; $50bed, Kitchen:Y, B'fast:N, Pvt.room:Y, Locker:Y, Recep:ltd; Note: resto/café, bag hold, forex, c.c. ok, old, central, some residents

Oslo Hotel Apts., Kjølberggaten 29, Oslo, Norway; *oslohotelapartments. com/*, T:24074003, *booking@kampenhotell.no*; $60bed, Kitchen:Y, B'fast:$, Pvt. room:Y, Locker:N, Recep:24/7; Note: resto/bar, parking, bag hold, linen fee, 'puter

Anker Hostel, Storgata 55, Oslo; T:22997200, *hostel@ anker.oslo.no/*; $40Bed, Kitchen:N, B'fast:$, Pvt.room:Y, Locker:Y, Recep:24/7; Note: café, bar, gym, lift, wh/chair ok, tours, bag hold, parking, safe dep, near trans/center

Oslo Vandrerhjem Holtekilen, Michelets vei 55, Stabekk, T:67518040, *oslo.holtekilen@ hihostels.no/*; $34Bed, Kitchen:Y, B'fast:Y, Pvt.room:Y, Locker:N, Recep:24/7; Note: gym, tour desk, bag hold, parking, suburbs

SARPSBORG is a city of 53,000 in the country's far southeast.

HI Sarpsborg Hostel, Tuneveien 44, Tuneheimen, Sarpsborg; T:69145001, *sarpsborg@ hihostels.no/*; $67Bed, Kitchen:Y, B'fast:Y, Pvt. room:Y, Locker:N, Recep:5>11p; Note: bikes, shuttle, laundry, parking, c.c. ok, maps, fax, lake

SOGNEFJORD is Norway's longest fjord and a UNESCO world heritage site.

Eplet Bed & Apple, Eplet, Solvorn, Sognefjord; T:41649469, *post@ eplet. net/*; $35Bed, Kitchen:Y, B'fast:N, Pvt.room:Y, Locker:N, Recep:ltd; Note: closed winter, bikes, minimart, bag hold, tours, parking, beach, ferry, Nature

STRYN is a village of 2200 and a municipality of 7000 at the head of the northern fjords. There is glacier skiing. There are also waterfalls, lakes, wildlife and a national park.

Stryn Hostel, Geilevegen 14, Stryn, *strynhostel.com/*, T:57871106, *strynvandrerhjem@hotmail.com*; $50Bed, Kitchen:Y, B'fast:Y, Pvt.room:Y, Locker:Y, Recep:4>8p; Note: skiing, bikes, resto, bag hold, parking, mart, tea/cof

TRONDHEIM is Norway's third city, with a population of 180,000, and has been an important trade center for a millennium at least. It was also the site of a Christian pilgrimage in the Middle Ages which still exists in some form to this day. There are several museums and an active music scene.

Singsaker Sommerhotell, Rogerts gate 1, Trondheim, T:73893100, *sommerhotell@ singsaker.no/*; $44Bed, Kitchen:N, B'fast:Y, Pvt.room:Y, Locker:N, Recep:24/7; Note: June>Aug, bar, gym, parking, central, castle, basement dorm

17) Sweden

Swedes were first out of the gates of Scandinavia, first pushing southeast to the Crimea in the early years of the Common Era, then as Goths on a similar trajectory before dividing into *Ostro* and *Visi* and founding the first successor states to the Roman Empire in Italy, Spain, and elsewhere in the sixth and seventh centuries; and finally as proto-Viking "Varangian" *Rus*, who apparently founded the first Russian/Ukraine state.

The modern state of Sweden finally began to emerge in the Middle Ages and by the 17th century, they had an empire to rival anyone in Europe. They lost all that, though, and today the emphasis is on quality of life, often regarded as the most egalitarian in the world. That comes with a price, of course. Sweden ranks high in science and engineering, with many inventions and patents, and the economy includes both services and manufacturing, much of it high-tech and oriented toward export (Ericsson, anyone?). Alfred Nobel invented dynamite here and instituted the Nobel Prizes. Politics are heavily social-democratic internally and nonaligned and neutral externally.

Sweden has managed to penetrate the English-speaking market for popular music and literature better than almost any other English-as-second-language country, with such popular music acts (all sung in English) as ABBA, Ace of Base, and Cardigans. Then there are the best-selling books of Stieg Larsson, not to mention the high art of playwright Strindberg or cineaste Bergman. Currency is the *krona*, phone code is +46, and the main language is Swedish, Finnish a second language.

8 Hostels) GOTHENBURG is on Sweden's west coast about halfway between Copenhagen and Oslo and is the major seaport of the region. As such, it has always occupied a strategic position. The Dutch and Scots for a long time wielded a major influence here. There is also a major film festival and book fair. Nearby islands are reachable by ferryboat. The cathedral and the Kristine Church are notable landmarks and there are cultural, maritime, and natural history museums. There are many parks and an amusement park, also. HINDAS is a small town of 2244 inhabitants nearby.

Ekgarden Kursgard och Vandrarhem, Tubbared Ekväg 17, Hindås; T:46/30119099, *aita@ ekgarden.org/*; $42Bed, Kitchen:Y, B'fast:$, Pvt.room:Y, Locker:N, Recep:ltd; Note: arpt trans, bikes, parking, tea/coffee, c.c. ok

Kville Hotel B&B, Kvilletorget 24, Göteborg; T:0317441440, *info@ kvillehotel.se/*; $40bed, Kitchen:N, B'fast:Y, Pvt.room:Y, Locker:N, Recep:ltd; Note: parking, laundry, a/c, c.c. ok, quiet neighborhood away from center

Backpackers Göteborg, Vegagatan 19, Göteborg; *sov.nu/*, T:+46/31426520

Slottskogens Y.H., Vegagatan 21, Göteborg; *mail@ sov.nu/*, T:031426520; $31bed, Kitchen:Y, B'fast:$, Pvt.room:Y, Locker:Y, Recep:ltd; Note: curtains on beds, laundry, luggage, forex

Linne Hostel, Vegagatan 22, Gothenburg; T:+46/31121060, *stay@ linnehostel.com/*; $32Bed, Kitchen:Y, B'fast:$, Pvt.room:Y, Locker:Y, Recep:3>5p (advise late); Note: wh/chair, maps, tea/coffee, c.c. preferred

STF Vandrarhem Stigbergsliden, Stigbergsliden 10, Göteborg; *hihostels. com/*, T:031241620, *vandrarhem.stigbergsliden@telia.com*; $29Bed, Kitchen:Y, B'fast:$, Pvt. room:Y, Locker:Y, Recep:4>6p; Note:lift, wh/chair ok, laundry

Hotel & Vandrarhem 10, Göteborgsvägen 64, Sävedalen; T:0313865030, *info@ hotel10.se*; $55Bed, Kitchen:N, B'fast:Y, Pvt.room:Y, Locker:N, Recep:ltd; Note: lift, laundry, bag hold, tour desk, parking

Göteborgs Vandrarhem, Mölndalsvägen 23, Göteborg; T:031401050, *Info@ goteborgsvandrarhem.se/*; $47Bed, Kitchen:Y, B'fast:$, Pvt.room:Y, Locker:N, Recep:8a>4p; Note: resto, minimart, tours, bag hold, parking, tea/coffee

HELSINGBORG is a city of almost 100,000 and the closest Swedish city to Denmark. There are stone churches, a medieval fortress, and pedestrian shopping mall. It is one of Sweden's oldest cities, and has traditionally profited on trade through the narrow straits.

Helsingborgs Vandrarhem Hostel, Hantverkaregatan 2, Helsingborg, T:042141565, *Info@ helsingborgsvandrarhem.com/*; $31Bed, Kitchen:Y, B'fast:N, Pvt.room:Y, Locker:N, Recep:3-6p; Note: @bus/train, wh/chair ok, lift, bag hold

KARLSTAD is a city of 62,000 on Lake Vanem in southern Sweden, with a reputation as the sunniest city in Sweden, no small item on the menu of a country famed for the murky interiors of cineaste Bergman. It has roots in the Viking Era, and was an ancient market place, Karlstad the lake's biggest port. Cycling is popular in summer, skiing in winter.

Karlstad Hostel, Kasernhöjden 19, Karlstad; *hihostels.com/*, T:054566840, *karlstad.vandrarhem@swipnet.se*; $41Bed, Kitchen:Y, B'fast:$, Pvt.room:Y, Locker:N, Recep:4>7p; Note: bikes, laundry, lift, gym, parking, wh/chair ok, hard find

3 Hostels) MALMO is a city of 300,000 and unofficial suburb to Copenhagen, just a hop-skip-and-jump across the sound in Denmark. Traditionally a shipbuilding town, Malmo is also rich in culture, with museums, theater, and music. There is diversity here. With more Iraqi nationals than Danes, Malmo gives new meaning to the term "border town."

Malmö City, Rönngatan 1, Malmö, *hihostels.com/*, T:46/406116220, *malmo.city@stfturist.se*; $39Bed, Kitchen:Y, B'fast:$, Pvt.room:Y, Locker:N, Recep:24/7; Note: mart, wh/chair ok, lift, laundry, luggage rm, tea/cof, central

Malmö Eriksfält, Backavägen 18, Malmö, *hihostels.com/*, T:04082220, *malmo.eriksfalt@stfturist.se/*; $36Bed, Kitchen:Y, B'fast:$, Pvt.room:Y, Locker:N, Recep:4>7p; Note: tea/coffee, laundry, bag hold, parking, not central

Rut & Ragnars Hostel, Nobelvägen 113, Malmö; T:+46/406116060, *Info@ rutochragnars.se/*; $28Bed, Kitchen:Y, B'fast:$, Pvt.room:N , Locker:Y, Recep:4>9p; Note: wh/chair ok, laundry, bag hold, parking, TV, not central

25 Hostels) STOCKHOLM is the capital of Sweden and the largest city in all of Scandinavia. It was fully a part of European history by the mid-13th century as a regular port for the trade of the Hanseatic League, complete with many German-speakers, and was capital of the Swedish Empire. Today it is one of Europe's most desirable cities, clean and green and polished to a high sheen. Its location surrounded by open water keeps its temperatures moderate, despite its sixty-degree northern latitude. There is an old town. Landmarks include the Royal Palace; the Church of St. Nicolas; the German Church; the House of Lords; the Stock Exchange; Riddarholm Church; The House of Parliament and the National Bank. Summertime rocks, with nightlife everywhere. This far north closing time is… never.

City Backpackers Hostel, Upplandsgatan 2, Stockholm; T:468206920, *info@ citybackpackers.se/*; $31bed, Kitchen:Y, B'fast:$, Locker:Y, Recep:8a>2a; Note: resto, bag hold, bike rent, c.c. ok, laundry, tea/coffee, tours

PART III: Scandinavia

Langholmen Hostel STF/HI, Långholmsmuren 20, Stockholm; T:087208507, *hotel@ langholmen.com/*; $33bed, Kitchen:N, B'fast:$, Pvt.room:Y, Locker:N, Recep:24/7; Note: member %, bar/café, bag hold, wh/chair ok, parking

Red Boat Malaren, Södermälarstrand Kajplats 10, Stockholm; T:086444385, *info@ theredboat.se/*; $42bed, Kitchen:N, B'fast:$, Pvt. room:Y, Locker:N, Recep:8a>1a; Note: resto/bar, bag hold, c.c. ok, on boat in water, bikes

Jumbo Stay STF/HI, Jumbovägen 4, Stockholm Arlanda Arpt; *hihostels. com/*, T:0859360400, *booking@jumbostay.com*; $73bed, Kitchen:N, B'fast:$, Pvt. room:Y, Locker:N, Recep:24/7; Note: resto/bar, bag hold, converted 747, shuttle!

STF/HI Fridhemsplan, St Eriksgatan 20, Stockholm; T:086538800, *info@ fridhemsplan.se/*; $47bed, Kitchen:Y, B'fast:$, Pvt.room:Y, Locker:Y, Recep:24/7; Note: parking, laundry, a/c, c.c. ok, wh/chair ok, lift, bag hold, central

Skanstulls Vandrarrhem, Ringvägen 135, Stockholm; T:086430204, *kontakt@ skanstulls.se/*; $33bed, Kitchen:Y, B'fast:N, Pvt.room:Y, Locker:Y, Recep:3p>8p; Note: max. stay 7N, bag hold, bikes, c.c. ok, no basement windows, laundry

Crafoord Place, Hälsobrunnsgatan 10, Stockholm; T:08337133, *info@ crafoordplace.se/*; $29bed, Kitchen:Y, B'fast:N, Pvt.room:N, Locker:Y, Recep:10a>6p; Note: 2N min., lift, parking, tours, a/c, c.c. ok, coffee/tea

Best Hostel City, Luntmakargatan 14, Stockholm; T:08218418, *city@ besthostel.se*; $43bed, Kitchen:Y, B'fast:Y, Pvt.room:Y, Locker:N, Recep:ltd; Note: luggage room, lift, laundry, c.c. ok, central

Best Hostel Old Town, Trangsund 12, Stockholm, T:46(8)4400004, $42

Best Hostel Old Town Skeppsbron, Skeppsbron 22, Stockholm; T:+46(8)4119545, *info@ besthostel.se/*; $34bed, Kitchen:Y, B'fast:Y, Pvt. room:Y, Locker:N, Recep:ltd; Note: bag hold, laundry, c.c. ok, coffee & tea, central

2kronor Hotel-City, Kammakargatan 62, Stockholm; T:+46/8229230

2kronor Hostel-Old Town, Skeppsbron 40, Stockholm; T:+46/8229230

2kronor Hostel-Vasastan, Surbrunnsgatan 44, Stockholm; T:+46/8229230, *info@ 2kronor.se/*; $35bed, Kitchen:Y, B'fast:N, Pvt.room:Y, Locker:Y, Recep:9a>6p; Note: laundry, luggage room, central, midday lockout

Interhostel, Kammakargatan 46, Stockholm, Sweden; T:084112311, *info@ interhostel.se/*; $30bed, Kitchen:Y, B'fast:N, Pvt.room:Y, Locker:Y, Recep:>2a; Note: linen fee, laundry, luggage ok, c.c. ok, no window in dorm

City Hostel - Central Station, Fleminggatan 19, Stockholm; *Info@ cityhostel.se/*, T:+46/841003830; $35Bed, Kitchen:Y, B'fast:N, Pvt.room:Y, Locker:Y, Recep:2>6p; Note: laundry, bag hold, maps, books, TV, central

Archipelago Hostel Old Town, Stora Nygatan 38, Stockholm, T:+46/8229940, *info@ archipelagohostel.se/*; $43Bed, Kitchen:Y, B'fast:$, Pvt.room:Y, Locker:Y, Recep:9a//6p; Note: central, TV, no lockout

Castanea Old Town Hostel, Kindstugatan 1, Stockholm; T:+46/8223551, *castaneahostel.com/*; $30Bed, Kitchen:Y, B'fast:N, Pvt.room:Y, Locker:Y, Recep:3>6p; Note: lift, luggage room, maps, c.c. ok, quiet/non-party

Lodge32, Hantverkargatan 32, Stockholm; T:086500032, *Info@ lodge32.se/*; $24Bed, Kitchen:Y, B'fast:$, Pvt.room:Y, Locker:Y, Recep:9a>6p; Note: bikes, wh/chair, lift, bag hold, cable TV, coffee/tea, central, long-stays

Zinkensdamm YH, Zinkens väg 20, Stockholm; *hihostels.com/*, T:086168100, *mail@zinkensdamm.com/*; $37Bed, Kitchen:Y, B'fast:$, Pvt.room:Y, Locker:N, Recep:24/7; Note: resto/bar, bikes, laundry, bag hold, parking, tea/coffee

Renstierna Hotel & Hostel, Renstiernas gata 15, Stockholm, T:086152135 *reservation@ hotelrenstierna.se/*; $41Bed, Kitchen:Y, B'fast:Y, Pvt.room:Y, Locker:Y, Recep:>8p; Note:laundry, bag hold, parking, coffee/tea, forex, SOFO 'hood

STF/IYHF af Chapman (Boat&House), Flaggmansvägen 8, Västra Brobänken; *hihostels.com/*, T:084632266, *chapman@stfturist.se*; $51Bed, Kitchen:Y, B'fast:$, Pvt.room:Y, Locker:N, Recep:24/7; Note: café, billiards, wh/chair ok, lift, central

Acco Hostel, Ansgariegatan 10, Stockholm, *accohostel.com/*, T:0760625700 *Acco.hostel@gmail.com*; $27Bed, Kitchen:N, B'fast:N, Pvt.room:Y, Locker:Y, Recep: remote (rec. sms codes); Note: no staff, laundry, bag hold, parking

PART III: Scandinavia

City Lodge Stockholm, Klara Norra kyrkogata 15, Stockholm, *citylodge. eu/*, T:08226630, *info@citylodge.se*; $28Bed, Kitchen:Y, B'fast:$, Pvt.room:Y, Locker:Y, Recep:>9p (get code for late arrival); Note:@train, bag hold, ctr, pasta

Hostel Bed & Breakfast, Rehnsgatan 21, Stockholm, T:08152838, *Info@ hostelbedandbreakfast.com/*; $52Bed, Kitchen:Y, B'fast:Y, Pvt.room:Y, Locker:Y, Recep:9a>9p; Note:basement/few windows, pool, luggage rm, prkng, center, linen $

Hostels By Nordic, Drottninggatan 83, Stockholm; T:0760-217101, *desk@ hostelsbynordic.se/*; $28Bed, Kitchen:Y, B'fast:N, Pvt.room:N, Locker:N, Recep:>6p M>F; Note: tea/coffee, laundry, tours, parking, windowless rooms, central

3 Hostels) SUNDSVALL is a city of 50,000 and twice that many if you count the surrounds, and in most-central Sweden, though far north of most of the population. It is an industrial city with roots in forestry and aluminum. There are several music festivals. KRAMFORS is a nearby town of 6000 — and falling. Though blessed with nearby High Coast landscape, the traditional timber and lumber bizniz is in decline, with no remedy. Timber tour, anyone?

Getberget, Jude 222, Ramvik, Kramfors: T:+46/61243090, *Info@ getbergets-vandrarhem.se/*; 30Bed, Kitchen:N, B'fast:Y, Pvt.room:Y, Locker:N, Recep:ltd; Note: bikes, luggage room, parking

Sundsvall City Hostel, Sjögatan 11, Sundsvall; Tel:+46(0)60126090, *bokning@ sundsvallcityhostel.se/*; $35Bed, Kitchen:Y, B'fast:$, Pvt.room:Y, Locker:N, Recep:ltd; Note: café, lift, luggage, c.c. ok, laundry, linen $, long-timers, central

Gaffelbyn Hostel of Sundsvall, N Stadsberget, Sundsvall; T:+46/60612119 *boka@ gaffelbyn.se/*; $25Bed, Kitchen:Y, B'fast:$, Pvt.room:Y, Locker:N, Recep:4>6p; Note: wh/chair ok, laundry, parking, linen $, not central

5 Hostels) UPPSALA is only forty minutes from Stockholm by train, so if the big city is booked up (no joke), then consider staying here. It's less than a half hour to Stockholm's airport. It was an early religious center, with a pre-Christian town 3mi/5km north. Besides the Gothic cathedral, there is a castle that is now the governor's residence, the botanic garden and house of

Carolus Linnaeus, and the Victoria Museum, with Egyptian antiquities. It's a university town, too.

Vandrarhem Centralstation, Bangårdsgatan 13, Uppsala; T:0761858485, *info@ hotellcentralstation.se/*; $31bed, Kitchen:Y, B'fast:$, Pvt.room:Y, Locker:N, Recep:24/7; Note: bag hold, bikes, c.c. ok, $11 linen fee, no windows, central

Vandrarhem Uppsala-Kungsangstorg, Kungsängstorg 6, Uppsala; T:0761858485, *info@ vandrarhemuppsala.se/*; $35bed, Kitchen:Y, B'fast:$, Pvt. room:Y, Locker:N, Recep:ltd; Note: central, staff scarce, linen $5, towel $5

STF/HI Uppsala/Vandrarhem, Kvarntorgsgatan 3, Uppsala; *hihostels.com/*, T:18242008, *kvarntorget@uppsalavandrarhem.se*; $30bed, Kitchen:Y, B'fast:$, Pvt. room:Y, Locker:Y, Recep:8a>7p; Note:fees, bag hold, resto/bar, no windows

Uppsala City Hostel, S:t Persgatan 16, Uppsala, T:018100008, *bokning@ uppsalacityhostel.se/*; $35Bed, Kitchen:Y, B'fast:$, Pvt.room:Y, Locker:Y, Recep:8a>11p; Note: wh/chair ok, bag hold, center

City Stay Uppsala, Trädgårdsgatan 5, Kvarntorget 3, Uppsala; T:018121000, *booking@ citystayuppsala.se/*; $35Bed, Kitchen:Y, B'fast:$, Pvt. room:Y, Locker:N, Recep:3>10p; Note: bikes, wh/chair, lift, laundry, bag hold, tea/coffee

PART IV: East Europe

East Europe includes much of the former Soviet Union, including Russia itself, the former Communist mastermind that kept the West up in arms for most of the 20th century. Fortunately that era is over now, and Europe is at peace, but unfortunately I think many Westerners, particularly Americans, are still hesitant to poke their toes across that imaginary line that once divided countries—and opinions. That's a shame, too, because this is the hottest travel destination in the world, hottest ticket I mean, not temperature. No, the temps are just fine, with cool latitudes and cool attitudes.

Hostels are generally of good quality, though few score straight Y's in the Big 5 qualifications that I monitor most closely in my listings, as you will soon see. They're hip to the modern 'flashpacker' trend, though, as much as anywhere in the world, and their English is as good as most anywhere where it's spoken as a second language, with Russia probably the weakest link in that chain. They CAN help you with the peculiarities of the Russian system, though, including LOI's and such. Except for Russia, trains, buses and planes are pretty much all integrated within the European systems. Russia has its own, so arguably best considered as a trip of its own. That's your decision.

18) Belarus

Belarus is the country variously referred to historically as Byelorussia, "White Russia" and so forth, and it emerged in the same phenomenon that included

Kievan Rus, the act of Varangians catalyzing local Slavs into political entities. The Mongol hordes destroyed all that, of course, but the culture reemerged intact and has been paired variously with neighbors Poland, Lithuania, and most of all Russia. That is the case in post-communist Europe, where Belarus has the reputation as least-changed of all the ex-USSR constituent states, due mostly to the autocratic rule of Alexander Lukashenko.

That in itself is tour-worthy, I suppose, but it might cost as much money and hassle as Russia, for a country much smaller. There are four world heritage sites, though, and it's on my list. A transit visa might work, three days to cross from Ukraine via Belarus to Lithuania or vice-versa sounds about right; train from Warsaw via Belarus to Moscow would also work. Belarusian *ruble* (BYR) is currency; Belarusian and Russian are the languages; calling code is +375.

GRODNO (Hrodna) is a city of 330,000 near the borders of Poland and Lithuania. It dates back a millennium.

Hello, Grodno!, ul. Gorodnichanskaya, 30-1, Grodno; *grodnohostel.by*, T:+375/152743308, *Grodno.hostel@gmail.com*; $12Bed, Kitchen:Y, B'fast:Y, Pvt. room:N, Locker:Y, Recep:24/7; Note: cash, 1pm checkout, tea/cof, tours

6 Hostels) MINSK is the capital and largest city of Belarus. It is also headquarters for the CIS, the union of ex-USSR members. It is documented from the 11th century and was a part of the Grand Duchy of Lithuania as well as the Polish-Lithuanian commonwealth. It was annexed by Russia in 1793 and became a Soviet Socialist Republic in the USSR. Minsk was always a center for foreigners, but WWII decimated the Jewish population and Soviet policies afterwards didn't help, so many have since left. Polish people still have a presence here. The major foreign presence is Russian, though, as Belarus still has a political relationship with Russia, and may in fact never totally break away. Tourism is in its infancy. There are many churches and cathedrals, but the main attraction is the general atmosphere of old-school Communism, still largely intact here.

Hostel Jazz, Mosirskaya St 37A, Minsk; *hosteljazz.by*, T:(8)333361633, *hostel.jazz@gmail.com*; $10bed, Kitchen:Y, B'fast:N, Pvt.room:Y, Locker:N, Recep:24/7; Note: bike rent, pool, tour desk, bag hold, TV

Hostel Postoyalets, Partizansky Ave. 147, Minsk; T:(8)172434981, *res@ postoyalets.by*; $14bed, Kitchen:Y, B'fast:N, Pvt. room:N, Locker:N, Recep:24/7; Note: central, TV, pool, luggage room

Viva Hostel Minsk, Zhukovskogo St, 4, Minsk; *Info@ hostelviva.by/*, T:+375/336271133; $18Bed, Kitchen:Y, B'fast:N, Pvt.room:N, Locker:Y, Recep:24/7; Note: arpt trans, bikes, hot tub, laundry, tour desk, TV, nr train

Kinghostel, Storozhevskaya 8-208, Minsk; *Info@ kinghostel.by/*, T:+375/295029460; $18Bed, Kitchen:Y, B'fast:$, Pvt.room:Y, Locker:Y, Recep:24/7; Note: arpt trans, lift, forex, parking, safe dep, cash only

Trinity Hostel, 12 Starovilenskaya Str, Minsk; *hostel-traveler.by/*, T:+375/293112783, *hostel-traveler@ gmail.com/*; $15Bed, Kitchen:Y, B'fast:Y, Pvt.room:Y, Locker:N, Recep:24/7; Note: cash, laundry, bag hold, hard find

Hostel Sky, 2b Leanida Biady, Minsk; *Info@ hostelsky.com/*, T:+375/293800045; $15Bed, Kitchen:Y, B'fast:$, Pvt.room:N, Locker:N, Recep:24/7; Note: hot tub, arpt trans, café, lift, bag hold, laundry, tours, parking

19) Estonia

Estonia shares much of the same history as its Baltic buddies Latvia and Lithuania, but that is mostly circumstantial, a sharing of the same events of the last millennium — Vikings, Hansesatic League, Germans and Russians, Nazism and Communism. Its genetic roots lie with Finland across the water — language and presumably DNA, united at a time in the past in a place to the east, a time and place that must have included the Magyars of Hungary in its orbit, if linguistic evidence is to believed.

That all predates the historic record, though, so must go back at least a few thousand years. Still I think it's reasonable to assume that the Finns and Estonians were here first, before the Indo-European Scandinavians.

Sami (Lapp) is another related language by the way. The Roman historian Tacitus mentions the *Aesti* as amber traders. Later evidence indicates a Viking presence here, though it's not clear in what capacity, as native Estonian "Osselian pirates" would seem to be their competition.

Later Teutons, Swedes, and Russians all pretty much had their way here as they did elsewhere in the Baltics. Then the citizens of all three Baltic countries united in a human chain to protest Soviet occupation in 1989. Today Estonia is a post-USSR success story, a "Baltic Tiger," ready to rock and ready to work. It has carefully been promoting itself as "Nordic," not "Baltic" (i.e.winners not losers). The economy is market-oriented. Politics are liberal and democratic. Protestant work ethic is strong, though hardly anyone is religious. Skype™ was developed here. Music and song festivals are an important tradition. Euro (EUR) is currency; Estonian is the language; phone code +372.

9 Hostels) TALLINN, formerly known as Reval, is the principal city of Estonia in every way. It was a Hanseatic city back in the day, and something like a time capsule today. If nothing else, communism can be depended on to stop the clock. It is also party central for mobile hip Westerners who like to descend on a budget-friendly member of their European hinterlands which has just been selected for further in-depth maneuvers of the social kind... all of which is to say that the women are friendly.

The city is cute as a bug, too, and a UNESCO world heritage site. Landmarks include the 13th C. Toom Church, the Gothic Oleviste and Niguliste churches, the Great Guildhall of 1410, the 14th C. Rathus, and much of the old castle. It is well-connected by ferry to Finland, Russia, and Germany, by bus to the south, and budget airlines to all over. Hostels are good, but please, "don't sleep drunk in the kitchen." And don't sleep on the router, either.

Red Emperor Hostel, Aia 10, Tallinn; T:58091576, *craig@ redemperorhostel.com/*; $11bed, Kitchen:Y, B'fast:$, Pvt.room:Y, Locker:N, Recep:24/7; Note: bar, parking, free tour, travel desk, laundry, luggage room, c.c. ok

Tallinn Backpackers, Olevimägi 11, Tallinn; T:6166754, *info@ tallinnbackpackers.com/*; $13bed, Kitchen:Y, B'fast:N, Pvt.room:N, Locker:Y, Recep:24/7; Note: bar, tours, laundry, bag hold, c.c. ok, parties

The Monk's Bunk, Tatari 1, Tallinn; T:6561120, *info@ themonksbunk.com/*; $13bed, Kitchen:Y, B'fast:N, Pvt.room:Y, Locker:Y, Recep:24/7; Note: bar, free tour/info, c.c. ok, bag hold, laundry, near center, party

Old House Hostel, Uus 26, Tallinn; T:+372/6411281, *info@ oldhouse.ee/*; $13bed, Kitchen:Y, B'fast:$, Pvt.room:Y, Locker:N, Recep:24/7; Note: parking, safe deposit, no bunks, in old town

Gidic Backpackers, 31 Tartu mnt, Tallinn; T:+372/6466016, *bookings@ gidic.ee/*; $14bed, Kitchen:Y, B'fast:$, Pvt.room:Y, Locker:Y, Recep:24/7; Note: bike rent, free tour, fax, luggage room, laundry, c.c. ok, parking

ALUR Hostel Tallinn Old Town, Lai 20, Kesklinn, Harju County; *hostel. alur.ee/*, T:6466210, *hostel.alur@gmail.com*; $13bed, Kitchen:Y, B'fast:$, Pvt. room:Y, Locker:N, Recep 24/7; Note: tours, bag hold, c.c. ok, old town

Flying Kiwi Backackers, Nunne 1, Tallinn; T:58213292, *info@ flyingkiwitallinn.com/*; $19bed, Kitchen:Y, B'fast:N, Pvt.room:Y, Locker:N, Recep:ltd; Note: sauna, travel desk, old town

16EUR Hostel, Roseni 9, Tallinn; T:+372/5013046, *info@ 16eur.ee/*; $13bed, Kitchen:Y, B'fast:$, Pvt.room:Y, Locker:Y, Recep:24/7; Note: pool, bar, forex, luggage room, tour desk, c.c. ok

The Dancing Eesti, Väike-Karja 1, Tallinn; *thedancingeesti.ee/*, T:53654382, *deniz@homemail.com*; $12bed,Kitchen:Y, B'fast:N, Pvt.room:N, Locker:Y, Recep:24/7; Note: bag hold, laundry, free tour/info, a/c, pub crawls, central

3 Hostels) TARTU is Estonia's second city and a university town, the intellectual and cultural counterpoint to Tallinn's political and financial orientation. First documented in the chronicles of Kievan Rus, it also went through the same phases in the Hanseatic League and regional rivalries as Tallinn. Architecture shows influence from Germans and Russians.

Terviseko, Raekoja Plats 10, Tartu; *terviseksbbb.com/*, T:+372/5655382, *terviseksbbb@gmail.com*; $20bed, Kitchen:Y, B'fast:Y, Pvt.room:Y, Locker:Y, Recep:ltd; Note: advise ETA, central, laundry, free printing

Looming Hostel, Kastani 38, Tartu, T:+372/56994398, *info@ loominghostel. ee/*; $20bed; Kitchen:Y, B'fast:$, Pvt.room:N, Locker:Y, Recep:ltd; Note: bike rent, luggage room, tour desk, parking, pets ok, eco-artsy

HIIE MAJA, *Hiie 10, Tartu*; T:+372/7421236, *info@ bed.ee/*; $20bed, Kitchen:Y, B'fast:$, Pvt.room:Y, Locker:N, Recep:ltd; Note: parking, camping ok, half hour walk to center

20) Latvia

Latvia is one of the three Baltic States, the middle one in fact, the others being Lithuania, with which it has been intimately related since time immemorial, and Estonia, which is more closely related to non-Indo/European Finland, unlike the majority of European nations. The three Baltic countries were the last of the modern states to join European civilization. The forebears of today's Latvians traded amber with the rest of Europe since antiquity, but weren't converted to Christianity until the 13th century, by force of the Teutonic Knights (What? You didn't know that Latvia was a Crusader state?). Inclusion in the Hanseatic League quickly followed.

Borders and alliances came and went — with Poland, Lithuania, Sweden, and Russia — until Latvia was forced to join the USSR at the point of a (very large) gun in 1940, along with the other two Baltic states, the last constituent republics of that empire to "join." It was brutal, of course, and Latvia was among the first to demand reconsideration during the period of *glasnost*. Full independence came in 1991. The problem of citizenship status for a large Russian minority has yet to be resolved. Latvia is rich in flora and fauna and is environmentally aware. Hundreds of former Soviet collective farms have been converted into eco-farms. Latvian is the language; *lats* (LVL) is the currency; the phone code is +371.

LIEPAJA is on the Baltic Sea and is Latvia's third largest city. It has gradually completed a transition from a military city to a modern port. There are beaches, historic architecture, and a secret military camp now open to the public.

Travellers Beach Hostel, Republikas Iela 25 (corner w/ Uliha) LV; *liepajahostel.com/*, T:371/28690106, *liepaja@hostel.lv*; $15bed, Kitchen:Y, B'fast:N, Pvt.room:Y, Locker:Y, Recep:24/7; Note: bar, prkng, tours, bag hold, laundry

11 Hostels) RIGA is the largest of the Baltic capitals and a member of the Hanseatic League from the 13th century. As such it had a large resident German population and German language until 1891. It was even a Swedish city for almost a hundred years, from 1625-1710, when Peter the Great besieged Riga and won. By the time that Russia gained influence, a national awakening occurred also, and a struggle between Russia and Germany was matched by a stuggle for Latvian identity and language dominance.

World War II was bad, with concentration camps and such, and so was Communism, with Russians occupying all positions within the country. They still haven't left, not all of them, anyway. With the arrival of budget airlines Riga is now well-connected to the rest of Europe and tourism is on the rise. The historic center is the main attraction, including the castle on the waterfront, the Doma Cathedral, and several medieval houses. It was designated a UNESCO World Heritage site.

Cinnamon Sally Backpacker's House, Merķeļa iela 1, Riga; T:22042280, *ieva@ cinnamonsally.com/*, $10bed, Kitchen:Y, B'fast:N, Pvt.room:Y, Locker:Y, Recep:24/7; Note: wh/chair ok, bar, laundry, bag hold, a/c

Blue Cow Backpackers, Torņa iela 4, Riga; *bluecowhostel.com/*, T:27736700, *info@bluecowbarracks.com*; $17bed, Kitchen:Y, B'fast:N, Pvt.room:Y, Locker:Y, Recep:24/7; Note: printer, bar, TV, bag hold, laundry, tours, ctr

Naughty Squirrel Backpackers, Kalēju iela 50, Riga; T:67220073, *info@ thenaughtysquirrel.com/*; $16bed, Kitchen:Y, B'fast:N, Pvt.room:Y, Locker:Y, Recep:24/7; Note: bar, TV, tours, laundry, bag hold, central

Funky Hostel, 25 Krisjana Barona St, Riga, Latvia; *funkyhostel.com/*, T:+371/29105939, *funky@hostel.lv*; $13bed, Kitchen:Y, B'fast:Y, Pvt.room:Y, Locker:Y, Recep:24/7; Note: bar, tours, laundry, bag hold, 4th Fl, central

RedNose Hostel, Jana Street 14, Old Town, Riga; T:+371/27721414, *info@ rednose.lv/*; $12bed, Kitchen:Y, B'fast:$, Pvt.room:Y, Locker:Y, Recep:24/7; Note: parking, c.c. ok, central

Riga Style Hostel, Alfrēda Kalniņa Street 4-11, *Riga;* T:67280830, *info@ rigastylehostel.com;* $13bed, Kitchen:Y, B'fast:$, Pvt.room:Y, Locker:Y, Recep:24/7; Note: TV, travel desk, 4th Fl no lift, near train/bus/old town

Central Hostel, Ernesta Birznieka-Upīša iela 20, Riga; T:22322663, *reception@ centralhostel.lv/;* $13bed, Kitchen:Y, B'fast:Y, Pvt.room:Y, Locker:N, Recep: 24/7; Note: laundry, luggage room, tour desk, parking, central

Dome Pearl Hostel, Tirgoņu iela 4 Riga; *dome-hostel.com/,* T:67212161, *info@hostelwelcome.com;* $14bed, Kitchen:Y, B'fast:N, Pvt.room:Y, Locker:Y, Recep:24/7; Note: luggage room, coffee & tea, central

Riga Old Town Hostel/Backpackers Pub, Vaļņu iela 43 Riga; T:67223406, *info@ rigaoldtownhostel.lv/;* $19bed, Kitchen:Y, B'fast:N, Pvt.room:Y, Locker:N, Recep:24/7; Note: café/bar, tours, laundry, bag hold, central

Best Hostel, Aleksandra Čaka iela 52, Riga; T:67314234, *info@ besthostel. lv/;* $16bed, Kitchen:N, B'fast:N, Pvt.room:Y, Locker:Y, Recep:24/7; Note: tours, forex, luggage room, c.c. ok

Riga Hostel, Merķeļa St 1, 4th Fl, Riga; T:67224520; *reception@ rigahostel. com.lv/;* $8bed, Kitchen:Y, B'fast:Y, Pvt.room:Y, Locker:Y, Recep: 24/7; Note: arpt trans, bikes, café, bag hold, parking, tours, old town nr trans

21) Lithuania

Lithuania is the largest of the three Baltic States. It shares much of the same history of the others, but its big claim to fame was the Grand Duchy of Lithuania and the commonwealth it shared with Poland for two centuries, before being finally dismantled and reduced to its current size, Russia grabbing most of it. So for much of the Middle Ages Lithuania was one of the largest and greatest countries in Europe, not bad for a nation that was only established in 1253, and for which Christianity clearly became national policy only upon the Grand duke's personal union with Poland in 1385.

Upon full establishment of the commonwealth, Lithuania underwent a Polonization. The Great Northern War with Sweden devastated the country, then Russia's ever-increasing power eventually tore the commonwealth asunder in a full partition, and a plan for Russification became official policy. It was the first Soviet state to declare independence in 1990. Future's bright. Currency is *litas* (LTL); language is Lithuanian; phone code is +370.

2 Hostels) KAUNAS is Lithuania's second largest city and a major industrial center. Unlike Vilnius it is almost purely Lithuanian. It has many museums and parks and a historic old town, with many historic buildings, such as the ruins of the castle at the confluence of the rivers, the Vytautas Church, the Holy Trinity Church, and the Jesuit Church.

R Hostel, Vytauto pr. 83-9, Kaunas 44238, Lithuania; *r-hostel.lt/*, T:(8)60123625, *r_hostel@yahoo.com*; $12bed, Kitchen:Y, B'fast:N, Pvt.room:Y, Locker:Y, Recep:24/7; Note: TV, laundry, luggage ok, parking, central, bikes, pub crawls

Hostel 10, Neries kr. 16, Kaunas, T:+370/37302218, *info@ hostel10.lt/*; $13bed, Kitchen:Y, B'fast:N, Pvt.room:N, Locker:N, Recep:24/7; Note: 30 min. walk to center, parking, a/c

6 Hostels) VILNIUS is Lithuania's main city and capital, and a picturesque one at that. Its origins are murky but by the time of the commonwealth with Poland city walls were being built, a university opened, and migrants were coming from all over. That all changed with the Russian occupation a few centuries later. Its Jews were massacred in WWII, and its intelligentsia deported afterward. Then ordinary citizens were deported and Russians moved in, until 1991. Today it is a modern European city.

Bigger than Tallinn, Vilnius is still easily walkable. The entire center is a UNESCO world heritage site. There are castles, cathedrals, genocide museums, the ruins of the Castle of Gediminas on Castle Hill, a 16th C. Gothic Church of St. Anne, a dozen 17th C. Baroque churches, notably the Church of SS. Peter and Paul, a cathedral that dates from 1387, and... a monument to Frank Zappa. It has not yet been colonized for Western parties. Give it another year or two.

Fortuna Hostel, Liepkalnio str, 2 Vilnius, *fortunahostel.lt/,* T:+370/62345050; *fortunahostel@lha.lt;* $10bed, Kitchen:Y, B'fast:N, Pvt.room:Y, Locker:N, Recep:24/7; Note: tours, parking, bag hold, c.c. ok, tea/coffee

Hostelgate, Sv. Mikalojaus 3, Vilnius; *hostelgate.lt/,* T:+370/63832818, *hostelgate@gmail.com;* $14bed, Kitchen:Y, B'fast:N, Pvt.room:Y, Locker:Y, Recep:24/7; Note: free tour/info, laundry, bag hold, parking, c.c. ok, central

Paupio Namai, Paupio St. 31a, Vilnius; *paupionamai.lt/;* T:+370/52643113; $20bed, Kitchen:Y, B'fast:N, Pvt.room:Y, Locker:N, Recep:24/7; Note: parking, laundry, forex, doctor/nurse on call, bag hold, central

Old Town Hostel, Aušros Vartų gatvė 20, Vilnius; *oldtownhostel.lt/,* T:+370/52625357, *oldtownhostel@lha.lt;* $10bed, Kitchen:Y, B'fast:N, Pvt.room:Y, Locker:N, Recep:24/7; Note: bikes, laundry, bag hold, parking, tours, central, tea/cof

Youth Hostel Filaretai, Filaretu St 17, Vilnius; T:+370/52154627, *info@ filaretaihostel.lt/;* $13bed, Kitchen:Y, B'fast:N, Pvt.room:Y, Locker:N, Recep:24/7; Note: HI member %, laundry, c.c. ok, uphill 15 min. walk <ctr, parking

A Hostel, Sodu str. 8 & Sodu str. 17, Vilnius; T:(8)69909903, *info@ hostelsvilnius.lt/;* $10bed, Kitchen:N, B'fast:$, Pvt.room:Y, Locker:Y, Recep:24/7; Note: laundry, café, bag hold, parking, tours, tea/coffee

22) Russia (Western)

The legacy of the USSR casts a long shadow over the image of Russia, but that's an image that will fade in proportion to the distance from that era. More than anything else Russia is huge, occupying more than ten percent of the planet's available land after the world's most massive migration ever, that of Russians east to Siberia and the Pacific. This all finally coalesced into a state so recently that it's fairly well documented, starting with the proto-Viking Varangian "Rus" (get it?) around Kiev in the ninth century AD and re-constituted in the Grand Duchy of Moscow's post-Mongol Era, when it fancied itself the "Third Rome" picking up the pieces after the fall of Constantinople.

Then followed the Enlightenment, Peter the Great's entry into Europe, and finally the 20th century, with its WWII catastrophe and its Communism. With the final demise of the USSR and a decade of ineffective leaders, local mafia, and decline, Russia is finally regaining its balance and status in the world (thanks at least in part to high oil prices). Unfortunately tourism doesn't seem to have changed much since the early days when commie paranoia was matched only by the need for hard currency. Currently they could not care less. Nobody will be waiting at baggage claim to buy your used Levis, and Russian women will not follow you down the street wanting to get into your used Levis.

Yet in Russia there is still a level of unnecessary formalities and bureaucracy almost unknown elsewhere. That means a super-expensive visa, which means a Letter of Invitation, basically just a meaningless extra formality and charge. Then once you get there, you're supposed to register everywhere you go, which carries with it another charge. Supposedly they check, but usually never do; still you never know. All this ups the price of an already expensive country. Now Moscow is certainly unique, and so is Saint Petersburg, but besides that, the big attraction is the trans-Siberian train… and Siberia itself, of course. Russian is the language; *ruble* is currency; phone code is +7.

KALININGRAD was a German city known as Konigsberg, going way back to the Knights Templar, Prussia and then Germany before the USSR decided to snatch it as the spoils of WWII. The German inhabitants were all evicted and forced to settle elsewhere. The *oblast* of the same name is an enclave even smaller in size than the Baltic countries, NATO nations which now separate it from not-so-motherly Russia. The city is a confusing conglomerate of modern Russian buildings and old German ones.

Amigos Hostel, Epronovskaya st. 20-102, Kaliningrad; *amigoshostel.ru/*, T:8(911)4852157, *kld.hostels@hotmail.com*; $19bed, Kitchen:Y, B'fast:N, Pvt. room:N, Locker:Y, Recep:24/7; Note: 13th fl, lift, bag hold, lift, bar, central

19 Hostels) MOSCOW is the heart of the beast, of course, documented from at least the mid-12th century and prominent since the 1300's as the Grand Duchy of Moscow. Before that it was just a village on the river Moskva. It lost some prominence in the 1700's with the founding of Saint Petersburg, but regained it in the Soviet era. It withstood the onslaught and sieges of Napoleon in the early 1800's, ditto Hitler in WWII, so naturally became a bit defensive about the challenge laid down by the US during the Cold War.

Already the head of a 15-nation USSR with a strong buffer zone in Europe's own Warsaw Pact, Moscow increasingly found itself at the center of an empire spreading (ideologically at least) all over the world, first China and Mongolia then North Korea, Cuba, Vietnam, Laos, Cambodia, with more to come, increasingly more totalitarian disctatorships than economic socialists — Angola, Ethiopia, Libya, Syria, Nicaragua, Afghanistan (sound of needle scratching long and hard on vinyl) — and the rest is history.

Communism fell, and after a rough start, Moscow's future is bright at the head of a reinvigorated Russia, as long as the Mafia gets their cut. It's more than a little bit ironic that twenty years after communism's fall, Moscow has more billionaires than any other place in the world, and I doubt that the GINI poverty index is so good, either. Moscow's Commie rep as a drab collection of khaki-colored comrades sipping cold soup in cement-grey cell-blocks is a thing of the distant past. Today Moscow puts the 'vibe' in 'vibrant' with the word 'nonstop' plastered all over, from café to pub to all-night disco. And of course they've always had some of the finest literature, music, dance, and art the world has ever seen. Catch the classic rock band Mumiy Troll. And there's still the Kremlin and St. Basil's and Matrioshka dolls just waiting to have their outer layers removed.

The Kremlin includes the Saviour (Spasskaya) Tower, leading to Red Square. Also on the Red Square is the St. Nicholas (Nikolskaya) Tower. The two other principal gate towers — the Trinity (Troitskaya) Tower, with a bridge and outer barbican (the Kutafya Tower), and the Borovitskaya Tower — rise from the western wall. Churches and other landmarks include the Cathedral of the Assumption, the Cathedral of the Annunciation, the Palace of Facets, the Armoury Palace and Armoury Museum. Hostels are good but not cheap, and then there are the regulatory hassles. Persevere. It's got to be worth it for that train, right?

Green ManGO Hostel, Novaya Basmannaya St 25/2, Moscow; T:4992611076, *gm.hostel@gmail.com*, $13bed, *facebook.com/greenmangohostel* /; Kitchen:Y, B'fast:N, Pvt.room:N, Locker:N, Recep:24/7; Note: bikes, lift, hard find, central

Godzillas Hostel, Bolshoi Karetnyy 6, Apt 5 (1st Fl), Moscow; T:+7(495)6994223; *info@ godzillashostel.com/*; $16bed, Kitchen:Y, B'fast:N, Pvt. room:Y, Locker:N, Recep:24/7; Note: luggage rm, laundry, tours

Chocolate Hostel, Degtyarny per. 15, Bldg 1, #4, I-com 004, Moscow; *contacts@ chocohostel.com/*, T:+7(495)9712046; $21bed, Kitchen:Y, B'fast:Y, Pvt. room:Y, Locker:Y, Recep:24/7; Note: bag hold, laundry, tours, central

Moscow Home Hostel, 2 Neopalimovsky Per. 1/12, (1st Fl), Moscow; T:+7(495)7782445, *info@ moshostel.com/*; $16bed, Kitchen:Y, B'fast:N, Pvt. room:Y, Locker:N, Recep:24/7; Note: bag hold, laundry, parking, tours, central

HM Hostel Moscow, #14, 4th Fl, M. Afanasyevskiy per 1/33, m. Arbat; T+7(495)7788501, *info@ hostel-moscow.com/*; $25bed, Kitchen:Y, B'fast:$, Pvt. room:N, Locker:N, Recep:24/7; Note: bar, tours, bag hold, laundry, central

TNT Hostel, 5 Zvonarskiy pereulok, 3rd Fl #6, Moscow; T:8(495)9730501, *info@ tnthostel.com/*; $14bed, Kitchen:Y, B'fast:N, Pvt.room:Y, Locker:N, Recep:24/7; Note: laundry, parking, c.c. ok, LOI, no signs outside, clubs & pubs

Moscow Style Hostel, Tverskaya St. 15 App.80, Moscow; *mos-style.com/*, T:8(926)4936225; $21bed, Kitchen:Y, B'fast:Y, Pvt.room:Y, Locker:Y, Recep:24/7; Note: bag hold, laundry, tours, central, homestay

Comrade Hostel, Maroseyka St, 11, 3rd Fl, Moscow; T:+7/4997098760, *info@ comradehostel.com/*; $21bed, Kitchen:Y, B'fast:N, Pvt.room:Y, Locker:N, Recep:24/7; Note: LOI, bag hold, laundry, prkng, no lift, central, tea/cof

Trans-Siberian Hostel, Barashevskiy Pereulok 12, Moscow; T:+7/4959162030, *info@ tshostel.com/*; $18bed, Kitchen:N, B'fast:Y, Pvt.room:Y, Locker:Y, Recep:24/7; Note: tours, bag hold, laundry, prkng, a/c, LOI, central, market

Napoleon Hostel, Maly Zlatoustinskiy St, Dom 2, 4th Fl, Moscow; *info@ napoleonhostel.com/*, T:8(495)6245978, $13bed, Kitchen:Y, B'fast:N, Pvt.room:N, Locker:Y, Recep:24/7; Note: LOI, resto/bar, tours, prkng, 4th Fl no lift

A la Russe Hotel & Hostel, 5, Voznesenskiy St, Moscow, T:8(495)6970503, *info@ hotelalaruss.com/*; $13bed, Kitchen:Y, B'fast:$, Pvt.room:Y, Locker:Y, Recep:24/7; Note: wh/chair ok, parking, long-stays, central

Suharevka Hostel, Bolshaya Suharevskaya Sq, 16/18 apt. 5, Moscow; T:89104203446, *info@ suharevkahotel.ru/*; $13bed, Kitchen:Y, B'fast:N, Pvt.room:Y, Locker:Y, Recep:24/7; Note: LOI, tours, bag hold, c.c. ok

Da! Hostel, (Old) Arbat, 11, Moscow; T:+7(495)6915577, *info@ da-hostel.ru/*; $17bed, Kitchen:Y, B'fast:N, Pvt.room:Y, Locker:Y, Recep:24/7, Note: arpt trans, lift, luggage rm, laundry, tours, central, no lift

Apple Hostel, Big Spasoglinitshevsky Lane 6/1, Moscow; *applehostel.ru/*, T:+7(916)3355333, *applehostel@mail.ru*; $21bed, Kitchen:Y, B'fast:N, Pvt.room:N, Locker:Y, Recep:24/7; Note: bikes, lift, bag hold, laundry, prkng

iVAN Hostel, Petrovsky pereulok, 1/30, apt. 23., Moscow; *ivanhostel.com/*, T:+7/9164071178, *ivanhostel@gmail.com*; $23bed, Kitchen:Y, B'fast:N, Pvt.room:Y, Locker:Y, Recep:24/7; Note: arpt trans, lift, bag hold, laundry, basic

Bear/Arbatskaya, Bolshaya Molchanovka 23, fl#5, *bh3@bear-hostels.ru*; $15

Bear Hostels/Mayakovskaya, Sadovaya-Kudrinskaya 32, Bldg.2, fl#4, Moscow; T:+7(495)5404361, *bh2@ bear-hostels.ru/*; $16bed, Kitchen:Y, B'fast:N, Pvt.room:Y, Locker:Y, Recep:24/7; Note: bikes, lift, bag hold, laundry, tours

Taganka Hostel, Marksistskaia St 34/2, Vorontsovskaya St 35B-2, Moscow; T:(495)9116969, *info@ tagankahostel.ru/*; $19bed, Kitchen:Y, B'fast:$, Pvt.room:N, Locker:Y, Recep:24/7; Note: café/bar, tours, pool, bag hold

Capital Hostel, 5/6, Malaya Ordynka, Moscow; T:+7/4959591347, *info@ capitalhostel.com/*; $26bed, Kitchen:N, B'fast:N, Pvt.room:Y, Locker:N, Recep:24/7; Note: arpt trans, lift, parking, bag hold, central, cozy

12 Hostels) ST. PETERSBURG is Russia's second city of course, both in population and importance. It is also one of the newest, purpose-built by Peter the Great (note the similarity in names) to serve as his western-looking imperial capital, a function it served except for four short years until 1917. So Peter captured the land from Sweden in 1704, and by 1712 it was serving as capital, though the treaty that ended the war wasn't in effect until 1721. Cool,

huh? Just take what you want, as long as you size up your competitor's, uh... army, first. Russia also moved the capital of Finland to Helsinki, just so the two capitals could be closer, any symbolism your own.

With WWI and Bolshevism in full swing, SPb was first renamed Petrograd (to not sound so German), then "Red" Petrograd (to sound more Commie), then finally Leningrad (to honor the architect of the matrix... er, I mean 'revolution'). St. Petersburg finally returned to its original name after "falling" to capitalism in 1991. Today it's still a great seaport and Russia's most Western city. Tourist sights include Palace square, the canals, and my favorite, the Hermitage Museum. Others are Decembrists' (or Dekabristovs') Square, the buildings of the former Senate and Synod, the Horse Guards Riding School, St. Isaac's Square and cathedral of the same name.

The main thoroughfare Nevsky Prospekt contains the Stroganov, Shuvalov, and Anichkov palaces and several churches, of which the most notable are St. Peter's Lutheran Church, St. Catherine's Roman Catholic Church, and the Kazan Cathedral. Hostels tend to want cash and the quality varies wildly. If you need a LOI, then that's a consideration, since not all do it, and charges vary. St. Pete is Russia's beer capital.

Acme Hostel, 11, Sadovaya Str, St. Petersburg; *info@ acme-hotel.com/*, T:+7(812)3371223; $16bed, Kitchen:Y, B'fast:N, Pvt.room:Y, Locker:N, Recep:24/7; Note: 4th Fl no lift, tours, bag hold, laundry, central, arpt trans, tea/cof

Apple Hostel Italy, Italyanskaya St. 12, 2nd Fl, St Petersburg; *applehostel. ru/*, T:8(812)4588830, *applehostel@mail.ru*; $17bed, Kitchen:Y, B'fast:N, Pvt. room:Y, Locker:Y, Recep:24/7; Note: prkng, tours, laundry, bag hold, cozy

Soul Kitchen Jr, Moika embankment 62/2 app 9, St. Petersburg; *soulkitchenhostel.com/*, T:7(965)8163470, *soulkitchenjunior@gmail.com*, $19bed, Kitchen:Y, B'fast:$, Pvt.room:Y, Locker:Y, Recep:24/7; Note: arpt trans, laundry

MIR Hostel, Nevsky Ave, 16, St. Petersburg; *mirhostel.com/*, T:8(812)5710641, *mirhostel@gmail.com*; $16bed, Kitchen:N, B'fast:Y, Pvt.room:Y, Locker:Y, Recep:24/7; Note: cash, LOI, arpt trans, bikes, tours, laundry, bag hold, no lift

Griboideva Hostel, Treasury St. 6/13, St Petersburg; T:(812)3156948, *reservations@ griboedova71.ru/*; $14bed, Kitchen:Y, B'fast:N, Pvt.room:N, Locker:Y, Recep:24/7; Note: parking, laundry, bag hold, TV, c.c. ok, central

Nevsky Hostel, Bol'shaya Konyushennaya ulitsa, St Pete; *nevskyhostels. com/,* T:+7(812)3121206, *booking@hon.ru;* $16bed, Kitchen:Y, B'fast:$, Pvt. room:Y, Locker:Y, Recep:24/7; Note: bag hold, laundry, tours, c.c. ok, arpt trans

St Petersburg-Location Hostel, 8 Admiralteisky Ave, St. Petersburg; T:+7(812)4906429, *info@ location-hostel.ru/*; $18bed, Kitchen:Y, B'fast:N, Pvt. room:Y, Locker:Y, Recep:24/7; Note: laundry, luggage rm, center

Cuba Hostel, Kazanskaya ulitsa, 5, Saint Petersburg; *cubahostel.ru/,* T:8(812)9217115, *cubahostel@gmail.com*; $16bed, Kitchen:Y, B'fast:N, Pvt. room:N, Locker:Y, Recep:24/7; Note: bar, parking, tours, laundry, bag hold

St. Petersburg Intl. Hostel, 28 3rd Sovetskaya St, T:+7(812)3298018, *ryh@ ryh.ru/*; $24bed, Kitchen:Y, B'fast:N, Pvt.room:N, Locker:N, Recep:24/7; Note: tour desk, luggage room, laundry, a/c, c.c. ok

Puppet Hostel, 12 Ulitsa Nekrasova, St Petersburg; T:+7(812)2725401, *info@ hostel-puppet.ru/*; $16bed, Kitchen:Y, B'fast:$, Pvt.room:Y, Locker:N, Recep:24/7; Note: tours, bag hold, free visa reg, lift, arpt trans

Sabrina Hotel, Voznesenskiy pros. 41, St Petersburg; T:+7(812)3147200, *reception@ sabrina-hotel.ru/*; $13bed, Kitchen:N, B'fast:Y, Pvt.room:Y, Locker:N, Recep:24/7; Note: parking, tours, laundry, bag hold, a/c

Hostel Metro Tour, 47 Blagodatnaya str, St Petersburg; T:+7(812)3696451, *admin@ hostelmetro.spb.ru/*; $13bed, Kitchen:Y, B'fast:N, Pvt.room:Y, Locker:N, Recep:24/7; Note: tours, laundry, bag hold, c.c. ok

23) Ukraine

After Russia, Ukraine is the second-largest country in Europe, and it is not only vast but diverse, with Black Sea Coast, Carpathian Mountains, rivers, castles, historic urban areas, and the broad fertile fields where people make wine and folk art and not enough babies. Ukraine has a demographic crisis that some countries could (or at least should) only wish for, a declining fertility rate and population. How did this all begin? The history is as interesting and diverse as the countryside, all the more so because it is so recent.

The best picture is that of Kiev as the center of a Slavic state founded in the 9th century led by Scandinavian Varangian "Rus" which endured for several hundred years. After the invasions of the Mongols, that proto-Ukraine was left divided between the Golden (Mongol) Horde, Lithuania, and Poland. The next major phase was in union with Russia as part of Austria-Hungary, and then as part of the USSR under Russian domination, until independence in 1991.

Of course that thumbnail sketch says nothing of the Greeks, Romans, Byzantines, Goths, Huns, or Bulgars who came before and who all moved on to other parts. And it says nothing of the Zaporozhian Cossacks, a self-styled warrior class who ruled something of a cowboy commonwealth of refugee Ukrainian serfs beyond the Pale of Polish control past the Dnieper River, called the "Cossack Hetmanate" or "Zaporozhian Host" (17th C).

And it says even less about the depradations of those same Mongols still lingering long through history (to nearly 1800) as the Crimean Khanate, whose economy was apparently heavily based on the trade of slaves from the Slavic lands ("slav" = "slave"), and Ukraine in particular. And it says absolutely nothing about the slights to status and sleights of hand inflicted throughout history from big brother Russia toward lil' bro' Ukraine, least of all the 1930's famines under the guise and guidance of the USSR that most likely could have been prevented and which many call genocide.

So now Ukraine is free, and still it is slow to thrive, at least demographically, the whys and wherefores of which would probably explain something about us all, and "Caucasians" in particular. Economically things are much better. After a rough early patch, things have been good the last decade and Ukraine is open for tourism. It is in fact my personal recommendation as a "starter kit" for the old USSR. No visas are required for Americans, it is linked by public transportation within and without, it is reasonably priced, AND it's big and beautiful. Embroidery is a splendid folk art in Ukraine. The Russian fleet still parks on Ukraine's coast. I don't think there was an option. Ukrainian (and Russian) is the language; *hryvnia* is the currency; phone code is +380.

CHERNIVTSI is, along with Lviv, one of the main cultural centers of western Ukraine. Historically, the city's population has been a mixture of Ukrainians, Romanians, Jews, Germans, and Armenians, as the chief city in the territory of Bukovina. It only became part of the USSR in 1940. Situated just north of the border with Romania, Chernivtsi still has a large Romanian minority and Russians as well. It's a UNESCO world heritage site.

Tiu Chernivtsi Backpackers, 2, Sheptytskogo Apt.3, Chernivtsi; T:+380/508857049, *info@ hihostels.com.ua/*; $9bed, Kitchen:Y, B'fast:N, Pvt. room:Y, Locker:Y, Recep:24/7; Note: luggage rm, laundry, parking, nr train/cntr

4 Hostels) KIEV (Kyiv) is the capital and largest city in Ukraine, and center of Ukrainian culture, located north and central on the Dnieper River. One of the oldest cities in Eastern Europe, myths attribute its founding to the legendary Kyi and his family. Documents indicate that it was an outpost for the Khazars at the time it fell to the Varangian "Rus." Turkic Pechenegs and Kipchaks harassed it before the Mongols devastated Kiev, affecting civilization in the region for centuries.

As a vassal to other empires, what Kiev lost as a regional capital it made up as a spiritual one, as an important Christian center attracting pilgrims. Growing Russification threatened it culturally, though, as Russian culture became the high one and Ukrainian the folk culture of the lower classes. Kiev industrialized rapidly under Russian tutelage and in 1934 it became the capital of Ukraine USSR. The Nazis killed more than a half million Ukrainians in the Battle of Kiev, and more than 30,000 Jews in the aftermath, but Kiev recovered in the post-war period.

The nearby Chernobyl nuclear catastrophe occurred in 1986. The tour is now a popular attraction. Others include St. Sophia Cathedral and the Monastery of the Caves. Then there are the Baroque church of St. Andrew, the ruins of the Golden Gate, the Zaborovskyy Gate, and the remains of the Desyatynna Church, or Church of the Tithes. Today Kiev is a blend of modern and ancient, green and clean. The historic center has been polished and shined. Summertime is festive.

D'Lux Kiev Hostel, 10 Observatorna, 6 Fl, Apt 6, code 1010, Kiev; *dlux-kiev-hostel.com/*, T:+38(097)8328888, *hostel.dlux@gmail.com*, $15bed, Kitchen:Y, B'fast:$, Pvt.room:Y, Locker:Y, Recep:24/7; Note: Jacuzzi, lift, bag hold, laundry

Dream Hostel, 47 Chervonoarmiis'ka St, 17, Kyiv city; T:(066)2441447, *booking@ dream-hostel.com/*; $12bed, Kitchen:Y, B'fast:$, Pvt.room:Y, Locker:N, Recep:24/7; Note: arpt trans, bar, lift, tours, bag hold, laundry, parking, tea/cof

Kiev Central Station Hostel, Gogolivska, 25 Apt 15, Kyev; T:(093)7587468, *info@ kievcentralstation.com/*; $9bed, Kitchen:Y, B'fast:N, Pvt.room:Y, Locker:Y, Recep:24/7; Note: arpt trans, bag hold, laundry, parking, tours, no lift

Magic Bus, 31 Saksahans'koho St, #3, Kyiv; *busofmagic@gmail.com*, T:(097)3360303, *facebook.com/magicbushostel/*; $13bed, Kitchen:Y, B'fast:N, Pvt. room:Y, Locker:Y, Recep:24/7; Note: arpt trans, laundry, tea/cof, center

6 Hostels) LVIV (Lvov, Lwow, etc.) is Ukraine's second city and is located in the far west, close to the border with Poland, and the easiest part of Ukraine to access from the west, with convenient bus and train connections. It has historically been a center of culture for Galicia — including Jews, Ukrainians, and Poles — whose various kingdoms and incarnations it has been attached to more than any other. It also had a major German phase as a part of the Habsburg Empire from 1772-1918.

In fact Lviv only returned to the Ukraine homeland after WWII and was at the forefront of those calling for a break with communism and the Soviet Union. Now it's rapidly becoming a center for tourism. Much of the architecture dates from the 13th century. The historic center is a UNESCO world heritage site. Prices are good and the people are friendly. It's famous for its beauty. There isn't much English, but everybody speaks Russian, so that helps.

Old City Hostel, 3 Beryndy St, L'viv; T:0322949644, *booking@ oldcityhostel. lviv.ua/*; $11bed, Kitchen:Y, B'fast:N, Pvt.room:Y, Locker:Y, Recep:24/7; Note: arpt trans, bar, lift, bag hold, laundry, tours, mart, parking, central

Soviet Home Hostel, 3 Drukars'ka St 13, L'viv; T:0322727611, *info@ soviethomehostel.lviv.ua/*, $12bed, Kitchen:N, B'fast:N, Pvt.room:Y, Locker:Y, Recep:24/7; Note: arpt trans, bikes, bag hold, laundry, tours, tea/coffee, central

Central Square Hostel, 5 Rynok Square, Lviv; *cshostel.com/*, T:(095)2256654, *cshostel@gmail.com*; $11bed, Kitchen:Y, B'fast:N, Pvt.room:Y, Locker:Y, Recep:24/7; Note: arpt trans, bikes, club, tour/info, bag hold, laundry, central

Coffee Home Hostel, Javorskogo Sq. 1, Lviv; *coffeehomehostel.lviv.ua;* T:0932399393, *coffee@homehostels.com.ua;* $11bed, Kitchen:Y, B'fast:N, Pvt.room:Y, Locker:N, Recep:24/7; Note: arpt trans, bikes, laundry, bag hold, tea/cof

Mister Hostel, Bankivska Str. 5, Lviv; *misterhostellviv.com/,* T:0964798567, *misterhostel@gmail.com;* $9bed, Kitchen:Y, B'fast:N, Pvt. room:Y, Locker:N, Recep:24/7; Note: bag hold, laundry, tea/coffee, tours

Cherry Hostel, Tadeusha Kostyushka St, 5 Lviv; *fruit-hostels.lviv.ua/,* T:(097)6055599, *cherryhostel30@gmail.com;* $13bed, Kitchen:N, B'fast:Y, Pvt. room:N, Locker:Y Recep:24/7; Note: bikes, café/club, bag hold, tours, tea/ cof, cntr

2 Hostels) ODESSA is Ukraine's third city and a major seaport on the Black Sea. It still shares something of a mixed Russian/Ukraine identity, and Russian is still the most common language spoken. Originally a Greek colony, it has at various times been claimed by tribal Pechenegs, the Golden Horde, the Crimean Khanate, the Grand Duchy of Lithuania, and the Ottoman Turks. It is probably most famous for the battleship Potemkin, and Sergei Eisenstein's reenactment of that famous battle and massacre.

Babushka Beach, 2nd Kostandi #4, *cside_grand@yahoo.com*, T:09309841356

Babushka Grand, 60 Mala Arnauts'ka St, 16, Odesa; *babushkagrand.com/,* T:(063)0705535, *babushka.grand@gmail.com,* $14bed, Kitchen:Y, B'fast:N, Pvt. room:Y, Locker:Y, Recep:24/7; Note: bag hold, laundry, prkng

SEVASTOPOL is on the Crimean peninsula that juts out into the Black sea, thus making it the warmest city in Ukraine and a favorite holiday spot for ex-USSR countries. There was originally a Greek colony there, before becoming Roman then Byzantine then Ukrainian. The Russian presence is still strong, as it is elsewhere in the region, since the Russian fleet is stationed there, by mutual arrangement (after some dispute) between the two countries.

Funny Dolphin Hostel, yl. V. Kuchera, Bldg 5, apt.2, Sevastopol; *funnydolphin.hostel.com/,* T:0955013343, *funny_dolphin@mail.ru;* $17bed, Kitchen:Y, B'fast:N, Pvt.room:Y, Locker:N, Recep:ltd; Note: arpt trans, bag hold, ctr

ABOUT THE AUTHOR

American ex-pat Hardie Karges took his first extended international trip at the age of twenty-one in 1975 and traveled to his first ten countries within two years, all for less than two thousand dollars. Thus began a way of life that has taken him to some 150 countries (and counting), living and working in a dozen of them, learning several languages and trading in folk art and cottage industry products. He has also published poetry and created videos, before finally deciding to write about what he knows best—travel. His first book, "Hypertravel: 100 Countries in 2 Years," was published in 2012. The full set of "Backpackers & Flashpackers" is projected to include eight to ten volumes and be completed in 2014.

If you would like more information, or to make an inquiry or just leave a comment, please visit our blog at *backpackers-flashpackers.net/* or our *BackpackersFlashpackers* page on FaceBook.

www.ingramcontent.com/pod-product-compliance
Lightning Source LLC
Chambersburg PA
CBHW070957040426
42443CB00007B/546